The Quality of … Europe

Public Preferences and Policy Reforms

ANDREW ROBERTS
Northwestern University

CAMBRIDGE
UNIVERSITY PRESS

CAMBRIDGE
UNIVERSITY PRESS

32 Avenue of the Americas, New York NY 10013-2473, USA

Cambridge University Press is part of the University of Cambridge.

It furthers the University's mission by disseminating knowledge in the pursuit of education, learning and research at the highest international levels of excellence.

www.cambridge.org
Information on this title: www.cambridge.org/9781107417571

First published 2010
First paperback edition 2014

A catalogue record for this publication is available from the British Library

Library of Congress Cataloguing in Publication data

Roberts, Andrew Lawrence, 1970–
The quality of democracy in eastern Europe : public preferences and policy reforms / Andrew Roberts.
p. cm.
Includes bibliographical references and index.
ISBN 978-0-521-11033-4 (hardback)
1. Democracy – Europe, Eastern. 2. Political participation – Europe, Eastern. 3. Government accountability – Europe, Eastern. 4. Europe, Eastern – Politics and government – 1989–
I. Title.
JN96.A91R63 2009
320.947–dc22 2009028977

ISBN 978-0-521-11033-4 Hardback
ISBN 978-1-107-41757-1 Paperback

The Quality of Democracy in Eastern Europe

Public Preferences and Policy Reforms

How does democracy work in the new democracies of Eastern Europe? Do the people actually rule as one would expect in a democracy or do the legacies of communism and the constraints of the transition weaken popular control? This book presents a new framework for conceptualizing and measuring democratic quality and applies this framework to multiple countries and policy areas in the region. It defines democratic quality as the degree to which citizens are able to hold leaders accountable for their performance and to keep policy close to their preferences. Its surprising conclusion, drawn from large-N statistical analyses and small-N case studies, is that citizens exercise considerable control over their rulers in Eastern European democracies. Despite facing difficult economic circumstances and an unfavorable inheritance from communism, these countries rapidly constructed relatively high-quality democracies.

Andrew Roberts is currently Assistant Professor of Political Science at Northwestern University and a Fellow at the Institute for Policy Research. He is the author of *From Good King Wenceslas to the Good Soldier Švejk: A Dictionary of Czech Popular Culture* (2005) and has published articles in numerous journals, including *Comparative Politics, Legislative Studies Quarterly, Electoral Studies, Party Politics, Slavic Review,* the *Journal of Public Policy*, and *East European Politics and Societies*.

Contents

List of Tables and Figures

TABLES

FIGURES

Preface and Acknowledgments

Like many of my peers, I went to Eastern Europe in the early 1990s to work as an English teacher. I spent the next three years giving lessons in conversation and learning about the people and culture in my new home. Although I was not in a position to follow politics very closely – I only started learning the language after I arrived – in many ways those years shaped my view of Eastern European politics.

My dominant impression from that time was of living in a normal democratic country. If there were worries about civil liberties and political rights, they were mostly on the margins. Citizens and the press – not to mention my students – were not afraid to criticize the government. Elections were usually closely fought affairs that featured real differences of opinion about policy. Parties appeared to take the views of the public seriously, though mainly because they knew that getting votes depended on it. And a rough sort of accountability prevailed, where incumbents perceived as corrupt or incompetent typically lost their hold on power.

These impressions were partially a result of living in Brno rather than, say, Bucharest, but frequent visits to Hungary, Poland, and even Slovakia – then something of a pariah – did not overturn this impression. Of course, citizens complained to me constantly about their corrupt and self-serving leaders – and scandals were not in short supply – but then again Eastern Europeans are consistently among the least happy people in the world.

It was these simple observations that shaped the research questions at the heart of this book. The political science literature I read in graduate school took a fairly dim view of the new postcommunist democracies. The overthrow of communism elicited nothing but admiration. But scholars had doubts about whether democracy was working in these countries. They worried about whether politicians were accountable to citizens and even whether citizens were competent to rule. The standard picture was of corrupt and self-serving politicians manipulating hot-button issues and their old connections from communism to stay in power and enrich themselves and their friends.

It was the dissonance between these evaluations and my own observations that stand at the root of this book.[1]

The book itself was composed in two separate parts, which I hope is less evident to readers than it is to me. My doctoral dissertation asked about the causes of social policy reforms in three countries – the Czech Republic, Hungary, and Poland. The remainder of this project can now be found in Chapters 6 and 7. The answers that I found were what inspired the rest of the book. It seemed to me that, at least in these countries and policy areas, politicians were making policy with an eye toward what the public wanted – that democratic responsiveness prevailed. This conclusion was not one of my original hypotheses – hopefully a sign of unbiasedness – which is what made my discovery of it even more surprising. I had initially thought that it would be economic pressures or ideological conviction or even political institutions that shaped reforms of the welfare state. My graduate training was strong.

When I returned to the dissertation with an eye toward publication, I worried that the conclusion might be confined only to these countries and policy areas. I also began to think more broadly about the functioning of democracy in the region and the ways that public opinion, elections, and policy interact.

This thinking led to two major additions to the manuscript. One was conceptual. What did it mean for democracy to be functioning or malfunctioning – for a country to be a high- or low-quality democracy? Was it just responsiveness to the public or were there other pathways? These thoughts produced Chapter 2, which outlines my preferred way of conceiving of democratic quality as the degree of popular control of government. The other was to expand the number of cases and the range of policies. Chapters 3, 4, and 5 now analyze three modes of citizen control in the ten Eastern European countries that have entered the European Union across a range of economic policies. Even under these tougher tests, my initial conclusions mostly survived as I found good evidence that citizens could control their governments.

Despite its relatively positive conclusions, I hope that the book is not seen as Pollyannaish. I do not wish to turn a blind eye to the many problems these countries face – from corruption to populism – though my focus on a particular aspect of governance has removed some of these problems from my purview. Furthermore, if a bias exists in comparative politics, it may be to judge countries too harshly (Americanists have sometimes had the opposite bias). It is more serious to find flaws and to criticize. I hope this study is seen in that context.

I have a number of people and institutions to thank for this book. My dissertation research was generously supported by an SSRC dissertation fellowship and an IREX Individual Advanced Research Opportunity fellowship. The Searle Foundation for Policy Research helped me to pursue the additions to the manuscript that I described earlier and Northwestern University

[1] I should add that post-2000 politics in the United States further shaped my opinions. Corruption, abuse of power, and nonresponsiveness in the United States actually made Eastern European democracy look good by comparison.

supplemented their grant to allow me a full year of leave. At Cambridge, I would like to thank Eric Crahan for his support and encouragement.

I have many scholarly debts and wish that I had accumulated more. Nancy Bermeo generously agreed to take me under her wing when it seemed like every other comparativist at Princeton was relying on her advice. Despite working in a different field, Doug Arnold never failed to point me in the right direction and showed more faith in me than I did in myself. Josh Tucker came in at a late stage to offer devastating critiques and still serves that function. Kathryn Stoner-Weiss did the same in addition to training me in comparative politics. Finally, Anna Seleny was there at the start of the dissertation and always had an open door for my ideas.

At Northwestern, Kathy Thelen has been as kind a mentor as I could ask for and colleagues like Dennis Chong, Jamie Druckman, Sean Gailmard, Ed Gibson, Ken Janda, Jeff Jenkins, Jim Mahoney, Ben Page, Will Reno, Jason Seawright, Hendrik Spruyt, and the sorely missed Mike Wallerstein provided both encouragement and much needed advice.

The entire project started with an email to Mitch Orenstein, and he has been a careful critic and faithful supporter since then. Among the many others whose advice and encouragement helped to make this a better work are Michelle Dion, Benjamin Frommer, Tim Frye, Sona and Matt Golder, Anna Grzymala-Busse, Marc Morjé Howard, Tomasz Inglot, Byung-Yeon Kim, Ron Linden, Petr Matějů, Eric McGlinchey, Monika Nalepa, Grigore Pop-Eleches, Richard Rose, Vladimir Tismaneanu, Gabor Toka, Hubert Tworzecki, Milada Vachudova, and Jiří Večernik. I wish I could also thank the many anonymous reviewers who read both the entire manuscript and some of the individual chapters that were submitted to journals. Although I still cannot open envelopes or emails with those reviews without steeling my nerves, they inevitably provide some of the most needed advice.

I also wish to thank Elseveier Limited for allowing me to reproduce analyses from the article "Hyperaccountability: Economic Voting in Central and Eastern Europe," which appeared in the journal *Electoral Studies* (2008).

On a more personal note, I thank my parents for not asking too many times when the book would appear. My wife, Lenka, was extremely patient with the progress of a manuscript whose content is not her cup of tea. And for my son Matthew, who prefers books with animals in them, I add this sentence: The crocodile ate the book I was writing, so I am going to have to start writing another one.

1

Introduction

On 9 December 1997, Václav Havel, then president of the Czech Republic, addressed his country's Parliament, Constitutional Court, and diplomats. His purpose was to deliver an assessment of the state of the country at the end of its fifth year as an independent democracy. His conclusions were disturbing.

He saw a society with two faces. The first face was everyday life – work, family, and leisure. This face he called incomparably better and more varied than that under communism.[1] But there was another face: "the relation of citizens to their own government, to politics and public life" – what might be called the state of democracy. In his words,

> This side of life indeed shows a rather gloomy face at the moment. Many people – the opinion polls corroborate this – are disturbed, disappointed or even disgusted by the general condition of society in our country. Many believe that – democracy or no democracy – power is again in the hands of untrustworthy figures whose primary concern is their personal advancement instead of the interests of the people.... The prevalent opinion is that it pays off in this country to lie and to steal; that many politicians and civil servants are corruptible; that political parties – though they all declare honest intentions in lofty words – are covertly manipulated by suspicious financial groupings. An increasing number of people are disgusted by politics, which they hold responsible – and rightly so – for all these adverse developments. As a consequence, they have begun to feel suspicious of us all, or even take an aversion to us – notwithstanding the fact that they freely elected us for our offices (Havel 1999).[2]

Havel's evaluation of citizens' attitudes toward politics hit a public nerve. His pithy phrase describing this face of society soon entered into everyday conversation. He said that the country was suffering from a *blbá nálada*, or bad mood.

[1] I use the term communism rather than socialism or state socialism for reasons of conceptual clarity laid out in Roberts (2005).

[2] English translation from http://old.hrad.cz/president/Havel/speeches/index_uk.html.

Havel was not alone in his gloomy assessment. Many scholars have expressed similar doubts about the functioning of the public sphere in the postcommunist democracies. In a book-length assessment of the nature of postcommunism, Richard Sakwa (1999: 116–7) wrote that "[t]he gulf between formal and substantive democracy is in most places the defining feature of postcommunist democratization." Jane Curry (1995: 55) found that "in these new democracies, there is an increasing absence of the demos, the population, in the political process... even when individuals do participate their desires are all too often not reflected in political debates and policy decisions, or their votes reflect little real understanding of the positions of parties and candidates."

It is easy to find anecdotal support for these judgments even today, more than fifteen years after the fall of communism. Consider the most recent elections in the three states that are considered the great successes of the transition. Poland's elections of September 2005 produced a coalition of the Christian nationalist Law and Justice party with parties of the extreme left and extreme right that proceeded to collapse amid allegations of both corruption and persecution of political opponents. In Hungary, the Socialists won elections in May 2006 only to be exposed as having lied about the state of public finances and their future plans during the campaign. The release of a tape of the prime minister confessing these lies precipitated the largest street demonstrations since the fall of communism. Czech elections two months later ended with an exact tie between the parties of the right and left (the latter including an unreconstructed communist party), which after seven months of deadlock was only resolved by the mysterious defection of two Social Democratic MPs to their archrivals.

Other scholars, however, deliver a more positive assessment of the postcommunist era. In surveying these same three countries, Hubert Tworzecki (2003: 3) writes that "[a]n optimistic observer witnessing Czech, Hungarian, and Polish elections of the late 1990s might have easily concluded that democracy in East-Central Europe had been practiced for a long time and had become quite routine."[3]

Turning away from scholarship – where talk is sometimes cheap – ten countries in Eastern Europe did meet some of the toughest real-world challenges head on.[4] All managed to survive recessions as large as the Great Depression along with the reconstruction of their entire economies and polities, and yet they rarely came close to suspending free and fair elections. Even where less-than-democratic rulers took power, they were almost invariably thrown out of office at the next election. These countries also managed to fulfill the rigorous accession requirements of the European Union (EU), which were often created *de novo* precisely to make things difficult for them. A mere decade and a half

[3] Tworzecki follows this with a skeptical perspective, but he inclines to optimism.

[4] The designation Eastern Europe is not a perfect one and I do not use it as a term of disrespect. Nevertheless, it is more specific than Central Europe – which usually includes Germany and Austria – and less of a mouthful than East Central Europe or Central and Eastern Europe. I use it here as a shorthand for the ten countries from the region who entered the EU.

after exiting some of the most repressive regimes that the world has seen, these countries had entered the most prestigious and exclusive club of democracies in the world and done so while navigating economic and social problems that might have crippled even an established democracy.

These observations illustrate the two puzzles that motivate this book. The first is how to reconcile the diverse assessments of democratic quality in Eastern Europe. Are these democracies working poorly or well? Are they disconnected from their citizens and prone to corruption and repression as the pessimists argue? Or have they coped well with the transition and become functioning democracies, more or less indistinguishable – at least politically – from their Western neighbors? Are they truly full-fledged members of the club of democracies or do they reside in a halfway house between democracy and dictatorship that Richard Rose and his colleagues (Rose et al. 1998: 218) label "broke-backed democracy"? The first puzzle addressed in this book is which of the divergent assessments of democracy in Eastern Europe better fits the facts.

The second puzzle is how these countries managed to do what they did. Even the pessimists admit that these countries have managed to meet most of the minimal requirements of democracy: maintaining free elections and civil rights. But how have they managed to overcome enormous hurdles to reach as far as they did? Forty years without any genuine political competition or public participation meant that the entire political life of these countries had to be created from scratch with few memories of anything other than dictatorship. Moreover, the legacies of communism created a suspicion and apathy toward politics and a preference for technocratic rather than democratic solutions. And this does not include the rigors of the transition and economic reform mentioned earlier.

Even if one sides with the democratic pessimists, it is a puzzle that these countries could maintain the level of democracy that they did. What accounts for the fact that these ten countries survived as competitive democracies even as their governments had to deal with problems that would test even established democracies?

1.1. THREE ISSUES

The resolution of these puzzles requires that we address three issues. The first is the meaning of democratic quality. What does it mean to say that democracy is working well or badly? What differentiates a high-quality from a low-quality democracy? What sort of politics characterizes a high-quality democracy? As Chapter 2 makes clear, one of the causes of disagreement over the quality of democracy in Eastern Europe is the lack of a common conception of democratic quality. Different studies use different standards and some leave their standards implicit.

An important part of this book is an attempt to produce a set of criteria for assessing the quality of democracy and ways for operationalizing these criteria to conduct empirical research. This book puts forth an explicit definition of democratic quality and uses the definition consistently to assess the nature of democratic processes in Eastern Europe.

The second issue is the nature and level of democratic quality in Eastern Europe. Having established a set of standards, the main portion of the manuscript uses these standards to evaluate the new democracies in Eastern Europe. Another reason for disagreement over democratic quality in the region is the fact that many evaluations have proceeded either piecemeal – looking at isolated incidents – or at too high a level of abstraction – cumulating failures in different aspects of politics across multiple countries.

This study instead aims for a semblance of comprehensiveness and concreteness. In the first place, it considers a fairly wide portion of Eastern Europe: the ten countries that have joined the EU. Thus, conclusions can be made about general trends and outliers can be identified. Temporally, the study considers these countries over the entire period of their democratic existence, insofar as data permit. Thus, it can ask whether democratic quality has improved or declined over the first decade and a half of transition. With this set of standards and assessments, it is hopefully possible to determine if Havel's diagnosis is accurate.

The third issue is what stands behind these levels of quality. Given a set of standards and an assessment, what are the causes of the particular levels of quality in Eastern Europe? Are they to be found in the legacies of communism – its treatment of civil society, political parties, and economic life? Did it matter that citizens were well educated and mostly middle class? Or should attention be focused on the transition and particularly the economic challenges it presented? Did international pressure affect the development of democracy? Or were domestic political institutions at work with different constitutional structures producing different sorts of democracies? In short, what factors explain the sorts of quality that emerged in these countries and what do they imply for the quality of new democracies elsewhere in the world?

1.2. WHAT IS DEMOCRATIC QUALITY?

I begin by considering the first of these issues. The study of democratic quality has exploded in recent years. As Figure 1.1 shows, the phrases "quality of democracy" and "democratic quality" are much in vogue in political science.[5] Relatively uncommon just a decade ago, their use in scholarly articles has ballooned in the early years of the new millennium. Yet, as I show in Chapter 2, most works have left the meaning of the concept vague or have stretched it to cover too many disparate phenomena. This book provides a clear definition of the concept of democratic quality. Although this definitional exercise is the subject of the next chapter, it may be helpful to briefly outline the argument of that chapter here so that readers know where the book is headed.

[5] I use these terms interchangeably throughout.

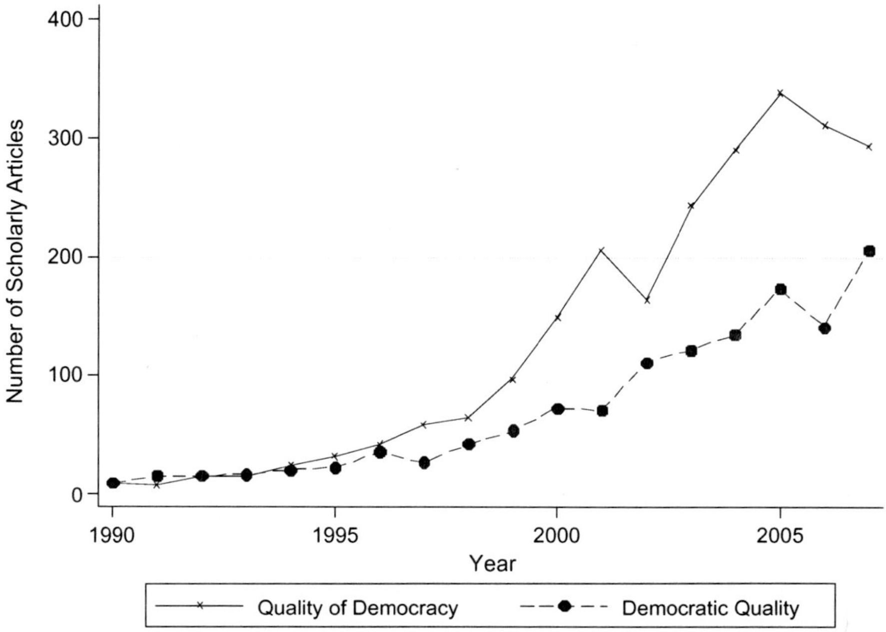

FIGURE 1.1. Scholarly articles mentioning "quality of democracy" or "democratic quality." *Note:* Numbers of scholarly articles using the given phrase in each year. *Source:* Google scholar, http://scholar.google.com, searched on 3 January 2009.

Democracy is unique as a system of governance in requiring formal institutions that permit citizens to influence their government. In the modern world, these institutions are free, fair, and regular elections and the civil rights that allow citizens to express their opinions to and about their government. Although citizens can influence the behavior of their government in other regime types, this influence does not come through formal institutions. Authoritarian rulers may deal with citizens as they see fit – revoking and granting rights, and ignoring and heeding petitions according to their whim. Only democracy formalizes and institutionalizes public influence over rulers. Indeed, this potential for influence epitomizes the commonsense view of democracy as citizen rule.

I would emphasize the word *potential* in the previous sentence. Democratic institutions give citizens opportunities to control their government, but they do not guarantee that citizens exercise such control. The institutions of democracy are in fact complex tools for citizen rule. Citizens may use them to punish incumbents, to select policy directions, and to petition rulers to address their needs. Such actions tend to give them the sort of government they want. But there is no guarantee that citizens take advantage of these opportunities or that politicians respond to the incentives they create. It is possible to have democratic institutions without citizens controlling their government. It is this observation that leads to the current concept of democratic quality.

I refer to the opportunities for citizen rule as linkages and define democratic quality as the strength of linkages or alternatively the strength of popular control. Strong linkages mean that citizens govern, as the commonsense understanding of democracy suggests; weak linkages mean that politicians escape popular control and rule as they themselves choose. Although strong linkages do not necessarily produce better government in the sense of better policy outcomes – a topic I explore later – they do produce more democratic government.

Three linkages are particularly important in allowing citizens to control and influence public policy, and they are the focus of the empirical analyses. Following Manin, Przeworski, and Stokes (1999), I call these links electoral accountability, mandate responsiveness, and policy responsiveness. Electoral accountability means that voters sanction politicians for producing outcomes that they do not approve of. These punishments should induce politicians to produce the outcomes that citizens want, lest they lose office. Mandate-responsive politicians present clear and distinctive programs in their campaigns, which they enact when elected. This gives citizens a means of ex ante rather than ex post control over policy. A policy-responsive government is one whose policy choices continually follow public preferences. The correspondence between public opinion and policy is perhaps the strongest sign of popular control.

By providing voters with the means to gain information about politics and express their opinions – whether at the polls or in other fora – democratic institutions should promote all three of these links. Voters have every incentive to punish or reward politicians according to their performance and to select and advocate their preferred policy directions, because then they can achieve the kind of government they desire. As long as voters are doing these things, politicians who wish to attain or retain office have every incentive to respond to voters' demands and to follow through on their programs. One would thus expect all of these links to be strong in a democracy.

Yet this outcome does not always happen, as Havel's diagnosis attests. Voters may be too ignorant of politics or incapable of acquiring enough information to adequately sanction and select their rulers. Politics may be in such flux that accountability targets are hard to find, public preferences nonexistent or unknowable, and campaign promises impossible to fulfill. Politicians for their part may choose to ignore the public, even if it costs them at the polls, or build support through alternative means like charisma. Trade-offs may also exist between these linkages: responding to current preferences may mean ignoring some election promises, and using the vote as a sanctioning mechanism may be at odds with using it as a selection mechanism. Democracy in the sense of democratic institutions does not always lead to popular rule.

1.3. WHY CARE ABOUT DEMOCRATIC QUALITY?

Does it matter whether the people rule? Recently critics have begun to express worries about the global expansion of democracy. Fareed Zakaria (2003: 248) writes, "What we need in politics today is not more democracy, but less."

Such critics doubt the ability of popular control to produce beneficial policies. High-quality democracy may not be a cure for the real problems that citizens face – whether poverty, disease, or physical safety – and may even make these problems worse. Is a focus on linkages then a diversion from the real issues and real problems of the current world?

Let me first lay out the critique. Even a high-quality democracy as defined here can produce disastrous policies. The reason is not the fecklessness of politicians – after all, in a high-quality democracy they are responsive to voters – but the incompetence of citizens. Many policies that promote human welfare are unpopular, hard to understand, or have short-run costs. As a result, citizens tend to oppose them and embrace populist fixes (Blinder 1997, Caplan 2006, Delli Carpini and Keeter 1996, Przeworski 1991). Indeed, a society might benefit from weakening linkages so that politicians are free to pursue "better" policies. The claim is that the ultimate test of a political system is whether it provides substantive representation – policies that serve the best interests of citizens – rather than popular control per se.

Several responses can be made to this critique. The simplest is that the study of democratic quality is a positive, not a normative, endeavor. Quality refers to the nature of democratic governance, not its worth.[6] Whatever the advisability of democratic quality, scholars wish to know what effect democratic institutions have. Despite the fears of critics, democracy is not only spreading to new countries but deepening in established democracies. As a result, understanding how democracy works is essential for making sense of politics in the world today. It may turn out that high quality is tantamount to poor policies, but it is important to know where and when high-quality democracy emerges to make this inference.

It is possible, however, to mount a stronger defense of popular control. Although this book remains agnostic on this defense until more evidence comes in, it does take seriously the possibility that high quality may be a good in itself. In the first place, evidence exists that citizens, especially in the aggregate, possess considerable wisdom about policy. If uninformed citizens choose among issue positions at random, their opinions should cancel each other and allow a small group of well-informed citizens to carry the day (Page and Shapiro 1992, Surowiecki 2004, but see Althaus 2003). Other studies show that citizens use heuristics and shortcuts to make good choices even when information is limited (Lupia and McCubbins 1998). Some evidence suggests that, even in complicated policy domains like foreign policy, citizens' opinions may be as reasonable as those of experts (Page and Bouton 2006).

Naturally, worries about the public are greater in new democracies, where citizens have less experience with politics and less access to unbiased information. Yet, even in these countries, there is cause for hope. In the first place, the excitement of the transition along with the high stakes of decisions may lead

[6] Although the phrases "high quality" and "low quality" have the appearance of value judgments, they are in fact empirical ones that rest on objective assessments of the strength of linkages.

citizens to become more informed about relevant policy choices. Moreover, the experience of dictatorship teaches citizens to be skeptical of the overblown claims and government propaganda through which they suffered for so many years.

This is not to say that the public is always "rational"; citizens are surely prone to hold false beliefs. But, even if these biases do exist, it is an open question of whether they are larger than the biases of rulers, particularly those unhinged from democratic control. A lack of popular control could certainly free expert politicians to pursue policies in the public interest, but it would also allow them to produce policies in their own personal interests. The course of mostly nondemocratic human history suggests that the latter path is more likely. Recent studies have in fact debunked the view that citizens are prone to manias and instead found that extremism is typically ignited by elites looking to improve their own fortunes (Bermeo 2003, Snyder and Ballentine 1996). The dangers of nonresponsiveness appear at least as large as the dangers of responsiveness.

Even if one grants that autonomous politicians could produce better policies, popular control may still provide a net benefit by increasing the legitimacy of rulers. Insofar as politicians ignore the preferences of the public, citizens lose confidence in the political system. Although this might lead citizens to simply tune out, it may also encourage antisystemic political activities like violence or riots or avoidance of beneficial actions like community service or paying taxes. Even if popular control produces some poor outcomes, it may help to avoid even worse outcomes by increasing the perceived legitimacy of collective decisions.

A final line of defense emphasizes one linkage in particular: electoral accountability. At the least, democratic quality implies that citizens remove leaders who perform particularly poorly and abuse the public trust. Indeed, fewer doubts exist about the ability of the public to throw the bums out than about the other linkages. Though detestable leaders have sometimes been able to win democratic elections, they have rarely, if ever, been able to win reelection in competitive contests. Although accountability has its downsides, little doubt exists that it limits the scope of true disasters.

Again, this is not to say that democratic quality is the be all and end all of political life in a democracy. Citizens of countries with low democratic quality may lead satisfying lives, and high quality is no guarantee against poor policy choices, sometimes with major consequences. Nevertheless, an important case can be made for popular control and, even absent that case, the empirical study of quality is necessary to provide a better understanding of the political system that for all its warts holds pride of place in today's world.

1.4. METHODOLOGY

This book uses a diverse set of tools to evaluate the quality of democracy. Three aspects of its methodology are worth comments: the use of mixed methods, the selection of cases, and the choice of policy domains. Although details about specific techniques and data sources are reserved for the empirical chapters where they can be described in context, this section describes the general methodology at work here.

1.4.1. Mixed Methods

This book follows the recent trend in political science of mixed methods research (Brady and Collier 2004, Lin and Loftis 2005). It uses both statistical methods to assess trends across a larger group of countries and structured, focused comparisons of a smaller number of cases. The justification for this approach is that it leads to better and richer causal inferences. The inferences are better because, if different techniques using different data produce the same conclusion, one can be more certain that the conclusion is valid. The inferences are richer because each method provides inferences about different aspects of democratic linkages.

Gerring (2004) has been the most eloquent writer on the relative benefits of the two methods. Large-N statistical analyses have the virtues of generalizability and identification of genuine causal effects. By looking at the full range of variation across a given dependent variable, these analyses can best identify the direction and magnitude of causal effects. Insofar as the goal is to assess the quality of democracy in Eastern Europe as a whole, a natural way to do this is to look at the full range of cases.

Eastern Europe is a particularly appropriate region for this sort of analysis. All of the countries transitioned to democracy at about the same time and faced a common set of external constraints. Without ignoring the diversity of communist and precommunist regimes in the region, very large internal similarities existed between these countries before 1989. In fact, due to the forced imposition of the Soviet model, they were probably more alike than any other group of countries in the world. As such, they present a particularly striking natural experiment that makes region-wide comparisons rewarding, as many others have found (Fish 1998, Frye 2002).

The statistical analyses, however, are incomplete in a number of ways. The necessity of dealing with a larger number of cases means that less attention can be paid to the development of valid concepts. Instead, the researcher has to rely on off-the-shelf indicators rather than ones that better fit the concept at hand with the attendant danger of conceptual stretching (Sartori 1970). The larger number of cases also risks the problem of comparing apples and oranges – or unit homogeneity, in technical terms. Perhaps most seriously, these analyses leave one without a good sense of what is actually happening within the countries at hand.

Case studies remedy many of these problems. In the first place, they provide "detail, richness, completeness, wholeness," without which a researcher has little sense of what is actually happening (Gerring 2004: 348). Indeed, it is hard to imagine that one could be persuaded that citizens control their rulers without considering the way politicians and citizens perceive and resolve particular controversies. This point is particularly important for democratic quality, where intentionality is central to the concept: are citizens trying to control politicians and are politicians listening to them?

In the same way, the case studies help to elucidate mechanisms connecting cause and effect (George and Bennett 2005: 21, Gerring 2004: 348). Although the statistical analyses may have uncovered genuine causal effects, scholars are interested not just in the direction and magnitude of effects but also in how they function. What, for example, are the mechanisms through which politicians respond to public opinion? Is it fear of electoral retribution or corporatist structures of interest intermediation or transmission belts within political parties? Detailed studies of individual cases also provide more guarantees that the indicators actually represent the concept at hand and indeed help researchers create both better indicators and better concepts (Goertz 2006).

One should not forget that case studies suffer from their own problems. It is difficult to choose cases that represent the full range of outcomes; therefore, inferences may be biased. It is also difficult to weigh the influence of a multiplicity of causes with this restricted variance. Combining case studies with statistical analyses, however, allows each method to correct the flaws of the other. The statistical analyses identify the average causal effects that apply across the region, whereas the case studies show how these effects work in practice and guard against spurious inferences.

1.4.2. Case Selection

The mixed method approach requires case selection at two levels – the larger set of cases for statistical analysis and the smaller set for the case study approach. The countries chosen for the statistical analysis are the ten Eastern European countries that had joined the EU by 2007: Bulgaria, the Czech Republic, Estonia, Hungary, Latvia, Lithuania, Poland, Romania, Slovakia, and Slovenia.

The reason for focusing on these countries is that they are the only ones in the region that have remained consistently democratic during the transition. A study of democratic quality only makes sense in countries that are procedurally democratic. In Eastern Europe, it was these states that quickly overthrew the communist regime and instituted elections widely regarded as democratic by organizations like Freedom House and Polity.[7] The two minor exceptions to this rule were Romania at the start of the transition and Slovakia in the mid-1990s, when allegations of authoritarian practices had some traction, but these interludes passed fairly quickly. More telling is that all of these countries had democratized enough to enter the EU, albeit Bulgaria and Romania were part of a second wave of expansion two years after the first. This sample of ten countries represents nearly the universe of democratic experience in Eastern Europe and certainly the universe of consistent democratic experience.

The case studies focus on three countries: the Czech Republic, Hungary, and Poland. It would be difficult to call these countries representative of the region

[7] Freedom House (2005) rated nine of the ten as "fully free" as early as 1991.

as a whole. They have widely been regarded as the leaders of the transition. They were the first to free themselves of communist rule and did so in a peaceful and negotiated way. All three quickly became models for the transition, adopting democratic institutions quickly and largely painlessly. As a result, they were at the forefront of accession to the EU and always composed its first wave.

In all of these senses, the three countries were somewhat atypical of the transition. Yet, this atypicality serves a purpose. On the practical side, because these countries have had the longest experience as consolidated democracies, they have provided the most evidence of how new democracies function. Similarly, the three quickly moved beyond the basic institutional reforms necessary for establishing a democratic capitalist system. As such they provide a better gauge of how "normal" politics works in the region.

More important, the similarities among these countries improve causal inferences. In the first place, the assumption of unit homogeneity can be more plausibly maintained. These three countries are far more similar to each other than to other states in the region. They share such important characteristics as levels of economic and human development, distance from the West, and relations with the EU. They also share much of the same history, whether in the deeper past under Habsburg rule or more recently as similarly positioned satellite states of the Soviet Union (Ekiert 1996).[8] These similarities also provide a way of excluding a number of potentially important causal variables from the analysis – an imperative given the limited number of cases.

1.4.3. Policy Domains

Because linkages relate public preferences with policy choices and outcomes, it is necessary to focus on particular choices and outcomes. Three domains are given particular attention in this book, though others are mentioned at certain points. These three domains are economic reform, pension policy, and housing policy.

The statistical analyses focus mostly on economic policy – the nature of economic reform and its effects on the macroeconomy. Economic policy is chosen for a number of reasons. In the first place is its salience in the region. Economic reform – defined as the liberalization and privatization of the state-run economy – was one of the first issues on the agenda of policy makers in the region and remained near the top at least until accession to the EU. It was also at the forefront of voters' minds. Economic reforms had massive effects, causing not only economic decline, inflation, and unemployment but also large sectoral shifts, rising inequality, and the end of traditional securities. The salience of these changes was reflected in political debates. Kitschelt et al. (1999: 389) note that "the centrality of conflict over economic reform,

[8] It is no surprise that many studies have chosen these countries for closer comparisons. See, for example, Orenstein (2001), Seleny (2006), and Stark and Bruszt (1998).

the divide between social protectionists and market liberals, is common to all postcommunist democracies."

Economic reforms and outcomes are also a useful domain because of their comparability. Statistics on economic outcomes are available with a fair degree of reliability for all countries and years in the sample. Comparable data exist even on the policy choices of governments. Because these countries adhered to a common communist model – albeit with some variations – they began their reforms at a similar baseline, further aiding comparison. Finally, considerable variation in economic reforms and outcomes existed across even this limited sample, which provides a basis for causal inference (Murrell 1996).

But these basic economic reforms were unique in ways that may limit what they can say about democratic quality in the region. They were often referred to as first-generation reforms because they set the basic structure of the economy and could then be ignored. They also took place in a distinctive environment. Many were adopted during a period of "extraordinary politics" (Balcerowicz 1994), characterized by public euphoria over the fall of communism and large uncertainty about interests, which granted politicians considerable leeway in formulating policy. The period was also marked by economic crisis, which often compelled particular policy choices. These choices, moreover, followed fairly clear guidelines set down by international institutions and the conventional wisdom of the economics profession (Williamson 1989). For all these reasons, the first generation of reforms might be expected to elicit distinctive and perhaps unrepeatable political dynamics.[9]

This is why the case studies focus on second-generation reforms that took place under circumstances more typical of future politics in these countries. Reforms of pension and housing policy were not one-time changes but have continually been the object of negotiation since the start of the transition. They were implemented under political conditions that look more like "ordinary" politics. Similarly significant is that choices in these areas were not dictated by international institutions or external pressures. Indeed, considerable doubts exist about best practice in all of them as evidenced by the variety of social policy models on offer within the EU alone. These policy areas also raise issues about the relationships between the state and market, which are at the heart of politics in all democracies and allow comparisons between politics in these countries and elsewhere.

As with economic reform, substantial differences in pension and housing policy choices across even this limited sample aid causal inference. Hungary and Poland partially privatized their pension systems, whereas the Czech Republic did not. Hungary undertook a massive housing privatization scheme, whereas the Czech Republic and Poland preserved a substantial public sector. These variations provide a good basis for drawing causal inferences about the

[9] These considerations of course do not make these reforms less worthy of study. Because of their importance it is essential to know how they took place. They do, however, limit what they can say about the general strength of linkages.

causes of the outcomes and therefore the existence or nonexistence of popular control.

1.5. THE CAUSES OF DEMOCRATIC QUALITY

The third question this book addresses is the cause of democratic quality. Why does democratic quality take the form it does in these countries? Because the study of democratic quality is relatively new, no standard set of theories exists to explain the relative strength of linkages. Scholars have long debated why countries become democratic (Geddes 1999), but a similar debate over the causes of democratic quality has yet to crystallize. Although this study was not initially designed to investigate this issue and is limited by its focus on Eastern Europe, it does at least try to provide an initial sounding of the roots of democratic quality.

This book considers five explanations for democratic quality. The first is authoritarian legacies. Communist regimes were among the most thorough dictatorships in the way that they tried to reshape society and even create a new type of man – what came to be called Homo sovieticus. It is more than likely that forty years of such attempts in these ten countries left some residue that would affect postcommunist politics (Bunce 1999, Kitschelt et al. 1999, Linz and Stepan 1996).

Most of these legacies should have a negative effect on democratic quality (Barany and Volgyes 1995). Communist repression produced citizens characterized by apathy toward politics, feelings of learned helplessness, and distrust of their fellow citizens (Jowitt 1992, Marody 1990, Schöpflin 1993). Similar worries existed about the political realm. Few prewar political parties survived communism and de novo parties had weak reputations and few ties to citizens. The individuals who led these new formations were moreover unschooled in the arts of compromise and accommodation necessary to democratic politics; instead their main experiences were with top-down control and following orders. In short, communist regimes left relatively poor soil from which democratic quality could grow.

A second explanation, with similar predictions, turns to the constraints of the transition. Offe (1991) calls it the triple transition because countries had to reconstruct political, economic, and state institutions, a daunting set of tasks for any country. Particularly salient for democratic quality was the economic transition. Largely as a result of communist rule, these countries entered the postcommunist era with their economies in a shambles. Not only did they have to pay back loans they took under communism and beg for new loans with the requisite strings attached, but they had to do so while suffering massive recessions with gross domestic product dropping by an order of one-fifth. Together these factors limited politicians' room for maneuver and, hence, the ability of citizens to control their actions (Greskovits 1998). EU integration could have similar effects as politicians came under pressure to implement EU policies rather than the policies desired by citizens (Vachudova 2005).

A third explanation draws more on existing work on democratization. It hypothesizes that socioeconomic modernization – the extent to which societies consist of educated, urbanized, middle-class citizens – affects the ability of citizens to control their rulers (Huntington 1991, Lipset 1959, 1994, Przeworski et al. 2000). Such citizens are more likely both to desire responsive government and to have the capabilities to select, sanction, and influence politicians. To a large extent, communist regimes succeeded in modernizing their societies. Education levels were high; a large portion of the population worked in skilled occupations and led middle-class lifestyles. These societies were also highly egalitarian – differences in wealth were small – which should limit the ability of a single class to dominate politics and give more power to the median voter. In short, citizens had the structural capacities to be effective citizens if they so chose.

A fourth explanation, however, emphasizes one aspect of postcommunist society that should limit democratic quality. Several recent scholars have posited that a strong and vibrant civil society is necessary for democracy to function (Putnam 1992, 2000). Civil society refers to the voluntary organizations that citizens join, from PTAs to sports clubs. They are hypothesized to create the tolerance, public-spiritedness, and organization that allow citizens to monitor politics and communicate their opinions to politicians. Largely as a consequence of communist legacies and transition constraints, civil society was extremely weak in Eastern Europe (Howard 2002). Communist regimes had almost completely eliminated civil society and tainted the very idea through forced mobilization of citizens in regime-sponsored organizations. The economic hardships of the transition further stood in the way of concerted civic action. This weakness should in turn have limited the ability of mass publics to control their rulers.

Finally, a number of scholars have found that political institutions affect democratic quality (Powell 2000). In particular, countries with institutions like proportional representation and multiparty systems tend to have stronger mandate responsiveness because they give citizens wider choices among party alternatives. Such systems, however, have only weak electoral accountability because it is unclear which party is responsible for policy outcomes. Conversely, majoritarian electoral laws and two-party systems limit mandate responsiveness because of the lack of choice over alternative programs, but they encourage electoral accountability because of the clear assignment of responsibility to the government. Although institutional explanations do not predict generally higher or lower levels of quality – both allow for popular control though in different ways – they do predict different types of control depending on a country's institutional configuration. As the postcommunist democracies have mainly chosen proportional institutional forms, they should fit that pattern.

1.6. FINDINGS

What are the answers to the empirical questions posed in this book? Rather than keep the reader in suspense, this section previews the main results. The headline finding is that democracy in Eastern Europe is working better than many scholars had expected. Politicians take considerable pains to try to please the public, and citizens are very capable of punishing politicians for poor performance. Although these findings are not universal, they do show up under some difficult tests. Reasonable levels of policy responsiveness and electoral accountability do, however, coexist with less positive results on mandate responsiveness, where citizens cannot expect politicians to present clear programs or to follow through on their campaign promises.

These results emerge most clearly in the statistical analyses of ten countries. The electoral performance of incumbents is strongly predicted by their economic performance. Governments that produced poor outcomes consistently did poorly in elections. Policy responsiveness also shows up clearly in the large-N analyses. Most impressive is the way that the pace of economic reforms followed public opinion quite closely. This outcome came as a surprise given that economic reforms are widely seen as incompatible with responsiveness because they cause intense social pain. The fact that responsiveness showed up specifically in this issue area and at an early point in the transition provides convincing evidence that politicians do try to follow public opinion.

To a large extent the case studies supported these results. On some of the key policy decisions in housing and pensions, politicians made choices in line with public preferences. This result may not seem surprising – politicians are known to step carefully in matters of social policy (Pierson 1994) – but it gains in interest when one considers the divergent paths taken by these countries. It is not just that politicians try to preserve the welfare state, as has been found in the established democracies (Brooks and Manza 2007). In fact, sometimes politicians cut back on the welfare state by privatizing housing or pensions and do so in responsive ways.

Policy responsiveness was not perfect. Politicians did sometimes engage in benefit cuts that citizens did not want. That they did so is not very surprising considering the economic straits in which they found themselves. Yet, this nonresponsiveness can be partially reconciled with democratic quality. In the first place, such cuts are typically characterized by nonresponsiveness in established democracies. Second, most of these cuts were accompanied by attempts to meet the public halfway – unpopular policies were watered down, postponed, and put into place only gradually. Whereas a cynical interpretation would note that politicians engaged in these tactics to deflect blame – which is surely true – such tactics are also common in established democracies and reflect a political class which does take the public seriously. The electoral connection matters for these politicians.

If a place exists where quality falls short, it is on mandate responsiveness. Compared to the established democracies – and here cross-regional data can be brought to bear – postcommunist party systems offered voters choices that were less clear and distinctive. Turning to specific promises, I found that they frequently went unfulfilled, and important policy changes were no where to be found in election programs. Although citizens could sanction politicians ex post for their performance and influence them in real time, they had a difficult time controlling them ex ante by selecting from among different programs.

What explains the relative strength of these linkages? The explanation most consistent with these results is socioeconomic modernization. It is the only explanation that predicts both the general strength of linkages and the particular strength of policy responsiveness. Just as theorists like Lipset (1959) predicted, societies with literate, educated, media-savvy citizens and relatively equitable distributions of wealth are best equipped to demand responsive and accountable governments. It is not just high incomes that matters here – in fact incomes dropped substantially during the transition – but a degree of agency among citizens and the capacity to understand politics and act on these understandings.

Modernization naturally is not enough to overcome all of the legacies of communism, nor is it sufficient in itself to produce democratic quality. The utter destruction of political society by communist regimes, for example, contributed to the weakness of mandate responsiveness. Modernization also depended on the introduction and maintenance of modern democratic institutions, which provided the incentives for responsiveness and accountability.[10] Yet, it does help to explain why the transition to democracy and markets in these countries went so much more smoothly than expected and why these countries weathered their transitions better than many countries in Latin America, which suffered from lower levels of education, wider gulfs between rich and poor, and greater existential poverty (Bunce 2001). The people who were able to engineer the people's revolutions in 1989 also proved capable of creating real democracies after 1989.

1.7. ORGANIZATION

The remainder of the book is organized as follows. Chapter 2 probes in detail the concept of democratic quality. It argues that the distinctive characteristic of democracy is institutions that allow citizens to influence their government and that an assessment of democratic quality should thus look at how citizens are linked to their government. The chapter then focuses on the nature of the three linkages: the ways they promote citizen rule, their virtues and vices, and possible interactions among them.

The empirical evidence on the quality of democracy begins in Part II of the book. The three chapters in this part present statistical evidence on the quality of democracy across the region. Chapter 3 considers whether incumbents are held accountable for their performance in office at election time. Chapter 4 looks at mandate responsiveness by evaluating both the clarity and the distinctiveness of election programs and the correspondence between programs and economic policy. Chapter 5 evaluates policy responsiveness, focusing in particular on the relation between public opinion and economic reform.

[10] Pressure from the EU to maintain democracy surely helped also.

Part III presents case studies of social policy in three countries. Chapter 6 focuses on pension policy – both changes in the parameters of the existing system and the decision to privatize. Chapter 7 considers several aspects of housing policy, including the pace of privatization and the regulation of rents. These studies focus mainly on policy responsiveness. They consider a wide variety of indicators that show whether politicians are listening to the public.

Part IV draws conclusions. Chapter 8 investigates the causes of democratic quality. Why do these countries have the type and degree of linkages that they do? Although data limit the reliability of this exercise, this chapter uses a set of three comparisons to draw preliminary inferences on the causes of quality.

Chapter 9 ties the results together and points the way forward. It probes the interactions between linkages, the nature of policy responsiveness, and the mechanisms through which citizens control their government. It also poses the larger question of whether governments in the region are substantively representative – does higher quality democracy mean a better life for citizens?

PART I

CONCEPTUAL ANALYSIS

2

Assessing the Quality of Democracy

For more than two decades, from the Carnation Revolution in Portugal to the Velvet Revolutions in Eastern Europe and beyond, the field of comparative politics has been preoccupied with the question of democratic transitions. The main issues are now well known: What factors lead a country to become democratic? Are transitions a product of social and economic changes or are they influenced by fortuitous events and strategic choices? And what, if anything, can the established democracies do to promote democracy around the world? So powerful was the paradigm that it even received its own name: transitology.

Although this research program has had its critics, its successes should not be overlooked. Studies of democratization have yielded a large number of powerful and subtle results derived from both large-N quantitative analyses and detailed case studies of individual transitions and nontransitions (Geddes 1999). Indeed, it would be hard to name a research program in comparative politics that has been as successful as the one looking into the causes of democracy and, more recently, the reasons for its persistence.

This chapter considers an unspoken assumption that underlies this paradigm. The assumption is that a transition to democracy inevitably leads to better political and social outcomes.[1] Promoting democracy means promoting better public policies, less corruption, and, central to the argument of this book, more responsive and accountable rulers.

The assumption is not ungrounded. Free and fair elections give leaders a powerful incentive to produce better policy. Failure to satisfy voters in a democracy typically costs politicians their jobs. By contrast, dictators can stay in office while presiding over disaster. Although democracy cannot be expected

[1] It would be unfair to say that most scholars explicitly endorsed this assumption. Although some bright-eyed democracy enthusiasts probably existed, political scientists on the whole tended to more sober assessments. The point is rather that the enormous energy put into this research program must have been inspired by such a normative vision.

to produce miracles overnight, one would expect a qualitative change in policy making as a country moved from unelected to elected leaders.

As the new democracies of the Third Wave mature, this assumption has come under the magnifying glass. Although a large number of these transitioning countries continue to hold free and fair elections, they also suffer from a variety of ills. Prominent among them are the weak entrenchment of the rule of law, high levels of public corruption, and serious economic problems. These problems have disappointed not just scholars but also citizens of the new democracies themselves, who in some cases have expressed skepticism about whether their transitions were worthwhile.[2]

These failures have led an emerging group of scholars to study what has been termed the quality of democracy. The idea is both a normative one (finding the correct standards for assessing the functioning of a democracy) and an empirical one (determining how democracies actually work and the degree to which they live up to these standards). This book falls squarely in this field of study. It asks whether democracy is doing what it should be doing in the new democracies in Eastern Europe. It puts forward a set of standards for assessing democratic quality and asks how well they are fulfilled. The aim of this chapter is to examine extant work on the quality of democracy and describe the conception of quality that guides the remainder of the book.

2.1. WHAT IS DEMOCRACY?

To assess the quality of democracy, it is first necessary to establish what democracy is. Democracy means the rule of the people. Democratic systems differ from others in that citizens have a central role to play in governing the polity. The fundamental principle of democracy is that ordinary citizens have an institutionalized place in governance.

This fundamental principle, however, leaves some questions unanswered. How exactly do the people rule? Until modern times, democracy meant the sort of institutions that prevailed in ancient Athens: citizens voted directly on policies and offices were filled by lot. Although a few might still endorse these principles, the scale of modern life makes them all but impracticable. Today's society is too large and specialized for citizens to gather and decide public issues in a public forum, and most citizens cannot easily put aside their careers to serve in government, nor do they have the skills to do so.[3]

Although debate still continues on the nature of democracy in the modern world, this book follows the procedural conception of democracy that has come to dominate political science. Developed by Joseph Schumpeter (1943) and given its most complete expression by Robert Dahl (1971), this conception

[2] Some of this disappointment can be attributed to asymmetries in the assessments of democracies and dictatorships. Because democracies are more open and transparent than dictatorships, their flaws are also more visible and criticism more abundant.

[3] For an argument that much higher levels of participation are still possible, see Barber (1984).

sees democracy as a set of procedures that allows citizens to select their leaders in a competitive process.

In this view democracy is founded on two main institutions. The first is free, fair, and regular elections for a country's most powerful policy makers, in which all adult citizens are allowed to participate on an equal basis, both as voters and as candidates. The second is a broad set of civil rights that allows these citizens to produce and obtain the information they need to participate effectively in these elections. As Huntington (1991: 7) puts it, a system is "democratic to the extent that its most powerful collective decision makers are elected through fair, honest, and periodic elections in which candidates freely compete for votes and in which virtually all the adult population is eligible to vote."[4]

I use this definition for two reasons. The first is its relative objectivity. Because it focuses on institutionalized procedures, outside observers can usually agree on whether a country is in fact democratic. Indeed, a variety of organizations and individuals use variants of this definition to rate whether countries are democratic and to a large extent have produced similar ratings (Goertz 2006). This achievement is not trivial in a world where the cachet of democracy is so high that virtually all countries regard themselves as democratic in some way or another. However, this is not to ignore the difficulties of recognizing whether elections are "free" and "fair" and citizens have "enough" freedom, but rather to say that this definition yields more reliable results than other definitions.

This objectivity is important because it makes little sense to evaluate the quality of democracy in nondemocratic countries. I call a country democratic if it meets a certain minimum threshold, and I use the rankings of organizations like Freedom House (2005) and Polity (Marshall and Jaggers 2001) to instantiate this decision. These rankings identify ten countries from Eastern Europe that have held recognizably free elections and upheld basic civil rights since the early 1990s. I exclude most of the former Soviet republics and successor states to Yugoslavia from my purview because they do not meet these standards.[5]

The second reason for using this definition relates to the study of democratic quality. By defining democracy as a set of institutions, I can begin to ask how it does and should work. As the literature known as the New Institutionalism has repeatedly shown, institutions create incentives that constrain, enable, and shape actions (Hall and Taylor 1996, Thelen 1999). By viewing democracy as a set of institutions, I can begin to see what sort of outcomes it is meant to promote and what outcomes it actually does promote.

Before moving on, I wish to respond to one objection to this conception of democracy. Some scholars have criticized the procedural definition as representing mere electoralism – an exclusive focus on choice in elections to the exclusion of other equally important values or institutions (Karl 1986).

[4] A more complete and analytic version of this definition can be found in Dahl (1989: 212).

[5] I do, however, consider the Baltic states and Slovenia.

Elections alone, they note, may coexist with high levels of lawlessness, corruption, and ineffective rule that are seen as incompatible with the ideal of the people ruling that is embodied in democracy. Some have proposed adding such conditions as rule of law and accountability to the definition of democracy (Schmitter and Karl 1991).

This critique is correct in the sense that free elections are not a cure-all for a society's ills. The problem is that adding these elements to a definition of democracy comes at the expense of understanding. Constructing a definition of democracy that includes, say, rule-of-law considerations produces a more varied palette for assessing democracies but masks the relations between concepts like elections and rule of law. The virtue of a parsimonious definition of democracy is that it leaves open the most interesting questions in comparative politics. Does democracy promote the rule of law or function better in its presence? A broader definition of democracy obscures these questions. Scholars end up producing competing ratings of how democratic a country is rather than asking what factors promote democracy and what the consequences of democracy are.[6]

2.2. FROM DEMOCRACY TO DEMOCRATIC QUALITY

Given this conception of democracy, how should one define its quality? Although the phrase "quality of democracy" has recently become popular, as shown in the previous chapter, few have ventured a clear definition of it. Gerardo Munck (2001: 129) notes in a recent review article that "[t]he key flaw with the concept of democratic quality is that it is simply unclear what it means. Indeed, the concept peppers the discussion in the literature without ever being clearly defined." In most cases, scholars skip the stage of conceptual elaboration and jump directly to indicators.

Moreover, given the high normative cachet of democracy, there is a tendency to equate democracy with all good things about a society. Thus, some accounts of democratic quality conceive it as a checklist of all social, political, and economic desiderata or, more commonly, as a checklist of potential undesirable outcomes that should be avoided (see, for example, Beetham et al. 2002, USAID 1998). These approaches, however, do not produce a clearly delimited concept. Without a conceptual anchor to hold these desiderata together, democratic quality expands until it covers just about any aspect of politics and society on which citizens or scholars have an opinion.

[6] As Samuel Huntington (1991: 9–10) puts it, "Elections, open, free, and fair, are the essence of democracy, the inescapable sine qua non. Government produced by elections may be inefficient, corrupt, shortsighted, irresponsible, dominated by special interests and incapable of adopting policies demanded by the public good. These qualities make such a government undesirable, but they do not make it undemocratic. Democracy is one public virtue, not the only one, and the relation of democracy to other public virtues and vices can only be understood if democracy is clearly distinguished from other characteristics of political systems."

A coherent concept of democratic quality should abide by two principles. First, it needs to distinguish democratic quality from democracy itself. Considerable research has gone into developing indicators to determine whether a country is democratic (Goertz 2006). Democratic quality, however, should be measured on a different scale from democracy itself. An assessment of democratic quality presumes that a country is already a democracy and then goes on to say something about how it functions. Measures developed to determine the existence or degree of democracy should not be used to assess how well these democracies are working. Indeed, such a transposition would lead to absurd claims, like calling China a low-quality democracy. A concept of democratic quality should go beyond a determination of whether democracy exists.

Second, because the concept is specifically of democratic quality, it should apply to an aspect of politics that is unique to democracies rather than applicable to all regime types. After all, the concept is of the quality of democracy, not the quality of governance in a country that happens to be democratic. For example, one would not want to judge the quality of a democracy by its level of prosperity because this measure could just as easily and justifiably be used to assess nondemocracies. Although economic development may improve the lives of citizens in a democracy, it arguably does the same for authoritarian regimes. Nothing about development is essential to democratic processes per se. The concept of democratic quality should focus on those aspects of politics that are intimately related to democracy itself.

I argue that this aspect of democracy is popular rule. The essence of democracy is that citizens have an institutionalized place in determining policy. Indeed, the main justification for democracy is precisely that all citizens have an inherent right to participate in binding collective decisions (Dahl 1989, 1998).[7] Whereas definitions of democracy describe the procedures that allow citizens to rule, assessments of the quality of democracy should go further and ask whether these institutions are doing what they are intended to do. In other words, democracy is a set of formal possibilities for citizen rule; democratic quality assesses whether citizen rule exists. Are citizens controlling their government or are they being ruled? I call this conception quality as linkages.

2.3. EXISTING STUDIES OF DEMOCRATIC QUALITY

Before considering this conception in more depth, I wish to return to existing conceptions of democratic quality. Although existing works do sometimes follow these principles, they often do not; instead they confuse democracy with

[7] Two other less common justifications exist for democracy. One advocates democracy because it produces better policy outcomes than other forms of government. Whether this is true remains an open question and thus constitutes a fragile defense (Przeworski and Limongi 1993). The other argues that citizens realize their true being through participation in collective decision making (Barber 1984). This view is more controversial and may not be practical under modern circumstances.

democratic quality, they apply to all regime types rather than simply democracies, and they do not focus on the essential core of democracy as popular rule through particular institutions. In short, they are not concepts of specifically democratic quality.

Although precisely defined conceptions of democratic quality are thin on the ground, one can make some progress in unpacking the implicit concepts behind existing works by considering their empirical referents. Because most studies provide a list of the dimensions of quality and often their empirical indicators, it is possible to identify what concept underpins these elements.

Table 2.1 presents the main empirical referents in several prominent studies of the quality of democracy (though not all of the studies use the term democratic quality). In Goertz's (2006) terms, these indicators are the secondary level (or sometimes even the indicator level) of the concept; the primary level is usually, but not always, left vague. These works are referred to in the discussion that follows.

Existing works, in fact, use three different conceptions of quality in addition to the quality as linkages approach that I advocate. I call these conceptions quality as procedures, quality as preconditions, and quality as societal outcomes. All of them are undoubtedly important, but none corresponds to the implications of the phrase "democratic quality."[8] Rather than asking about the consequences of democratic institutions for rule by the people – my conception of democratic quality – they focus instead on whether democracy exists, what is needed for democracy to work well, and whether public policies achieve a particular conception of human welfare.

2.3.1. Quality as Procedures

Procedural quality may be the most familiar way of studying gradations in democracy. It begins with the procedural definition of democracy mentioned earlier, but it also stops there. It asks to what degree elections are free and fair and if civil rights are genuinely protected.

Whereas at first glance a focus on procedures leads to a clear break between countries that are democratic – they fulfill these criteria – and those that are not, most scholars recognize that there is a continuum. Some countries, for example, may allow competition between certain parties but not others. Or, as all democracies did in the past, they may restrict suffrage to only a certain class of citizens. Or, due to state controls, citizens may not have access to all relevant political information they need to make informed choices.

The existence of such gradations has led to a number of attempts to assess procedural quality. The best known of these attempts are the indices of democracy produced by Freedom House (2005) and Polity (Marshall and Jaggers 2001). These indices measure the degree to which elections are free and fair

[8] Scholars often combine all three of these standards with the conception of quality as linkages introduced later.

TABLE 2.1. *Existing Standards for Assessing Democratic Quality*

Altman and Pérez-Liñán (2002)	**Beetham et al. (2002)**	**Diamond and Morlino (2005)**	**Lijphart (1999)**	**O'Donnell (2004)**	**Putnam et al. (1994)**
Effective civil rights	Citizenship, law, and rights	Rule of law	Democracy	Elections	Policy process
Effective participation	Representative and accountable government	Participation	Women's representation	Government	Policy pronouncements
Effective competition	Civil society and popular participation	Competition	Political equality	Legal system	Policy implementation
	Democracy beyond the state	Vertical accountability	Electoral participation	State and government	
		Horizontal accountability	Satisfaction with democracy	Courts	
		Freedom	Government–voter proximity	State institutions	
		Equality	Corruption	Social context	
		Responsiveness	Popular cabinet support	Human development	
			Kinder and gentler qualities	Human rights	

and citizens are guaranteed particular civil rights (sometimes along with other desiderata).

Some scholars have used these scales as indicators of the quality of democracy. Thus, Altman and Pérez-Liñán (2002) produced a measure of effective civil rights that is equivalent to the Freedom House measure. These ratings are also employed in Lijphart's (1999) assessments of quality. Similar measures of other aspects of procedures are also common. For example, a number of studies (Altman and Pérez-Liñán 2002, Schmitter 2005) look at measures of voter turnout as an indication of quality, when turnout is to a large extent a consequence of electoral procedures.

The procedural account of quality has much to recommend it. It produces a fairly objective set of indicators to measure the quality of procedures (although see Bowman et al. 2005, Goertz 2006, Munck and Verkuilen 2002). Moreover, these indicators flow directly from a widely accepted definition of democracy. By focusing on objective, measurable, and widely held standards, this conception can command considerable support, and for this reason it has been widely adopted.

The main argument for not identifying this approach with the quality of democracy is that it is mainly concerned with determining whether democracy exists – whether a particular regime fits the definition of a democracy. It does not say how or how well democratic institutions work, only whether a country is a democracy. Indeed, it is for this reason that procedural measures of democracy are frequently used in a dichotomous way to distinguish democracies from nondemocracies (Przeworski et al. 2000).[9]

2.3.2. Quality as Preconditions

A second approach to assessing democratic quality starts from a more normative conception. Its concern is that, without certain preconditions, democratic procedures do not fulfill their promise. Their promise is construed in a variety of ways – for example, to maximize individual agency, equalize influence on policy, or promote human development.

To give an example, O'Donnell (2004) argues that, unless a country has achieved a certain level of human development, citizens are not able to exercise the agency on which democratic procedures are based; therefore, human development is a part of democratic quality. Likewise, Diamond and Morlino (2005: xv) justify including the rule of law as part of democratic quality, with the argument that, when the rule of law is weak,

> participation of the poor and marginalized is suppressed; individual freedoms are tenuous and fleeting; civic groups may be unable to organize and advocate; the resourceful and well-connected have vastly more access to justice and power; corruption and abuse of power run rampant as agencies of horizontal accountability are unable to function

[9] Most indicators of democracy suggest a cut point where democracy begins.

properly; political competition is distorted and unfair; voters have a hard time holding rulers to account; and thus, linkages vital to securing democratic responsiveness are disrupted and severed.

Among the most commonly cited preconditions are the already cited rule of law and human development (Beetham et al. 2002, Diamond and Morlino 2005, O'Donnell 2004), participation and civil society (Altman and Pérez-Liñán 2002, Diamond and Morlino 2005, Rose-Ackerman 2005), socioeconomic equality (Diamond and Morlino 2005, O'Donnell 2004), and corruption (O'Donnell 2004). Space prohibits a discussion of how these factors achieve the desired ends of democracy, but what they all do have in common is that they are seen as necessary for democratic procedures to work in the proper way or to produce certain desired outcomes.

These effects, however, are often assumed rather than shown. Although it seems more than plausible that greater economic inequality or less secure access to courts would diminish the influence of certain groups of citizens on elections and policy, the existence and, more important, the magnitude of these effects must always be carefully confirmed.[10] In addition, it is not implausible to think that a country without certain preconditions – a poor one, like India, or one with a weak civil society, like Hungary, or one with high levels of corruption, like Italy – might have a vibrant democracy.

In any case, although such preconditions quite likely affect the functioning of democracy (or any other regime for that matter) and are probably desirable in their own right, they are analytically distinct from democracy itself. The decisive objection to equating these factors with democratic quality is that they are only indirectly related to the central idea of democracy: the idea of the people ruling and the importance of elections and rights in allowing them to do so. They surely do affect how the people rule and how policy emerges, but they are not the democratic process itself. In short, these factors may affect democratic quality but they are not democratic quality.

2.3.3. Quality as Societal Outcomes

A third way of looking at democratic quality focuses on the policies or societal outcomes that democracies produce. Scholars typically pick an objective and presumably desirable outcome that they believe is broadly beneficial for citizens. Thus, they might evaluate the quality of a democracy by its rate of economic growth, the percentage of its citizens in prisons, or its level of corruption.

This conception also has much to recommend it. For many citizens the quality of their country's democracy is equivalent to the policies and outcomes it produces. Indeed, in standard theories of voting, citizens decide whom to vote

10 Furthermore, it is likely that conceiving of quality in this way ignores trade-offs. For example, overly aggressive efforts to reduce corruption are likely to have negative effects on civil rights. Strict adherence to the rule of law may limit the domain of democratic decision making.

for based on their assessment of past policies or their desired future policies (Downs 1957). If citizens judge democratic officials by their policy achievements or goals, then it is not amiss for scholars to judge them in the same way.

Measures of policy or outcome quality have become increasingly common in political science. One of the best-known recent efforts is Robert Putnam et al.'s (1994) rating of Italian regional governments based on measures of their policy process, policy pronouncements, and policy implementation.[11] Lijphart (1999) also favors outcome measures, although his measures, somewhat controversially, focus on the "kinder, gentler" side of democracy. Accordingly, he looks at such variables as welfare effort, environmental policies, incarceration, and foreign aid. Schmitter (2005: 20), who ostensibly focuses on accountability as a measure of democratic quality, in fact chooses indicators that are, in his own words, the "likely and desirable product of well-functioning democratic institutions." These indicators include electoral turnout, answers to survey questions about interest in politics, the extent of protests, and the timeliness of the passage of legislation.[12]

Although studies in this tradition may be among the most valuable in the social sciences – for they can potentially find ways to improve human welfare – it would be a mistake to associate them with the quality of democracy. One reason is that the outcomes they study are not specific to democracies. Most of Putnam and Lijphart's variables could just as easily be applied to nondemocracies as to democracies. Although it would be quixotic to assess how completely fraudulent elections affect popular rule (though see Blaydes 2007 and Gandhi 2004), it is certainly worthwhile to consider levels of social policy effort, economic growth, and corruption in nondemocracies.

A stronger reason for rejecting this approach is that democracy does not imply particular kinds of policy. It does imply a government that is responsive to citizens, but it leaves citizen preferences open. Although citizens likely do favor higher growth, they may wish to trade some growth for more environmental regulation. In such a case, economic growth in democracies might be lower than in dictatorships, but the quality of democracy is high because the government does what citizens want. Scholars can certainly make a case that some outcomes are unequivocally better than others, but, insofar as this is the case, democracy

[11] Although Putnam does not explicitly refer to democratic quality, his book's title, *Making Democracy Work*, indicates that it is his focus. Whereas most of Putnam's indicators are outcome variables in the sense described here, one – his measure of clientelist relations – fits more comfortably in the conception of quality as linkages.

[12] One may even include citizen assessments of the quality of their country's democracy in the category of outcome quality. Although these assessments should not be ignored, it is likely that citizens judge their democracy's quality more by the sort of standards I described earlier than by the extent to which it encourages rule by the people. See Cullel (2004) for the potential of such assessments.

loses its luster. If the correct policy is clear, it would make sense to adopt that policy and limit democracy as much as possible.[13]

2.4. QUALITY AS LINKAGES

None of the aforementioned conceptions in short follows the principles set out earlier: moving beyond democracy itself and addressing phenomena specific to democracies. I argue that conceiving of quality as linkages follows these principles. In this conception, the quality of democracy is equivalent to the degree to which citizens control their rulers or alternatively the strength of linkages between citizens and policy makers.[14] Strong linkages mean that citizens have greater influence on the behavior of politicians – they are controlling them – and so democratic quality is higher. Weak linkages imply that politicians pursue their own interests without regard for the public and that democratic quality is low.[15] To simplify somewhat, high quality is popular rule.

Focusing on popular rule fits the two criteria laid out earlier. First, it moves beyond democracy because it considers not just the existence of democratic institutions, but also how these institutions actually work. Do they promote citizen rule or not? It also focuses on an aspect of politics specific to democracies. Democracy is a system of government that institutionalizes popular influence through elections and civil rights. It makes sense, therefore, to ask whether popular influence does, in fact, exist in democracies. Do citizens use democratic institutions to control their rulers?

One may expect democratic institutions to automatically create strong linkages and popular rule. After all, elections and civil rights seemingly put citizens in charge. Thus, citizens should naturally use elections and civil rights to rid themselves of politicians who do not act in their interest, choose politicians who share their interests, and make their preferences and judgments known to public officials all the while. In doing these three things, they not only get the politicians they want, but they simultaneously give them an incentive to stay in touch with public preferences because this would be the only way to achieve and remain in office.

[13] One additional problem with this conception is that it easily blurs into the conception of quality as preconditions. As O'Donnell (2004) points out, many of the outcomes he wants democracy to provide are also preconditions for democracy to work well. He suggests that this duality leads to virtuous and vicious circles.

[14] This conception differs from the previous ones in conceiving of quality as a causal relationship rather than a simple scale and accords with the view of democracy as an institutionalized relationship between two groups – citizens and policy makers. Although one could assess the quality of democracy by focusing only on voters (e.g., through measures of participation or civil rights as studies in the quality-as-preconditions vein often do) or only on officials (e.g., through measures of policy outcomes as studies in the quality-as-societal-outcomes vein do), it is in keeping with the spirit of democracy to focus on both sides of the relationship.

[15] Strong linkages could also imply that politicians are controlling citizens rather than vice versa. The question of reverse causality is considered in Section 2.7.

But these consequences are far from inevitable. The superficially simple institutions of democracy can produce a variety of results. Although they can promote rule by the people and strong linkages, everything depends on how citizens and politicians actually use them.

Consider the ambiguous power of elections. On the positive side, citizens may use their vote to sanction incumbents for poor performance, to choose desired policy directions, or to select good character types. In these ways elections promote popular rule. They install policy makers that citizens prefer and give them incentives to act as citizens desire. But that is not the only way that elections may work. On the negative side, citizens may sell their vote for money or other goods or they may vote for charismatic ciphers (Schaffer 2007). If this happens, politicians have little reason to act in anyone's interest but their own. Politicians, for their part, can promote or confound these behaviors, on the one hand, by contesting elections on clear and distinct platforms or, on the other, by offering side payments, nominating celebrity candidates, or libeling their rivals.

Civil rights have similarly ambiguous effects. On the one hand, they may be used to exchange views about the best election choices and to monitor the actions of incumbents, behaviors which should keep politicians responsive to the public. On the other hand, wealthy citizens may form pressure groups that attempt to purchase policies through campaign contributions, or political leaders may try to demonize their rivals and incite ethnic hatred, to name just a couple of possibilities.[16]

Clearly, some of these behaviors enhance the rule of the people. That is, they produce policies close to what citizens want. Others do not. Elections and rights work as intended when they encourage politicians to consider the desires of citizens in formulating policy. By forcing politicians to submit themselves to voters' judgments at elections and to hear their complaints between elections, democracy ideally serves as a mechanism for ensuring that politicians follow the preferences of citizens. The danger in any political system, as Madison (Madison et al. 1987) pointed out, is that rulers may abuse their power for their own ends. Frequent free elections and civil rights are an attempt to counteract this tendency. The study of democratic quality asks whether they do so.

2.5. THREE LINKAGES

Moving down a level of abstraction, democratic institutions promote popular rule in three different ways, which I call the three linkages at the heart of democratic quality.[17] Elections and rights give citizens three different powers: (1) the power to sanction incumbents, (2) the power to select new officials,

[16] On the potential dangers of free elections and civil rights in newly democratizing states, see Chua (2003) and Snyder (2000).

[17] In Goertz's (2006) framework these are the secondary levels of the basic concept of quality as linkages. I introduce the data/indicator level in the empirical chapters.

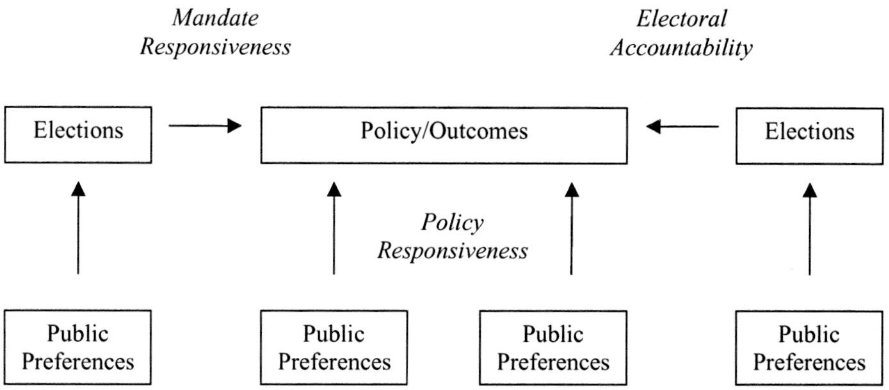

FIGURE 2.1. Linkages between citizens and policy makers.

and (3) the power to petition the government in between elections. All three powers enable citizens to control policy makers. If democracy promotes citizen rule, these linkages should be strong.

Figure 2.1 produces a graphic representation of these links with the italicized phrases indicating modes of influence on policy makers.[18] First, on the right-hand side, voters can reward or punish incumbents for their past performance at election time, which removes unsuccessful governments and provides incentives for politicians to listen to the public. I refer to this linkage as electoral accountability. Second, on the left-hand side, citizens have the power to select new officials whose policy views or personal characteristics they prefer. This gives rise to the linkage I call mandate responsiveness. Finally, the previous two linkages, combined with citizens' rights to petition their government, should lead to a linkage I call policy responsiveness, which is pictured in the center of the figure. Policy responsiveness means that the public's preferences determine day-to-day policy decisions. This linkage is almost tantamount to democratic quality because it measures popular control directly.

The quality of democracy lies in the strength of these linkages.[19] Democratic institutions are a set of potentialities that give citizens the opportunity to govern themselves and to control their representatives. Such control occurs, I argue, when citizens hold politicians accountable, when they select politicians who work to fulfill clear programs, and when these behaviors along with others lead to responsive politicians.

[18] See Przeworski et al. (2000: 9) for another graphical representation of this process, from which I have borrowed liberally.

[19] It is worth noting some ways that these linkages differ from each other. Mandate and policy responsiveness both measure the direct effect of citizens on politicians. Electoral accountability, by contrast, measures both a direct effect – the removal of bad politicians and the retention of good ones – and an indirect effect – the incentive that such actions give politicians to perform well.

TABLE 2.2. *Virtues and Shortcomings of Three Linkages*

	Virtues	Shortcomings
Electoral accountability	Easy for citizens Strong punishment Keeps politicians guessing	Politicians may feel pressure to overreach Officials have a free hand between elections Fails to utilize all of citizens' knowledge Backward looking
Mandate responsiveness	Forward looking Can deliver subtle signals Continues to hold after elections	Higher knowledge requirements for voters Deals poorly with unforeseen circumstances Limits leadership
Policy responsiveness	Closest to idea of people ruling Functions constantly Most limits discretion of politicians	Politicians may have more information than citizens Public opinion may be manipulated Citizens typically profess to dislike Limits leadership

Must all three linkages be present for a country to count as a high-quality democracy? I am hesitant to go so far. Many paths to popular rule exist. Sanctioning and selecting politicians (i.e., electoral accountability and mandate responsiveness) are two routes. Policy responsiveness may be viewed as a necessary condition and in some sense equivalent to popular rule. However, insofar as policy responsiveness refers to the various ways that opinion can influence policy – through letter-writing, protests, or lobbying – it may be seen as constituting a set of additional routes.

This book's view, therefore, is that not all three of these links have to be present in their maximal form for a country to be a high-quality democracy. Furthermore, some aspects may be able to substitute for others – high accountability may make up for weak mandate responsiveness and vice versa. Citizen rule can be achieved through multiple combinations of these linkages. What is uncertain is the exact combinations that work best or even well. This is a question I leave to future scholars.

In the following sections, I look more closely at the three linkages. For each, I focus on two issues: (1) how it works and (2) its virtues and shortcomings for democratic rule. Table 2.2 summarizes the discussion of virtues and shortcomings.

2.5.1. Electoral Accountability

Electoral accountability is the most basic way for citizens to influence policy. Scott Mainwaring (2003: 7) defines accountability as "relationships that formally give some actor the authority of oversight and/or sanction relative to public officials."[20] Because the present conception of democratic quality focuses on the links between citizens and politicians and on behavior rather than formal rules, I define accountability here as the degree to which citizens punish and reward officials at the polls according to their performance in office.

This conception differs from Mainwaring's in two respects. First, it focuses on the existence not of formal relationships of authority but of the actual exercise of sanctions. All democracies give voters formal power to sanction public officials; this is what free elections are. The question is whether citizens actually use this formal power to sanction officials for cause.

A second difference is that I focus only on electoral accountability – the existence of sanctions through elections. Thus, I ignore a relationship called horizontal accountability (O'Donnell 1998), which refers to the accountability of politicians to other political actors like courts.[21] Horizontal accountability is certainly important for the quality of governance in a democracy; if politicians can evade the law, it is likely that they are not producing policies in citizens' interests.[22] However, horizontal accountability is not a link between citizens and politicians. Indeed, some high-quality democracies – for example, Westminster systems – have very few mechanisms for horizontal accountability, suggesting that it may be an optional element of democracy.[23]

The main way that citizens hold politicians accountable in the present conception is elections. Voters decide whether to reelect incumbents or remove them from office. The less common institution of recall, where voters can vote to remove individual sitting politicians before general elections, should also be mentioned.[24] Nevertheless, the essence of electoral accountability is the ability to throw the bums out. To distinguish this limited conception from broader versions, I refer to it as electoral accountability.

Electoral accountability functions when there is a direct relation between the actions of politicians and voters' judgments at the polls; that is, incumbents suffer significantly at the polls when they perform poorly in office and do better when they perform well.[25] Distinguishing good and bad performance is a tricky question and is discussed in Chapter 3. It is sufficient to say that, insofar as

[20] Another definition of accountability emphasizes that politicians give an accounting or justification for their actions. It is unclear, however, what counts as a reasonable accounting. Almost all politicians provide some public justification for their actions, but it is often difficult to say which justifications are reasonable.

[21] O'Donnell (1998: 117) defines it as "the existence of state agencies that are legally enabled and empowered, and factually willing and able, to take actions that span from routine oversight to criminal sanctions or impeachment in relation to actions or omissions by other agencies or agencies of the state that may be qualified as unlawful." For an attempt to explain failures of horizontal accountability in Eastern Europe, see Krause (2006).

[22] I would thus include it in the rubric of quality as preconditions.

[23] Moreno et al. (2003) further argue that problems with horizontal accountability stem mainly from weak electoral accountability.

[24] Potentially one could study the degree to which citizens are able to force the resignations of politicians.

[25] The question of the standards citizens use for assessing performance is an important one. I return to it in Chapter 3.

citizens care about an issue, reasonably assess performance on that issue, and vote on that basis, then accountability functions.

Most would agree that it is a poor democracy where officials are rewarded for pursuing misguided policies and punished for producing generally beneficial ones. Yet, it is certainly empirically possible, and political scientists have not always had an easy time showing that a link between government performance and election results exists even in established democracies (see the literature review in Powell and Whitten 1993).

The virtues of accountability are thus easy to enumerate. Functioning accountability is a powerful disciplinary mechanism for politicians. Accountability has two beneficial effects on policy. The first is to rid the polity of incompetent and self-serving leaders who can be summarily removed from office. Equally important is that the threat of electoral accountability sets up incentives for rulers to do as the public wishes. If politicians wish to stay in power, accountability forces them to care about voters' judgments of them. Indeed, the incentive can be quite strong. Although voters may deliver only a gentle scolding – where a governing party loses a few percentage points of its previous vote share – they may also choose to remove a party from all public offices. As a harsh punishment, electoral accountability is likely to elicit a strong reaction (Mansbridge 2004).

Electoral accountability also has simplicity on its side. Voters merely need to know the answer to a few simple questions: Am I better off today than at the last elections? Has the current government done as well as it could have? Although these questions are relatively simple for voters to answer, they exercise considerable force over politicians.[26] Because politicians cannot know exactly what they have to do to satisfy voters (i.e., to produce positive answers to these questions), accountability forces them to try to do as well as possible to avoid the risk of losing office.

Nevertheless, accountability is not infallible.[27] One of the dangers of accountability is in fact that, because of its harsh verdict, politicians overreach before elections. For example, political systems that emphasize accountability are more likely to have political business cycles: politicians try to pump up the economy before elections to ensure their reelection (Persson and Tabellini 2003). Electoral accountability is also sometimes difficult to practice, as noted earlier; voters have to recognize who is responsible for specific outcomes, which in some political systems is not an easy task.

Another shortcoming of accountability is that it gives politicians a free hand between elections. Although politicians concerned with reelection likely think about their "accountability moment" throughout their term, they are free to pursue the sort of policies they wish up until election day. Thus, accountability has sometimes been characterized by the bon mot that voters are free

[26] Some scholars doubt that most citizens are capable of making more discerning judgments.

[27] Schmitter (2005) refers to the ambiguous virtue of accountability. For the case against accountability, see Mansbridge (2004).

only one day a year – election day. Moreover, if politicians are unconcerned with or prohibited from reelection, accountability has little effect on their decisions.

One may also worry about the crudity of the signal that accountability gives to politicians: a simple thumbs up or thumbs down. Although many voters are uninformed about politics, others do have enough information to send politicians a more subtle message about the particular policies they desire.[28] Moreover, the signal that is sent via accountability is entirely backward-looking. If voters wish to control their government, they would be better advised to look to the future and ask which party or candidate will ensure the best policies in the future.

Despite these drawbacks, accountability is widely seen as the key mechanism that voters can use to control politicians. Several prominent conceptions of democracy equate it almost entirely with the idea of accountability, either because they see it as the essence of control or as the only feasible means of control (Riker 1982, Schmitter and Karl 1991).

2.5.2. Mandate Responsiveness

Nevertheless, the simple institutions of democracy are sufficiently complex to do more. Voters may use elections not just as referenda on incumbents but also to choose future policy directions. In fact, it is rational for voters to consider not the past, which cannot be changed, but the future, which can. A rational voter might thus ask which of the competing parties would produce the best policies, regardless of what they have done in the past. Voters may want to act like forward-thinking bankers rather than backward-looking peasants (Erikson et al. 2002).

These considerations suggest that elections can be conceived of not just as sanctioning but also as selection mechanisms. Selection may take two different forms. The first is the selection of types. Voters may try to choose candidates who are smarter or more honest and avoid those who lack these characteristics (Ferejohn 1999). By choosing such candidates, voters ensure that their government behaves well. However, even though this sort of selection is undoubtedly important, it is difficult to study because it depends on judgments of variables like competence or honesty, which resist objective measurement.

The other type of selection is the selection of future policy directions. Voters can choose those parties or candidates that represent the policy directions they prefer, whether it be lower taxes or higher spending, pro-choice or anti-abortion. The parties who assume the reins of office should then enact the policies they have advocated. I call this linkage mandate responsiveness (Stokes 2001a). A politician or party is mandate responsive if it makes clear campaign promises and fulfills these promises once in office.

[28] Some recent studies have shown that the public in the aggregate is well informed (Erikson et al. 2002, Page and Shapiro 1992).

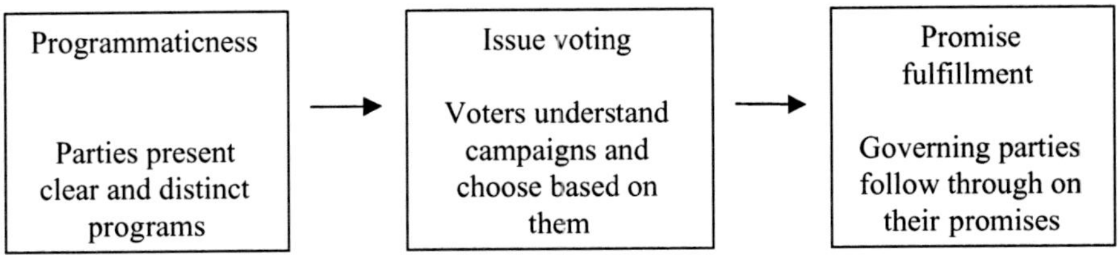

FIGURE 2.2. Elements of mandate responsiveness.

For this sort of selection to be an effective means of control, three conditions must hold, as shown graphically in Figure 2.2. First, elections should feature parties with clear and distinctive policy proposals; otherwise nothing exists for voters to select from. Another way of putting this is to say that the party system should be programmatic; it should feature parties who compete on the basis of alternative policy programs (Kitschelt et al. 1999). Second, voters should be well informed about these options and should choose on the basis of differences among them; this is often termed issue voting (Kessel 1972, MacDonald et al. 1995). Without it, voters are not truly selecting the policy directions they desire. Third, parties who win a share of power should do their best to follow through on their promises. It is a poor choice that voters make if promises apply only to campaigns. Only if parties do what they promise are election choices something more than shots in the dark. The mandate conception thus sees voters as choosing among distinctive programs that elected parties do their best to fulfill.

Some of the virtues of this linkage have already been mentioned. The mandate conception allows voters to send more subtle messages to politicians than a simple thumbs up or down. They may indicate their preferences for specific policies. Voters are, however, constrained to choose among the packages of policies offered by individual candidates or parties and cannot combine their preferences willy-nilly.[29] These messages, moreover, allow voters to influence the course of future policy rather than merely respond to the past.

And these signals from voters bind politicians in between elections. Because politicians must follow through on their campaign promises, they cannot simply pursue their own interests. The mandate conception may give citizens more direct control over politicians than electoral accountability, and doing so offers citizens a degree of predictability. Citizens can better make long-range plans because they have a good idea of how politicians will behave when elected.

A problem with this conception, however, is that it is not always clear what message voters are sending to politicians. How can one determine what policies voters wanted when they chose a particular party?[30] This issue has given rise to a wide-ranging debate in political science on whether mandates exist and

[29] Countries with more parties and electoral systems that allow more choices can enable more subtle messages.

[30] Referenda may be a more powerful version of the mandate conception because they bind politicians to enact or not enact certain policies.

how to identify them (e.g., Dahl 1990, Kelley 1983). This concern may be partially allayed by public opinion polls and by elections that feature clear policy alternatives. The civil rights guaranteed by democracy typically make the debate over the mandate a public one (Conley 2001): citizens may also have their say.

One may also worry if voters are capable of distinguishing between the policy programs of different parties and candidates. Studies of voters' knowledge of the issues of the day have not produced encouraging results (Delli Carpini and Keeter 1996), although others have noted that voters can use simple heuristics (Lupia and McCubbins 1998) and that uninformed voters may cancel each other out (Erikson et al. 2002, Page and Shapiro 1992). Concerns about citizen knowledge are even more severe in a new democracy, where parties have weak reputations and the media – an important force for informing voters – is still developing. Moreover, in order to enforce promise fulfillment, voters must both evaluate whether parties fulfill their promises and punish those who do not, two additional hurdles for voters (Ferejohn 1999).

Finally, one may worry how this conception fares in a world of considerable uncertainty. How should politicians react to changed conditions, such as an economic crisis, that would make promise fulfillment prohibitively costly? Should they break their promises in order to produce better outcomes or stick to their promises despite the possible ill effects (Stokes 2001a)? Again, this dilemma is even more applicable to the volatile circumstances of new democracies. Despite these drawbacks, the mandate conception has prominent advocates among theorists of democracy and voting (Erikson, et al. 2002, Downs 1957).

2.5.3. Policy Responsiveness

The third and final linkage between citizens and voters is policy responsiveness.[31] Policy responsiveness might be called the ur-linkage of democratic quality. If democracy is the rule of the people, then public policies should follow the preferences of the people. If the majority of citizens want a particular policy, then the government should give it to them.[32] This approach implies that governments both pay attention to issues the public cares about and do what the public wants with regard to those issues.

[31] This linkage is often called representation, but I reserve that term for a different use (see Section 2.8).

[32] One area that is ambiguous is corruption. If quality is the degree to which citizens control their rulers, then corruption can be seen as an indicator of low quality because politicians are escaping control and pursuing their own interests. I think this argument is mistaken on two counts. First, it is not clear how important corruption is to citizens. In some cases it may be more acceptable than others. Second, I would distinguish corruption from explicit policy choices. I characterize responsiveness in terms of policy choices following public opinion, but I am not convinced that corruption (as distinct from anticorruption policies) is a policy choice on which politicians necessarily can be responsive.

One may ask to which public politicians are responding. In what follows, I equate the public with the median voter on a particular dimension. One can make a strong case that if politicians respond to anyone, it should be the median voter (Powell 2000: 163–5). Because half of the polity sits on either side of the median voter, the median voter always sits with the majority.[33] If citizens voted directly on policies, the position of the median voter would win these referenda. Alternatively, "choosing the position of the median voter minimizes the number of voters opposed to the chosen position" (Powell 2000: 164). Although these arguments are not definitive, they do give the median a normatively privileged position.[34]

Policy responsiveness in this definition is distinct from participation by citizens in the policy-making process or the existence of channels of access for interested parties.[35] Although such participation may encourage policy responsiveness, it may also privilege more vocal groups over less vocal ones, direct beneficiaries of policies over indirect ones, and it may overload the government with policy issues. Which of these effects predominates is in the end an empirical issue and should be held analytically distinct from the question of whether policy follows public preferences, which may occur with or without direct participation of citizens in the policy process. I would include the matter of direct participation in the study of the preconditions or causes of quality rather than democratic quality per se.

Policy responsiveness partially follows from the previous two linkages. If citizens sanction governments who stray from their preferences, then politicians have strong incentives to need their wishes. Similarly, mandate responsiveness should produce a certain amount of policy responsiveness because newly elected governments are by definition aligned with public preferences. In this case, however, policy responsiveness lasts only as long as citizens' preferences remain relatively stable.

The rights and freedoms necessary for democracy are just as strong a factor in producing responsiveness.[36] As noted earlier, basic freedoms such as speech and assembly are a part of the definition of democracy, because elections can hardly be free and fair without citizens being allowed to express their opinions and obtain information. These rights also apply to the periods between elections, when citizens are allowed to make their views known, form pressure groups, and lobby their government, all actions that should help to induce policy

33 Provided the policy space is unidimensional and voter preferences are single-peaked.

34 One issue with this standard is that some citizens feel their preferences more intensely than others. Another is that politicians should take into consideration the entire distribution of opinions. For more theoretical discussion, see Achen (1978).

35 For the opposite point of view, see Rose-Ackerman (2004), who writes that "full democracy cannot be attained unless the policy-making process is accountable to citizens through transparent procedures that seek to incorporate public input."

36 These rights may also promote accountability, such as when public outcry forces scandal-ridden politicians to resign. Rights may also promote mandate responsiveness as when citizens demand answers to questions about a politician's intentions in office.

responsiveness.[37] Indeed, it is not an easy task for politicians to know what citizens want. A free society enables them to obtain this information at a fairly low cost (Hanson 1991).[38]

Some of the virtues of policy responsiveness have already been sketched. High policy responsiveness may be the closest thing to the direct rule of citizens. Consistently following the public's preferences puts very strong limits on the ability of elected officials to pursue their own interests. Policy responsiveness is also not confined to election time; it links citizens and politicians at all moments in time.

On the other hand, policy responsiveness is an ambiguous virtue. Politicians may be systematically better informed about policy than are citizens and thus may produce better policy by being freed from the dictates of the public. Indeed, some scholars have worried about what they call pandering – politicians trying to please voters with policies they know will have negative effects (Canes-Wrone 2006, Jacobs and Shapiro 2000). On the other hand, even better-informed politicians may choose not to act on their information if doing so does not benefit them. Responsiveness is also worrisome if public opinion is unstable, incoherent, or manipulated by politicians. If these dangers are very great, however, they call into question the institution of democracy itself. Why should citizens rule if they are systematically uninformed or slaves of propaganda?

Policy responsiveness, and to an extent mandate responsiveness, also reduces the role for leadership. One is reminded of the anecdote of the radical leader who, upon seeing a demonstration march by his café, sits up and says, "Those are my followers, now I must run to their head and lead them." Jacobs and Shapiro (1994), however, have outlined the possibility of what they call responsive leadership, where there are strong mutual influences between politicians and citizens. Finally, citizens themselves typically profess to dislike responsiveness, such as when they decry government by opinion poll. But even with these flaws, major theorists of democracy see responsiveness as almost tantamount to democratic quality (Dahl 1971, 1989).

2.6. TRADE-OFFS, COMPLEMENTARITIES, AND INSTITUTIONS

Although all these linkages are modes of popular control, potential contradictions exist between them. As political scientists are taught in graduate school, not all good things go together. Figure 2.3 outlines some of the trade-offs. Electoral accountability and mandate responsiveness require that citizens use a single vote to send two different messages: a verdict on the incumbents and a choice over future policies. It is unclear whether a vote can successfully carry

[37] Of course, there are biases in which interest groups form and how much influence they have (Olson 1965). In a democracy, however, numbers often beat organization.

[38] Dictators sometimes fall because repression makes it hard to know what citizens are thinking (Kuran 1991).

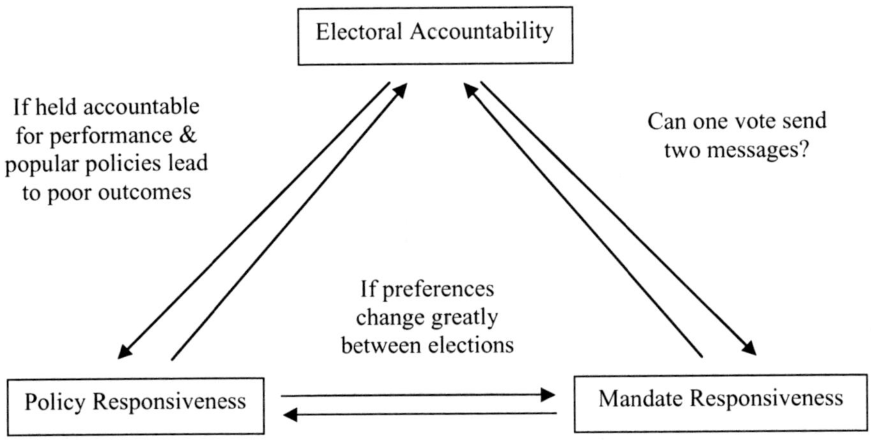

FIGURE 2.3. Trade-offs between linkages.

both messages. Politicians may take advantage of this dichotomy by emphasizing either their past performance or their future plans, depending on which produces better results (Stokes 2001a).

Contradictions may also exist between mandate responsiveness and policy responsiveness. When public opinion changes, a government that wishes to be policy responsive may have to ignore parts of its mandate. This creates a dilemma for voters, who want officials to be both faithful and responsive. Finally, if, as suggested earlier, citizens dislike a government that is too responsive and want one with more backbone, or if policy responsiveness leads to poor outcomes because public opinion is misinformed, politicians may have to choose between following public opinion and producing a record that guarantees victory on the grounds of accountability.

I do not take these contradictions lightly. As a number of scholars have noted (Huber and Powell 1994, Powell 2000), citizens may have to choose between the values represented by these links. However, I suggest that some of these contradictions are exaggerated and that these linkages may also coexist with, if not reinforce, one another.

Figure 2.4 presents some of these complementarities. To reconcile electoral accountability and mandate responsiveness, one can imagine a system where citizens use their vote first to render a verdict on incumbents and, after having done so, to choose among the remaining policy directions on offer or to mix these two motives in some proportion. Surveys of public opinion may help to distinguish the weight of each motive.

It is also not hard to imagine a system where campaigns present clear options to which politicians adhere in office, but that leave room for flexibility in responding to changed public opinion. Parties in high-quality democracies should make clear promises in areas where it is reasonably certain that unexpected contingencies would not force them to change their position and to be

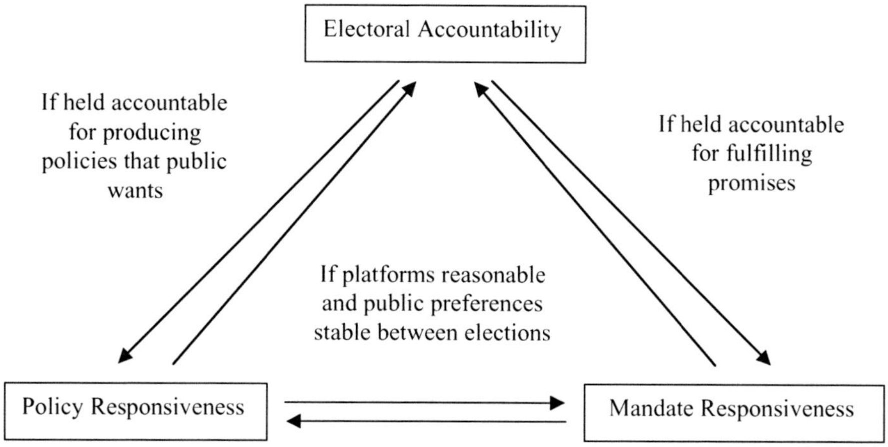

FIGURE 2.4. Complementarities between linkages.

circumspect with promises they believe cannot or should not be fulfilled.[39] In this way, they might avoid the trade-off between mandate and policy responsiveness. Finally, a public well informed about policy should leave only a small gap between the policies produced by a policy responsive government and those produced by one concerned about its performance on accountability grounds.

These linkages may even reinforce one another. As Stokes (2001a) finds, citizens may punish parties for deviating too far from their programs, which should induce parties to adhere to their programs. Electoral accountability may encourage mandate responsiveness. As noted earlier, electoral accountability and mandate responsiveness should support policy responsiveness. If voters punish politicians for straying too far from public preferences, then governments may take greater care to be policy responsive.

A number of scholars have suggested that institutions may affect these trade-offs and complementarities. As Lijphart (1984, 1999) and Powell (2000, also Huber and Powell 1994) have shown, constitutional designers can choose between two ideal types in creating political institutions. The consensus or proportional vision finds institutional expression in proportional electoral systems, coalition governments, bicameralism, and strong parliamentary committees. It favors a large number of parties who represent diverse points of view and encourages them to negotiate with each other in making policy. Conversely, the majoritarian vision is represented by first-past-the-post elections, single-party majority governments, unicameralism, and a weak committee system. It tries to produce a single-party government with control over most levers of policy.

[39] George H. W. Bush's "Read my lips: no new taxes" is a promise that should not be made for exactly this reason.

As Powell makes clear, these two visions have important consequences for the strength of individual linkages. The majoritarian system encourages accountability. It gives voters a clear target of responsibility, which they can blame or reward for policies and outcomes. In a proportional system, by contrast, it is difficult for voters to know which among the many parties participating in policy making is responsible for individual policies and outcomes. On the other hand, the proportional system provides citizens with a wider palette of choices in elections, encouraging mandate choices. First-past-the-post elections in majoritarian systems may, by contrast, lead to Downsian centripetal competition and a lack of real choice between parties – the well-known "not a dime's worth of difference." However, to the extent that parties in majoritarian systems do present distinctive programs, they have the power to fulfill their campaign pledges. The presence of numerous veto points in consensus systems may prevent parties from following through on their promises.

Both systems, however, should produce policy responsiveness, though in different ways. Centripetal competition in majoritarian systems should lead to both parties representing the median voter. Granting proportional power to all points of view should do the same in proportional systems. Powell finds considerable evidence that these differences do emerge in twenty established democracies – majoritarian designs produce high accountability and proportional ones provide more choices – though majoritarian governments are somewhat less responsive than proportional ones.[40]

2.7. REVERSE CAUSALITY

The three linkages of democratic quality are intended to run in one direction – from citizens to politicians. Citizens hold politicians accountable and endow them with mandates; politicians for their part are induced to respond to citizens' preferences and to follow through on their mandates.

Yet, one may worry about the directionality of these linkages. Evidence of strong linkages may be a consequence of reverse causality. For example, a high degree of responsiveness may in fact indicate that politicians have manipulated citizens' preferences in the direction of their own. On the accountability criterion, misleading campaigns may lead voters to believe they are rendering accountability verdicts when they are not. On the mandate criterion, a well-produced campaign could give the illusion of substance while in fact promising little at all. Effective political spin may thus give the appearance that citizens and politicians are in tune, when in fact citizens are being tuned.

This possibility figures strongly in one of the most widely accepted theories of public opinion. John Zaller (1992) argues that public opinion emerges

[40] I would add that Powell's results are not iron laws. One can imagine two-party systems where citizens can choose between different policy options (in fact, Downsian competition does appear to be limited) or a proportional system where citizens can discover which parties are responsible for outcomes.

from elite cues. When elites are united in favor of a particular policy option, citizens are likely to adopt their outlook (although when they are divided, citizens have more freedom to create their own preferences). If Zaller's theory is true, it is possible that strong linkages indicate not popular but rather elite control.

I cannot dismiss this possibility a priori. Indeed, the mass media and civil society – the two places citizens may expect to hear alternative opinions – were fairly undeveloped in Eastern Europe. And Eastern European parties have sometimes been portrayed as forming a cartel in collusion against the public. What I try to do in the empirical chapters that follow is to look very closely at the origin of public preferences. Did citizens have access to a wide variety of points of view and alternative sources of information. Were public preferences balanced evaluations of current circumstances or reasonable deductions from past experiences? In short, were they exogenous to the political process? Only if the answers to these questions are positive and preferences were not shaped by political actors can one conclude that quality is high.

2.8. SUBSTANTIVE REPRESENTATION

I suggested in the previous chapter that some critics dismiss linkages as epiphenomenal or unnecessary. They would argue that a political system should produce not policies that citizens want but policies that are best for citizens. I follow Manin, Przeworski, and Stokes (1999) in calling a government substantively representative if it produces policies in the best interests of citizens. (This criterion corresponds to the conception of quality as societal outcomes, presented earlier.)

Substantive representation is difficult to study. How does one know what is in the public's best interest? If citizens are the best judges of their own interests, then substantive representation becomes policy responsiveness. But few would make this claim absolutely. Citizens are often uninformed or misinformed about the consequences of public policies. But given that citizens may not know their own best interests, how can others know them? And even if they could be known, how should conflicts between the interests of individuals or groups be resolved?

Various standards have been put forward to square this circle. The best known is the Pareto criterion: policies are to be preferred if they make at least someone better off, but no one worse off. One can easily find objections to this criterion: Who judges whether someone is made better off? What if the status quo is very unjust? Does it preclude changes that make many much better off and just a few a little worse off?

Rather than engage in these debates here – which would take the discussion very far afield – I do want to flag this issue and keep in mind whether the linkages considered earlier are producing substantively representative government (Manin et al. 1999). The hope of all democrats is that strong linkages produce substantive representation.

TABLE 2.3. *Linkages and Substantive Representation*

Linkage	Leads to Substantive Representation if ...
Electoral accountability	Citizens hold politicians to highest standards they are capable of and accurately judge performance relative to possibilities.
Mandate responsiveness	Some platforms include good policies, citizens are aware of the consequences of policies, and conditions do not change greatly between elections.
Policy responsiveness	Citizens are well informed about policy options and their likely consequences.

I do not, however, include this criterion in my conception of the quality of democracy. Although substantive representation is normatively desirable, it does not follow directly from the definition of democracy suggested earlier. Indeed, adherents of other forms of government have argued that these forms produce greater substantive representation.[41] Democrats naturally argue just the opposite, claiming that democratic linkages lead to policies in the best interests of citizens.

For strong linkages to lead to beneficial policies, a number of conditions must be met. Table 2.3 summarizes these conditions. Electoral accountability produces strong incentives for good government when citizens set high but attainable standards for politicians and are good evaluators of performance. If standards are too low or too high, incumbents lose their incentive to perform as well as possible because it is too easy or too hard to win reelection. If citizens misperceive policies and outcomes, then politicians may win elections without substantive representation. Mandate responsiveness produces good policies when citizens are well informed about the consequences of policy choices, at least some parties offer "good" programs, and circumstances do not change radically between elections. If citizens are not well informed, they may choose platforms that do not represent their interests. If circumstances change, politicians may follow through on policies that are no longer best. Policy responsiveness likewise leads to good government if citizens are well informed about policies and their consequences. If not, politicians will enact flawed policies that citizens unfortunately desire.[42]

Although my research design does not allow me to trace the connections between linkages and representation, I do want to see whether policy making in the region is producing good results on some fairly unobjectionable criteria like prosperity and security. What degree of substantive representation do countries in the region achieve and does it occur because of or in spite of the

[41] The foremost advocate of this view is Plato (1966).

[42] As one colleague remarked to me, "What if a country has bad citizens?" For a recent discussion, see Caplan (2006).

linkages I find? My test of substantive representation is weak, but I do not want to avoid it.

2.9. SCHOLARLY DEBTS

I argued earlier that most studies of the quality of democracy have focused on quality as procedures, preconditions, and outcomes rather than linkages. Nevertheless, the concept of quality as linkages does draw from a number of studies in political science that I would be remiss not to mention. In the interests of exposition, this chapter has ignored a number of major works that have taken similar courses. This section tries to remedy these omissions.

Two works that have put forward similar concepts of democratic quality are those of Przeworski, Stokes, and Manin (1999), and Powell (2000). The first focuses on the degree to which elections produce substantive representation – the problem flagged in the previous section. The editors of that volume produce a scheme of three major linkages almost identical to the one here (in fact, I borrow their terminology). The difference is that their goal is to determine the degree to which these linkages encourage substantive representation rather than popular control. Nevertheless, their basic setup is the direct inspiration for the way I have conceived the quality of democracy.

In several recent works, H. Bingham Powell (2000, 2004, 2005) has also considered the incentives provided by free elections and outlined what he calls the chain of responsiveness. In *Elections as Instruments of Democracy* (Powell 2000), he focuses on the degree of electoral accountability and policy responsiveness in the established democracies. In "The Chain of Responsiveness" (Powell 2004), he adds to those linkages others – the link between citizen preferences and vote choices and the link between governments and policy – which I do not consider because they do not directly connect citizens and policy makers.

I would add three other sets of authors who advocate similar conceptions of democratic quality. Lawrence Jacobs and Robert Shapiro (1994) recommend that scholars focus on what they call "substantive democracy," which they equate with the links between citizens and politicians, mainly in the form of policy responsiveness. Herbert Kitschelt (2000, Kitschelt et al. 1999) and his collaborators have also emphasized a conception of democratic quality that privileges linkages. His main focus is the mandate linkage – whether parties offer clear programmatic alternatives or gain support through clientelism – although he also looks at the responsiveness of parties to voters. In a series of works, Susan Stokes (2001a, 2001b) has explored the conceptual underpinnings of the mandate and accountability linkages, with particular attention to the circumstances of new democracies.

Finally, I would make note of the many studies on American and sometimes Western European politics that have accumulated around each of the three linkages. This book owes a considerable debt to these works. What is noteworthy is that only in exceptional cases have these literatures looked at new democracies – the places where the greatest doubts exist about the strength of linkages. Indeed, the lion's share of work on linkages focuses on the United States, which is in many ways an atypical democracy. Nevertheless, these studies provide both models of how to study linkages and a point of comparison for the strength of linkages. I discuss them in more detail in the chapters that follow.

I would also be remiss to ignore several political theorists who have explored these issues in considerable depth. The classic work on the subject is Hanna Pitkin's (1967) *The Concept of Representation*, while a key recent contribution to the subject is Jane Mansbridge's (2003) "Rethinking Representation."[43] Both describe multiple mechanisms through which democratic institutions affect governance.

In short, the conception of democratic quality as linkages owes a considerable debt to previous work. Although, with the exception of Kitschelt, none of these scholars refers explicitly to the quality of democracy; their aims and methods are similar to the present volume and in fact inspire it. The scope of this book is only possible because it stands on the shoulders of these giants.

[43] It may be worth quickly relating my conception of quality to these works. Pitkin identifies four types of representation. Her formalistic representation corresponds to both the procedural definition of democracy – how representatives are chosen – and electoral accountability – whether representatives can be sanctioned. Her substantive representation – whether representatives act in the best interests of the represented – exactly corresponds to the present use of the term. Symbolic representation – whether citizens approve of the work of their representatives – might also be included as a measure of substantive representation. If citizens know their own interests, then their approval or disapproval indicates whether representation is occurring. Her descriptive representation – whether representatives resemble the represented – does not have a place in the scheme here. Indeed, there is a wide-ranging debate on whether descriptive representation is a good thing (for a recent discussion see Dovi 2007). Mansbridge's categories are weaker fits because she is primarily concerned with the way that representatives decide on particular actions rather than on how citizens control representatives. Her promissory representation corresponds to mandate responsiveness, whereas her anticipatory representation might fit with electoral accountability. Neither gyroscopic representation (where representatives look within themselves to derive a basis for action) nor surrogate representation (where representatives represent those outside of their districts) have good equivalents in the present scheme.

PART II

STATISTICAL ANALYSIS

The following three chapters conduct statistical analyses of the three linkages at the heart of democratic quality. Each chapter considers a single linkage in ten Eastern European countries over approximately the first fifteen years of the transition. The countries are Bulgaria, the Czech Republic, Estonia, Hungary, Latvia, Lithuania, Poland, Romania, Slovakia, and Slovenia. They were chosen because they represent the most consistent democratic experience in the region. The goal of these analyses is to determine if citizens exercise control over their rulers in the region as a whole. The results should thus be seen as average effects or the typical degree of popular control of policy makers through each of the three linkages. Indeed, producing unbiased estimates of average effects is the main advantage of large-N analysis. Consideration of the substance and mechanisms of these effects is reserved for the case studies in Part III.

3

Electoral Accountability

The fate of the former Polish ruling party represents a microcosm of trends in electoral accountability in Eastern Europe. In the partially competitive elections of 1989 that marked the transition from communism in Poland, the Polish United Workers' Party (PZRP), which had governed the country since 1945, faced competition for only 35% of the seats in the lower house of parliament and all one hundred seats in a newly created senate. The communist leaders were confident that even with the limited competition they would do well in these elections; after all, they held myriad organizational advantages over the opposition.

In fact, the elections proved disastrous for them. They lost every competitive seat and could not even muster a majority for some of the seats reserved to them. Their dismal showing in these elections indicated that their time had come and, after further negotiations, many of their elected deputies defected to the opposition and allowed the leaders of the opposition Solidarity union to take power.

After this crushing defeat, the party transformed itself into a European-style left-of-center party called the Democratic Left Alliance (SLD). The party purged the hardliners who had been active in the repression of the 1980s and tried to present itself as a modernizing, democratic party (Grzymala-Busse 2002). When it faced the electorate again in Poland's first truly free elections in 1991, the SLD did somewhat better, winning 12% of the votes in a crowded field and finishing in second place.[1] But for many this was the party's last hurrah; mass support for the former communists was nowhere to be found.

Yet, in 1993, SLD achieved a stunning electoral victory. Running on a platform of "Things don't have to be like this," they defeated the ruling right-wing parties who had presided over Poland's transition from communism, its dramatic shock therapy reforms, and a severe recession and dramatic upsurge in unemployment. The SLD was the leading vote-getter in these elections with

[1] The crowding was mainly on the right. The 12% thus represented a fairly unified left vote.

20% of the vote, which translated into 37% of seats and a dominant role in the new coalition government.[2]

The four-year rule of the SLD produced an economic boom in Poland. Whether this was due to their policies or to the reforms of the previous government is a matter of dispute, but the results were clear. The growth rate hit 6.8% and unemployment fell from 16 to 11%.[3] By almost all accounts, the SLD was guiding Poland through a successful transition to a market economy. Yet when they faced the electorate again in 1997, they could not hold onto their position in government. Although their vote share increased from 20 to 27%, they saw their seat percentage drop by a point and they lost the elections to a newly unified right, which was able to put together a governing majority.

After four years in opposition, the SLD was then well placed to take advantage of a stumbling economy and record unemployment – which had risen to 18% – to win another landslide victory in 2001, taking home 47% of the vote and a near majority of seats. Although the following four years saw creditable but not outstanding economic performance, the party found itself entangled in numerous corruption scandals. Most prominently, Rywingate – named for a well-known film producer – saw the government charged with offering legislation in exchange for campaign contributions. The verdict of voters in the elections of 2005 was merciless. SLD's vote share fell by 36% and they finished in fourth place, behind even a protest party.

The fortunes of the SLD graphically indicate some of the main trends in electoral accountability in Eastern Europe. Like most former ruling parties, they were punished heavily during the first free and semifree elections. Their victories, always occurring when they were in the opposition, show the severity of electoral retribution for governing parties and the desire for change when economic performance was poor. Their near loss in 1997 indicates how even incumbents who produced enviable economic outcomes found it almost impossible to win reelection. And their dramatic loss in 2005 shows how important corruption had become to voters.

This chapter looks in more detail at trends in electoral accountability across Eastern Europe. In particular, it tries to determine whether a relation exists between the performance of incumbents in office and their election results. Are poorly performing politicians punished and successful ones rewarded? And which aspects of performance, if any, do voters use to assess the performance of incumbents?

3.1. THE STUDY OF ELECTORAL ACCOUNTABILITY

Electoral accountability means that citizens sanction governments at election time for poor performance. But what is a sanction and what is poor performance? At election time, voters have only one way of sanctioning parties whose

[2] The disproportion between votes and seats arose because about one-third of votes went to parties that did not exceed the newly instituted 5% threshold for entry into parliament.

[3] Unless otherwise stated, all economic statistics are from EBRD (1995–2009).

performance they disapprove of: they can withhold their vote for those parties. Thus, a government or party can consider itself sanctioned if it loses vote share relative to its previous performance. All else being equal, a loss in vote share means that a party would dispose of fewer seats in parliament, would be less likely to serve in government, and would have less political power.[4] A party that loses vote share should feel that it has been punished.

What counts as poor performance? One issue is the aspects of government performance that matter. Most research has focused on economics. Thus, the school of retrospective economic voting analyzes whether past economic performance affects the electoral results of incumbents (for a review see Lewis-Beck and Stegmaier 2001). The focus on economics is because it is one of the most consistently salient issues for voters and has a large effect on human welfare.[5]

Voters, however, may care about other aspects of government performance besides the economy. As the case study at the beginning of the chapter indicated, allegations of corruption against governments are rife in Eastern Europe and, according to journalistic accounts, have hurt many incumbents. Another possibility is that breaking campaign promises hurts governing parties (Stokes 2001a). From the perspective of democratic quality, what is important is that voters hold incumbents accountable for some consequential aspect of their performance over which they have control because this both rids the polity of incumbents who harm the public in consequential ways and gives them an incentive to perform well in this domain. If these conditions are met, electoral accountability is functioning.

Another issue involves whose judgments of performance are taken into account. Performance might be measured by voters' subjective impressions of a party or government. Indeed, much work on economic voting has taken this approach. It uses survey data and correlates citizens' vote intentions or reported vote choices with their perceptions of the economy. Citizens who perceive the economy to be performing poorly should be more likely to vote against the incumbent and vice versa (Duch and Stevenson 2008).

This method has several shortcomings. In the first place, it is difficult to make comparisons over space and time because surveys are conducted in different formats at different places and times.[6] More important, the connections derived from survey analysis may not capture the concept of accountability. One reason is that survey respondents may not accurately predict or remember their voting decisions, and the survey sample may not perfectly reflect the electorate. More

[4] Of course, all else is not equal. Whether a party loses power depends on electoral rules – how votes are converted into seats – how other parties perform, and how the government formation process plays out. These factors, however, are extraneous to the message that voters send with their vote.

[5] An important issue in the literature is whether voters judge their own economic situation or the general state of the economy. Most studies find that voters' judgments are based on the general state of the economy; in the jargon they are sociotropic rather than egocentric.

[6] Time-series analysis solves one part of this problem, but only short and inconsistent time series exist for the ten countries in the present sample. Time-series analysis also usually focuses on government approval rather than on election results.

problematic is that citizens may be misinformed about the true state of the economy (Blendon et al. 1997, Caplan 2006, Holbrook and Garand 1996). As a result, findings that perceptions of the economy influence vote choice can be found even if actual economic conditions do not affect the performance of incumbents.

For these reasons, this chapter focuses mainly on a second method of evaluating accountability. It considers the relation between objective measures of performance and actual election results. These real and aggregate connections give a better view into whether politicians are genuinely held accountable. Does poor economic performance lead to actual vote losses and governments being removed from office? Indeed, just such a connection is necessary for accountability to produce incentives for better economic policy. I argue in the conclusion to this chapter that even this connection may not be enough.

Somewhat surprising is that cross-national studies of retrospective economic voting in the advanced democracies using these methods have produced fairly weak results. In most cases, general economic conditions do not determine whether incumbents are rewarded or punished (Lewis-Beck 1988, Paldam 1991, Przeworski and Cheibub 1999, but see Hellwig and Samuels 2007 and Wilkin et al. 1997). Only in certain delimited contexts, described later, do economic conditions affect vote shares (Powell and Whitten 1993, Whitten and Palmer 1999). The question is whether incumbents in Eastern Europe are held accountable for their performance. Although a fair amount of research has addressed this question, little of it has looked at outcomes at the national level and objective performance indicators where accountability matters most.[7]

3.2. FIRST ELECTIONS

Before turning to this analysis, it is worth looking at the first contested elections in Eastern Europe. These elections are not included in the larger statistical analysis that follows because they are of a qualitatively different type. In these elections, voters were asked for the first time in forty years to render a verdict on their rulers. Although this made them in some sense the epitome of accountability moments, they featured incumbents who were anything but normal incumbents. Communist parties had ruled for more than forty years, had never been legitimated in free elections,[8] and had in previous sham elections received upward of 99% of the vote.

[7] Existing studies of Eastern Europe have delivered a mixed message. The most consistent findings have used subnational data and found that voters sanction according to party type. Citizens punish reformists and reward former communists for a poor economy whether or not they are incumbents (Bell 1997, Fidrmuc 2000a, Jackson et al. 2005, Powers and Cox 1997, Tucker 2006). A handful of other studies have found evidence for standard retrospective economic voting, usually using survey data (Anderson et al. 2003, Duch 1995, 2001, Pacek 1994, Przeworski 1993, 1996). Several of these studies are discussed later in more detail.

[8] With the possible exception of the Czechoslovak election of 1946.

It is this last point which is key. It was inevitable that these parties would lose votes. But one cannot say with certainty the extent of their punishment because their actual level of support under the old regime is an unknown; who can say what percentage of votes they would have received in free elections. Additionally, the forty years of rule means that it is difficult to pin down what voters were holding them accountable for. Their recent performance likely played in voters' judgments, but myriad events in the past certainly mattered also.

If citizens judged the communist incumbents solely based on their records, they would almost certainly have been turned out of office. These regimes had violated human rights on a massive scale – not only imprisoning many of their citizens for political offenses, but severely restricting such basic freedoms as speech, press, and assembly. Even focusing more narrowly on economic and social performance, at best, all of these countries had been experiencing economic stagnation for a decade; at worst, they were in the midst of serious economic crises at the time of the first free elections. Judging them over the longer term, they had all produced far less economic prosperity than similarly situated European countries,[9] which is not to mention the ubiquitous corruption of political leaders resulting from their iron grip on power.

Yet the communists held several very real advantages even where these first elections were entirely free. In the first place, they brought to bear an impressive set of organizational resources. They boasted membership rolls far higher than any opposition party even after a massive exodus of members. Their candidates often enjoyed high name recognition, whereas representatives of the opposition were usually unknown to the public. And these parties still controlled considerable financial resources that they could use to mobilize voters.

Even economically, incumbents had something of a leg to stand on. Decades of communist propaganda had tried to convince citizens that communist policies sheltered them from unemployment and gave them the benefit of economic security. Although newly opened borders showed voters how far their economies lagged behind those of their Western neighbors (if they did not know already), some of the propaganda about homelessness and poverty in the West was not easily dispelled and was even partially confirmed by the disastrous consequences of early reforms. Finally, the communists were often able to dictate the timing of elections to showcase these factors to their best advantage. Indeed, these advantages were enough to lead many communists to believe that they would do well in free elections.[10]

How then did this battle between performance failures, on the one hand, and organizational superiority and past propaganda, on the other hand, play out in the first competitive elections? Table 3.1 presents the performance of the former

[9] Czechoslovakia had an income similar to that of Austria at the end of World War II but was far poorer by the end of communism.

[10] For more on these successor parties, see Grzymala-Busse (2002) and Bozóki and Ishiyama (2002).

TABLE 3.1. *Performance of Successor Parties in the First Elections*

Country	Successor Party	Year	Vote Share
Bulgaria	Bulgarian Socialist Party (BSP)	1990	45.1
	Bulgarian Socialist Party (BSP)	1991	33.1
Czech	Communist Party of Czechoslovakia (KSČS)	1990	13.5
	Left Bloc (LB)	1992	14.0
Estonia	Joint Council of Work Collectives	1990	26.0[a,b]
	Estonian Social Democratic Labor Party	1992	0.0
Hungary	Hungarian Socialist Party (MSZP)	1990	11.9
	Hungarian Socialist Party (MSZP)	1994	33.0
Latvia	Communist Party members	1990	21.5[a]
	Latvian Socialist Party	1993	0.0
Lithuania	Lithuanian Communist Party	1990	16.0[a,b]
	Lithuanian Democratic Labor Party (LDDP)	1992	44.0
Poland	Polish United Workers Party (PZRP)	1989	0.0[a,b]
	Alliance of the Democratic Left (SLD)	1991	12.0
Romania	National Salvation Front (FSN)	1990	66.3[a,b]
	Democratic National Salvation Front (FSDN)	1992	27.7
Slovakia	Communist Party of Slovakia (KSS)	1990	13.5
	Party of the Democratic Left (SLD)	1992	14.7
Slovenia	League of Communists	1990	17.3[a]
	United List of Social Democrats (ZLSD)	1992	13.8

[a] Semifree elections. [b] Seat percentage.
Sources: Project on Political Transformation and the Electoral Process in Postcommunist Europe, Berglund et al. (1998), Rose and Munro (2003).

ruling parties in all ten countries for the first two competitive elections.[11] In most of the new postcommunist democracies, citizens used elections to deliver devastating verdicts against the ruling communists. From winning greater than 99% of the vote and all the seats in communist-era parliaments, the ruling communist party or its hastily cobbled together successor became only one of a plethora of parties – and not the most successful one at that.

The first semifree elections in Poland, mentioned at the beginning of the chapter, were perhaps the starkest illustration of the rule, but reconstructed or unreconstructed communist parties in the Czech Republic, Estonia, Hungary, Latvia, Lithuania, and Slovenia fared just as poorly, typically winning vote shares in the mid-teens in the first free or semifree elections. The exceptions to this rule were Bulgaria and Romania. The Bulgarian Communist Party renamed itself the Bulgarian Socialist Party (BSP) and put in a strong performance, winning 45% of the votes in June 1990. More problematic is the Romanian National Salvation Front (FSN), who used the organizational resources of the

[11] In more than half the countries – Estonia, Latvia, Lithuania, Poland, Romania, and Slovenia – the first elections were not completely free. This circumstance should favor the communist successor parties.

former Romanian Communist Party to resoundingly win elections in May 1990 with 66.3% of the vote even while proclaiming to have overthrown the communists. Although questions have been raised about the fairness of these elections, particularly in Romania, both parties repeated their success in more open elections in 1991 and 1992.

These results are telling in a number of ways. In the first place, a massive drop-off appears for almost all parties who inherited the communist mantle even when they proclaimed their distance from it by changing their name or program as they did in just about every country except the Czech Republic. This drop-off occurred despite very real organizational advantages over the opposition. Citizens were clearly able to sanction these parties for their performance despite significant obstacles.[12]

It is also worth noting that the second free elections in these countries often took on a very different character. While former communists remained marginal in the Czech Republic, Estonia, Latvia, Slovakia, and Slovenia, they posted victories in Hungary, Poland, and Lithuania and continued to do well in Bulgaria and Romania. By then, parties of the former opposition were running on a real platform rather than just opposition to communism, and they faced their own accountability moments.

3.3. THE COSTS OF GOVERNING

What happened in later elections? Unlike the communist rulers in the initial elections, these governments had the legitimacy of a democratic election on their side and ruled under democratic conditions. Thus, they should not have received the nearly universal punishment of the communist parties. Instead, rational voters should distribute punishments and rewards in about equal measure. By distributing rewards to governments that performed above average and punishments to those that performed below average, voters give governments an incentive to seek above-average performance. Such incentives would disappear if punishment was automatic or punishment and rewards were not correlated with performance.

Such an array of outcomes has been found in established democracies, where the typical government experiences marginal vote losses – on the order of about 2 to 3% – but can often be expected to improve its performance (Paldam 1991).[13] Thus, costs of governing exist – incumbents do lose slightly more often than they win – but the are not overly large.

The electoral fate of democratically elected incumbents in Eastern Europe from the start of the transition until 2006 presents a very different result. Figure 3.1 shows the difference between their vote shares at the beginning and

[12] Fish (1998) argues that the results of the first elections were key for democratization and economic reforms.

[13] For reasons why punishment is stronger than reward, see Nannestad and Paldam (2002).

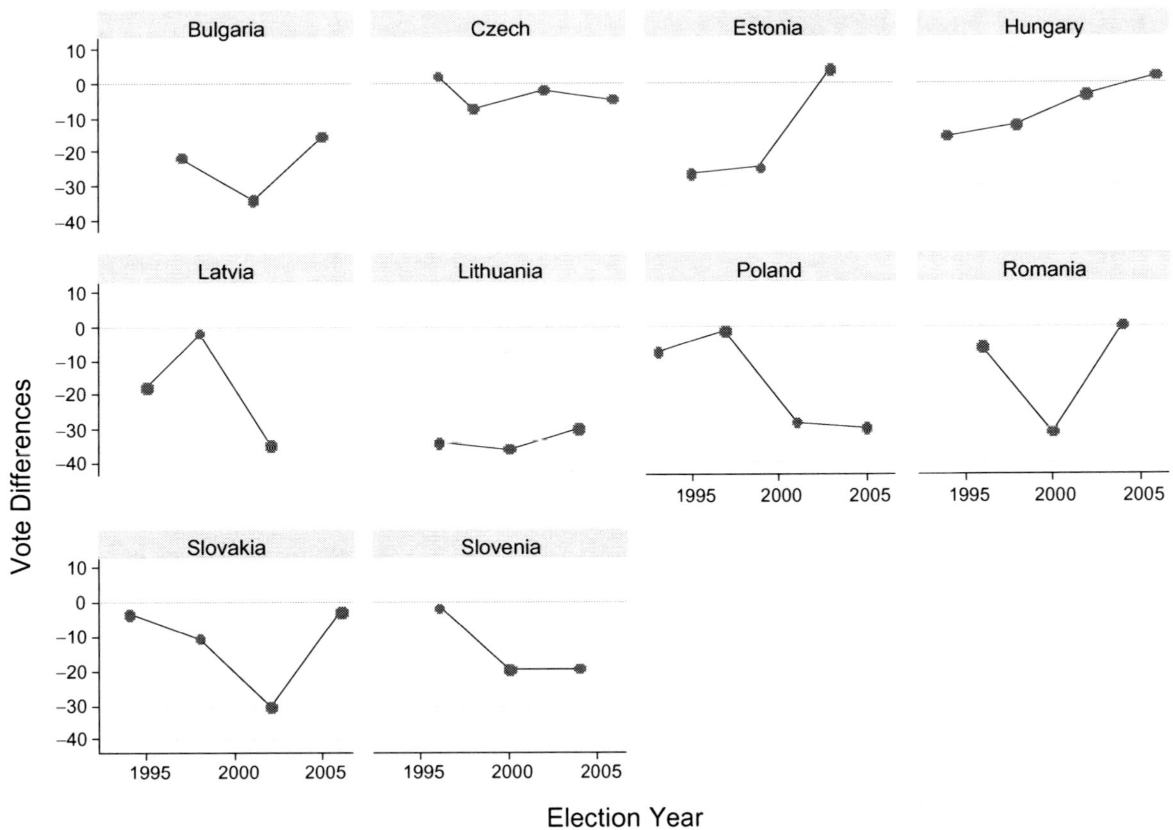

FIGURE 3.1. Trends in vote differences.

end of terms for all governments in the region.[14] Positive numbers indicate that governments improved their vote share and negative numbers that they lost vote share. In almost all cases, incumbents lost votes compared to when they were elected. Of the 34 governments, 30 of them lost votes. And in most cases, they lost a very large number of votes. The average government in the region saw its vote share decline by 15% – more than five times the level of vote losses seen in established democracies. The typical government earned 43% of the vote when it was elected and received 28% when it faced the electorate again.

Some of these losses were truly dramatic. In Lithuania, for example, every incumbent government lost more than 30% from its previous vote total. As mentioned in the introduction to this chapter, the ruling Democratic Left Alliance in Poland saw its vote share drop from 47 to 11% between 2001 and 2005. Indeed, with the exception of the Czech Republic and Hungary, every country saw the average government lose more than 10% from its previous vote total. By contrast, the victories of incumbents were less than overwhelming. The four governments who did manage to gain vote share saw only minimal improvements, ranging from 0.2 to 3.8%.

These losses had real consequences. Incumbent parties were rarely able to enter the first government formed after elections. There were seventy-three parties who sat in government at election time and only twenty-two (about 30%) joined the government formed immediately after elections. And in only two cases out of thirty-four did a sitting government manage to return to power intact after elections. Elections, in short, produced large changes in the composition of parliaments and governments.

It may be possible that these large losses were something other than the punishment of incumbents. Instead, voters may have punished all parliamentary parties and given their votes to brand new parties not previously represented in parliament. Rose and Munro (2003) and Birch (2003) pointed to the emergence of new parties and the disappearance of established parties as one of the distinctive phenomena of party politics in Eastern Europe. The aformentioned anti-incumbency results may thus capture the flux of party politics in the region. Yet, the average opposition party in parliament improved its vote share by 2.3% in the following election.[15] Voters do distinguish between incumbents and the opposition and they more strongly punish incumbents.[16]

[14] I coded as incumbents parties who sat in government at the time of elections. If there was a caretaker government at the time of elections, I considered the nearest partisan government. One exception was Bulgaria between 1991 and 1994, which was eliminated from the data set because it was ruled for two years by a caretaker cabinet. I also eliminated the 1992 election in the Czech Republic and Slovakia because the party system had changed so dramatically between 1990 and 1992 with two large forum parties disappearing from the scene, the 1992 elections in Romania because the 1990 elections were not entirely free, and the 1991 elections in Bulgaria because the 1990 elections led to an explicitly temporary government. Data on election results are taken from the Project on Political Transformation and the Electoral Process in Postcommunist Europe at the University of Essex, www.essex.ac.uk/elections. Data on government composition are from Müller-Rommel et al. (2004).

[15] I considered only parties with greater than 2% of the national-level vote.

[16] Regression analyses confirm these differences.

The anti-incumbent mood may also be temporally confined. In particular, punishment might be harsher at the start of the transition. Voters may turn against early incumbents because of large transitional recessions or the pains of introducing a market economy. However, the average vote differences of governments across the first, second, third, and fourth accountability elections do not show any obvious trends. Vote losses were high – greater than 10% – in all four elections.[17] Inspection of Figure 3.1 shows few obvious trends – vote losses sometimes increase, sometimes decrease, and sometimes fluctuate. I return to this phenomenon later in the chapter.

3.4. ECONOMIC VOTING

These results are problematic from the perspective of accountability. Merely punishing incumbents would not tend to produce good government. Indeed, if incumbents knew in advance that they would lose elections, they would have every incentive to shirk their duties and steal from the public till. What would they gain from expending effort on producing good policy and forego-ing opportunities for self-enrichment? For elections to produce incentives for representative government, it would have to be the case that voters distinguish between good and bad performance. Are variations in vote losses explained by differences in performance?

Perhaps the most important aspect of performance is economic policy. Three measures of economic performance are common in studies of accountability: unemployment, inflation, and growth. There are good reasons to believe that voters prefer lower levels of unemployment and inflation and higher levels of growth. Indeed, economists devote much of their research to explaining the dynamics of these variables precisely because of their importance for human welfare. If material conditions matter to them, voters should reward govern-ments that best achieve these outcomes and should punish those that do not. I thus add measures of these three variables to the electoral outcomes data set for the period just before elections.[18]

It is worth mentioning that election-year economic indicators are quite vari-able in Eastern Europe; growth rates range from −9.4 to +8.3%, unemploy-ment from 4 to 19%, and inflation from 1 to 123%, indicating the roller-coaster ride of economic performance in the region.

[17] Coding of these elections is not obvious because of the presence of some semifree elections, the breakup of two countries, and elections without an incumbent. Other coding schemes, however, produce similarly weak trends.

[18] Data on economic variables are taken from the EBRD's (1995–2009) *Transition Reports*. One would typically measure the level of these variables for the period immediately preceding elections; voters' memories of economic performance are usually short. Most works use lags of one year or less (Lewis-Beck and Stegmaier 2000). In fact, only annual (rather than quarterly) data are available. Thus, I use the level of the variable for the election year if the election took place in the second half of the year and the level of the variable in the previous year if the election took place in the first half of the year. Achen and Bartels (2004) suggest that these short memories are problematic for promoting good performance and popular control.

I begin with a rough measure of accountability: were governments that presided over economic disasters punished more than other governments? I define a disaster as the presence of two of the following three conditions during an election year: growth less than 2%, inflation greater than 20%, and unemployment greater than 12%. Eight elections in the sample took place under these conditions and in them the government lost 23% of the vote versus 13% in other elections. A rough justice does prevail.

Although these differences suggest a possible influence of economic conditions on election results, they do not include controls for other factors affecting vote shares. For more reliable inferences, I turn to regression analysis. The dependent variable in these analyses is the vote share of governments. The lagged vote share is included as an independent variable to account for temporary swings in vote share and autocorrelation (Whitten and Palmer 1999).[19] The main independent variables of interest are the three indicators of economic performance.[20] The growth and inflation variables are highly correlated with each other ($r = .76$). Whether the variables were included together or separately, however, did not affect the results.

Table 3.2 presents the results of ordinary least squares (OLS) estimates. Model 1 shows that unemployment has a strong and significant effect on election results. Greater unemployment reduces the vote share of incumbents. Although the coefficients on the growth and inflation variables both point in the expected direction – high growth helps incumbents and high inflation hurts them – neither is precisely estimated.

The following models probe the robustness of these results. In model 2, I add time dummies for the first, second, and third accountability elections in each country (leaving out the fourth) to control for trends in electoral accountability. The results remain almost equivalent to earlier results. Model 3 introduces a far tougher challenge because country dummies are added to the regression (leaving out Slovenia) to control for unobserved country differences in electoral performance. This adds nine new variables to an already small data set. Again, unemployment remains a significant predictor of vote shares, though now at the .10 level.

Models 4 and 5 consider the possibility that these results are driven by small, ephemeral parties that play only a minor role in politics. Model 4 isolates the largest party in each government and model 5 all of the other governing parties.[21] Economic performance has a far greater effect on the large

[19] Although Whitten and Palmer (1999) recommend a more sophisticated method to account for the panel nature of the data, their corrections may not be justified for a data set where the time-series component consists in most cases of only three observations. Moreover, their estimates with the more sophisticated procedure mirror the OLS estimates.

[20] I also experimented with a control variable measuring the change in the number of effective parties because a declining number of parties may artificially inflate the performance of incumbents. This variable was not significant and did not affect the impact of the other independent variables.

[21] Model 5 clusters by election and uses robust standard errors to account for the fact that multiple parties competed in several elections.

TABLE 3.2. *Effect of Economic Conditions on Vote Shares*

	Model 1	Model 2	Model 3	Model 4	Model 5
	All Governments			Largest Governing Party	Other Governing Parties
Prior vote	0.261	0.272	0.183	0.261	0.667**
	(0.182)	(0.212)	(0.188)	(0.161)	(0.168)
Unemployment	−1.433**	−1.450**	−1.643+	−1.263**	−0.107
	(0.381)	(0.393)	(0.834)	(0.358)	(0.171)
Growth	0.647	0.645	1.681***	0.418	0.226
	(0.788)	(0.814)	(0.880)	(0.747)	(0.424)
Inflation	−0.052	−0.032	0.108	−0.027	0.014
	(0.116)	(0.129)	(0.139)	(0.108)	(0.068)
Constant	31.296**	35.781**	30.176	24.68**	0.346
	(11.012)	(12.692)	(14.543)	(8.336)	(2.997)
Time dummies		Yes			
Country dummies			Yes		
Observations	34	34	34	34	39
Adjusted R^2	0.36	0.32	0.53	0.27	0.29

** Significant at .01, * significant at .05, + significant at .10.

Note: Standard errors in parentheses for models 1–4. Robust standard errors with clustering on elections for model 5. Dependent variable is the percentage of the national vote.

parties than on the smaller ones. Unemployment has a strong and significant effect in model 4, but not in model 5. This result is encouraging because these large parties hold more political power and thus play a greater role in governing (Druckman and Roberts 2005); they are the parties who should be held accountable.

The effect of unemployment in all of these regressions is also substantively important. A 1% higher unemployment rate reduces vote share by something more than 1%. A party who managed to reduce unemployment by 5% could expect to increase its vote share by 7%.

In short, the vote for incumbents in Eastern Europe was strongly influenced by the state of the economy. Indeed, the effects were even stronger than in Powell and Whitten's study of established democracies, where economic variables had a significant effect only in certain delimited situations. Eastern European voters did hold governments accountable for their economic performance, in particular for the level of unemployment, and they did so in a clear and direct way.

3.5. UNEMPLOYMENT AND VOTING

It is curious that, of all the economic variables, it was unemployment that had the largest effects. Other work on electoral accountability does not always single out unemployment as the key economic variable. The work closest in subject matter is Remmer's (1989) analysis of the economic determinants of the vote in Latin America soon after the transition to democracy in that region. Her main finding is that incumbents were punished for high inflation and currency devaluations, not for high unemployment. Powell and Whitten (1993) meanwhile found that it was sometimes inflation and sometimes unemployment that mattered to voters in advanced democracies.

Yet these varied results make sense. During the 1980s and early 1990s, the most salient economic issues in Latin America were monetary in nature. Many countries suffered through bouts of hyperinflation, which were cured through tight monetary policy and currency devaluations. Likewise, in advanced industrial economies, a trade-off often exists between inflation and unemployment, which helps to explain the varying results in these countries.

More to the point, there are good reasons why unemployment was politically significant in Eastern Europe. One of the signal achievements of communism was full employment (Baxandall 2000). All citizens who wished to work (and even some who did not) were given jobs. Moreover, this achievement was a major tool in communist propaganda.

It was for this reason that unemployment and particularly high unemployment came as such a shock to citizens after the transition. Lack of experience with unemployment, years of communist propaganda, and the uncertainty of newly created safety nets combined to make unemployment the specter haunting these countries. Although citizens surely fretted over high inflation and low growth, these specters were familiar from communist times and were ones to which citizens had learned to adjust. It is no wonder then that voters punished governments who presided over high unemployment. Indeed, Przeworski (1993) found that government approval in Poland closely tracked the evolution of the unemployment rate.

These reflections lead to a more general point. Economic voting depends on the salience of particular economic conditions. More probing of the salient economic issues in the established democracies may explain why economic voting analyses have found such weak results. It is possible that the salience of particular economic conditions differs by country and time period, which may explain why no single economic variable has a consistent effect on vote shares across countries.

3.6. OTHER INFLUENCES: CLARITY OF RESPONSIBILITY, TIMING, AND PARTY TYPE

A number of studies have suggested that the strength of economic voting differs across space and time. In this section I consider some of these possibilities, both to guard against the possibility that omitted variables have biased the results and to probe further the nature of accountability.

The most prominent of these hypotheses is that economic voting differs according to clarity of responsibility (Powell and Whitten 1993). In situations where it is obvious who is in charge, voters should be able to attribute economic performance to incumbents and to hold them accountable. By contrast, where responsibility is blurred – perhaps because of coalition governments or separation of powers – voters may not know whom to hold accountable for given outcomes. Politicians may add to this opaqueness by blaming each other for poor results.

The main factor that blurs responsibility in Eastern Europe is cabinet type. Minority governments may escape responsibility because they can only make policy with the help of other parties who thus bear some of the responsibility for economic performance. Coalition governments are in a similar position because it is unclear which of the members of the coalition is responsible for economic outcomes.[22]

Rerunning model 1 for separate samples of coalition, single-party, minority, and majority governments (but not combinations of the types because of the small number of data points) yields weak results (not shown). Unemployment significantly and negatively affects all government types, although the effects are somewhat stronger for single-party and majority governments. Counterintuitively, growth and inflation have a larger effect on coalition and minority governments, but these results are typically insignificant.[23] In short, citizens in Eastern Europe did enforce somewhat more accountability where they could clearly attribute responsibility for policy to the government, but they were able to sanction even minority and coalition governments for their performance.[24]

Another factor affecting accountability is time. Several recent works have argued that in new democracies retrospective economic voting should develop only over time. Two variants of this argument exist. Duch (2001) argues that lack of information and trust in politicians may impede electoral accountability. Uninformed voters have difficulty making attributions of blame to those responsible for policy, whereas voters lacking trust in politicians are unlikely to apportion reward and blame in line with performance. Duch argues that over time citizens should become more informed and more trusting, which should strengthen economic voting.

Stokes (2001b) suggests a different mechanism for temporal effects. She argues that, early in the transition, voters are likely to forgive incumbents for poor results because they attribute poor performance to the old regime or see

[22] Other factors that blur clarity of responsibility like bicameralism, strong committee power, and separation of powers, were not prominent in the region. Four of the ten countries have bicameral assemblies, but only in Romania does the second chamber possess a real veto on legislation (Roberts 2006). A recent study of parliamentary committees in the region also presents a picture of general weakness (Olson and Crowther 2002). No country has a presidential regime.

[23] Using the entire data set and interaction terms yields similar results – the interactions between government type and economic outcomes are correctly signed but not precisely estimated.

[24] The relative dearth of single-party majority governments in the region (only three of thirty-four governments) and the relative frequency of minority, coalition, and surplus majority governments meant that voters in most countries were in the same boat as far as clarity of responsibility is concerned.

TABLE 3.3. *Economic Voting over Time and by Party Type*

	Model 6	Model 7	Model 8	Model 9
	Pre-1998 Governments	Post-1998 Governments	Old Regime Parties	New Regime Parties
Prior vote	0.550	0.284	0.742**	0.706**
	(0.320)	(0.237)	(0.178)	(0.126)
Unemployment	−0.891	−1.987**	−0.646+	−0.697**
	(0.529)	(0.555)	(0.360)	(0.223)
Growth	0.528	1.410	−0.664	0.804*
	(0.972)	(1.344)	(0.826)	(0.391)
Inflation	−0.093	−0.396	−0.071	0.127
	(0.138)	(0.263)	(0.132)	(0.080)
Incumbent party			−8.397*	−9.263**
			(3.629)	(2.205)
Constant	17.842	33.209*	17.269*	9.904*
	(17.285)	(14.831)	(7.596)	(3.790)
Observations	15	19	43	71
Adjusted R^2	0.35	0.47	0.34	0.41

** Significant at .01, * significant at .05, + significant at .10.
Note: Standard errors in parentheses for models 6 and 7. Robust standard errors with clustering by election in models 8 and 9. Dependent variable is percentage of the national vote.

it as the price that must be paid for future growth. In either case – she calls the responses exonerating and intertemporal – economic voting should be weak at the start of the transition, when incumbents are not punished and may even be rewarded for a weak economy.

To test these possibilities, I divided the sample into two parts near the midpoint of the data. This produces a group of pre-1998 and post-1998 elections. Models 6 and 7 in Table 3.3 presents the standard economic voting regressions for the two samples. In line with the timing hypothesis, there is a stronger relationship between economic conditions and vote shares in the latter period. Unemployment has a significant effect on vote shares only in the post-1998 period. Its substantive size is also larger, as is the amount of variation explained by the economic variables. The results are less supportive of the Stokes hypothesis, which predicts a reversal of economic voting early in the transition; the signs on the economic variables do not reverse.[25]

Nevertheless, even for the earlier period, unemployment has a nearly significant effect on vote shares ($p = .12$) and a reasonably sized substantive effect. Furthermore, moving the cutoff date to 1997 increases the size and significance of the unemployment coefficient for the earlier period. Finally, the regression for the pre-1998 period explains a significant portion of the variation in vote

[25] The cutoff date of 1998, however, may be too late for the sort of effects expected by Stokes. Isolating the first accountability election in each country, however, yields similar results.

shares. Taking into account the small sample size, one can say that even early in the transition there is a reasonable amount of economic voting.[26]

Finally, I consider a variable that has been found to affect economic voting in established and new democracies alike. Voters may calibrate their attributions of responsibility by the type of party in power. Powell and Whitten (1993) found that left-wing governments tend to be held responsible for unemployment, whereas right-wing governments are held responsible for inflation. Voters distinguish between governments according to their performance on the issue, which is part of their perceived core competence.

In Eastern Europe, left and right are less associated with particular economic goals. Party competition appears to be more structured around attitudes toward the communist experience than the traditional question of state intervention in the economy. Tucker (2006) has shown that the distinction between old and new regime parties can structure economic voting (also Fidrmuc 2000b, Powers and Cox 1997). In particular, when economic conditions are poor, voters appear to punish reformists and reward parties associated with the old regime. The logic is that poor performance vindicates the communist era – and by extension the former communist parties – and calls into question the reformists. Good performance has the opposite effect. Curiously, these effects occur without regard to incumbency status as voters link parties with their type rather than with their responsibility for policy in the present.

This idea, however, has not yet been explored at the national level (most tests use subnational or survey data). To see whether it applies, all of the parties in the data set were coded as "new regime," "old regime," or "neither."[27] Models 8 and 9 in Table 3.3 present the standard economic voting regressions for old and new regime parties. Because of heteroskedasticity in this data set – sometimes more than one party of each type competed in a single election – these estimations were clustered by election and robust standard errors applied. Controls were added for parties that sat in government at election time since incumbency did affect election results. As Tucker predicted, unemployment has a significant and negative effect on new regime parties, but it also has a less significant though substantively similar effect on old regime parties; the sign does not reverse. Growth reverses its sign in the direction Tucker would expect and has a significant effect of new regime parties, though not for the old regime parties. Inflation has only weak effects in both samples.

Therefore, some evidence exists that voters treat different party types differently, though the effect is weaker than in Tucker's study of regional economic

[26] A robustness check on these results uses the entire data set and interacts a dummy variable for post-1998 elections with the main economic variables. None of the interaction terms are significant, although their signs fit the Duch–Stokes hypothesis. The main-effect unemployment variable usually remains significant in these regressions.

[27] For the four countries covered by Tucker, I followed his codings. For the remaining six countries, I attempted to replicate his coding scheme using information about the parties from Bugajski (2002).

voting. The main impression, however, is that incumbents are held accountable for their economic performance. Although voters may take party type into account in their decisions, they also judge all governing parties by a strict standard based on their economic performance. This fact is encouraging because Tucker's party-type voting does not produce strong incentives for good performance. Whereas new regime parties should strive for better outcomes whether or not they are in government, old regime parties should do the opposite; because they benefit from poor economic conditions, they have little incentive to want the economy to perform well. It is heartening then that unemployment has a similar effect on both party types.

3.7. OTHER PERFORMANCE INDICATORS: ECONOMIC REFORM AND CORRUPTION

It is encouraging that governments are held accountable for economic performance across a wide range of conditions. But the economy is not the only aspect of performance that matters. Are governments punished for other performance failures?

Probably the most salient political issue in the region was economic reform – the liberalization and privatization of the economy. Moreover, economic reforms caused considerable short-term pain through higher inflation and unemployment and, thus, may be unpopular with voters who associated it with these effects. Are more reformist governments subject to greater punishment?

To test this idea, I added to the regressions a variable that captures the amount of reforms achieved by each government. Depth of reform is measured as the percentage change in the European Bank for Reconstruction and Development (EBRD) reform scores for the duration of each government (EBRD 1995–2009).[28] This variable, however, showed virtually no relation to the vote shares of governments. In fact, the sign indicates that faster reform improved the performance of incumbents, although the effect is imprecisely estimated (Bunce 2001). Reform per se does not affect election outcomes, although it may matter through its effect on the economy.

The anecdote at the beginning of this chapter identified corruption as a major influence on election results. Many studies have documented the high level of corruption in postcommunist countries (Treisman 2003). Citizens share this opinion (Krastev 2004). The World Values Survey (1995–1998) showed that, in nine of the ten countries, greater than 65% of respondents expressing an opinion viewed either most or almost all politicians as corrupt (the exception is Slovenia).

Unfortunately, sufficient data on corruption do not exist to subject this variable to regression analysis. Although Transparency International and the World Bank have begun to produce ratings of corruption in postcommunist countries, their assessments either cover only a short time series or do not

[28] These scores are discussed in more depth in the following chapters.

correspond to election years.[29] One can, however, look at expert assessment of individual elections. The journal *Electoral Studies* published election summaries for most of the elections in the sample. These summaries were written by country experts according to a fairly standard format that considered the major issues at play in each election.

Such election summaries exist for twenty-eight of the thirty-four elections. In fourteen of these twenty-eight cases (or exactly half), corruption is mentioned as an important campaign issue. In the elections where corruption is mentioned, vote losses were nearly twice as high (20 versus 10%) as in elections where corruption is not mentioned. A difference-of-means test suggests that the vote losses for "corruption-oriented" elections are higher than for others ($t = 2.07, p < .03$). Again, these results should be taken with a grain of salt. The evaluations in *Electoral Studies* are impressionistic and not intended for comparative purposes, but they are revealing about the importance of corruption in election campaigns and their potential significance in hurting incumbents. More research is necessary to confirm these conclusions.

3.8. ECONOMIC PERFORMANCE AND PARTICIPATION IN GOVERNMENT

One may worry that the focus on vote shares in this chapter does not capture the full force of electoral accountability. Parties might care more about participation in government than vote share for this gives them greater access to power and money. If this is true, they have incentives to perform well only if performance affects their likelihood of remaining in government.

A first concern then is whether changes in vote share are related to entering government. Are parties whose electoral performance worsened less likely to serve in government than those whose performance improved? It would be a perverse set of incentives if voters punished parties at the polls and yet found them more likely to enter government. Although such a situation is improbable in a majoritarian, two-party system, it is easily attainable in a parliamentary system where postelection bargaining admits multiple outcomes.

To test this proposition, I performed a logistic regression of a party's participation in government – a dichotomous variable that takes a value of 1 if the party participated in the first postelection government and a value of 0 if it did not – on the change in the party's vote share from the previous election to the current one. I added a control variable for participation in the incumbent government to determine whether incumbents were able to entrench themselves in power beyond what their performance warranted.

Table 3.4 presents the results. Model 10 shows that government participation did respond in the expected way to changes in vote shares. The positive

[29] Correlating average vote losses in each country with average corruption scores yields the correct directional associations – higher corruption is associated with greater losses – but insignificant coefficients.

TABLE 3.4. *Determinants of Government Participation*

	Model 10	Model 11
Sample	**All Parties**	**Incumbent Parties**
Vote difference	0.08**	
	(0.02)	
Incumbent	0.34	
	(0.35)	
Unemployment		−0.13**
		(0.06)
Inflation		−0.09⁺
		(0.05)
Growth		0.08
		(0.15)
Constant	−0.75**	1.04
	(0.20)	(1.10)
Pseudo R^2	.08	.15
Log likelihood	−116.4	−38.1
Observations	198	73

** Significant at .01, * significant at .05, ⁺ significant at .10.
Note: Logistic regressions, standard errors in parentheses. Dependent variable is participation in government (1 = participated).

and significant sign on the vote difference variable indicates that parties who improved their vote share were more likely to serve in government, whereas those who lost votes were less likely to serve. Electoral performance did matter for participation in government.

Does economic performance have a direct effect on participation in government? Are poorly performing governments less likely to retain office? Model 11 shows the results of a logistic regression of government participation on the three major economic variables for all incumbent parties. All three economic variables have the expected signs – higher unemployment, higher inflation, and lower growth reduce the likelihood of government participation – and unemployment has a statistically significant effect whereas inflation has a nearly significant effect ($p = .052$).[30] Incumbent parties who presided over poor economic conditions are less likely to return to government, particularly if they lose vote share. In sum, whether parties desire votes or office, they have an incentive to produce good economic performance.

3.9. UNIVERSALITY OF PUNISHMENT

The results so far leave one large puzzle. Although vote totals do respond to economic conditions, virtually all governments lost votes. This is worrisome.

[30] Adding a control for the change in vote shares slightly weakens these results, although the vote share variable is itself insignificant.

If governments expect to be thrown out of office, then they lose much of their incentive to perform well. What do they gain from better performance? Indeed, Przeworski et al. (1999) call this the "nightmare scenario."[31]

What explains the near universality of punishment? Can any of the variables considered thus far account for this phenomenon? To explain the consistency of punishment across the region, it is necessary to find a factor that consistently reaches a high value across the region and is evaluated negatively by voters.

Does economic performance fit the bill? It is true that many governments governed during periods of high unemployment, low growth, and high inflation, but a significant number of governments produced quite respectable economic outcomes. The average results for election-year performance in the sample are 3.7% growth, 15.8% inflation (including one value over 100%), and 11.3% unemployment. These values also include the very poor performance of countries early in the transition. It is hard to believe that this level of performance justified such consistent punishment unless voters' standards were very high.

Two more candidates to explain universal punishment are economic reform and corruption. Although differences in reform rates do not explain variations in electoral results, the generally high rate of reform in the region (relative to, say, Western Europe) may explain high rates of punishment. Virtually every government had to remove some popular economic securities. A similarly high level of punishment characterized Remmer's (1989) sample of reforming countries in Latin America, where the average president lost 13.4% from his previous vote total.

A similar calculation applies to corruption. Again, corruption was relatively high across the region and was certainly perceived as high by citizens in all ten countries. Citizens may have been punishing all governments for their perceived corruption. This level of corruption was at least partially related to economic reform. Massive privatization, not to mention other reforms, opened large opportunities for rewarding supporters and rent-seeking (Hellman 1996).

In the same vein, one may argue that the new rulers of Eastern Europe scored low on absolute measures of competence. Few had experience in governing and almost none had knowledge of the market reforms they were required to undertake. It is more than likely that they made avoidable mistakes. While voters should set a baseline standard of competence equal to the average competence of politicians and reward those more competent and punish those less competent, it is likely that postcommunist citizens set far higher standards than this average. Holmes (1997) even calls overly high expectations for leaders one of the fundamental characteristics of the transition.

These expectations may have flowed from the euphoria of the transition – the idea that everything has changed and good times were around the corner – and from comparisons with Western Europe. Not only did politicians promise

[31] Page (1978: 222), by contrast, argues that "to err on the side of forgiveness would leave voters vulnerable to tricky explanations and rationalizations, but to err on the draconian side would only spur politicians on to greater energy and imagination in problem solving."

a "return to Europe", but citizens also saw firsthand the prosperity and peace of their Western neighbors. Their own politicians could only come up short in these comparisons, leading them to believe that most governments were below average in competence.

3.10. EXPLAINING ELECTORAL ACCOUNTABILITY

What explains the relatively high degree of electoral accountability in the region (aside from the universality of punishment)? The causes of democratic quality are explored in Chapter 8. But here it is worth pointing out several circumstances in the region that helped citizens hold their rulers accountable.

One circumstance is the depth of the changes taking place. Massive economic reforms and dramatic swings in economic conditions had large effects on the lives of citizens. Almost no one was blind to what was going on economically, and with good reason. The scope of changes meant that failure to hold policy makers accountable could do enormous damage. If citizens left a failed government in power, they would possibly suffer another four years of negative growth, hyperinflation, and rising unemployment. This situation contrasts with the muddling-through sort of politics characteristic of established democracies. As shown in Chapters 8 and 9, citizens were in fact more interested in politics and more likely to follow political news than their counterparts in established democracies; they were aware of and concerned with what was happening.

At the same time, they lacked means other than elections to affect policy (see Section 9.3). Parties were mostly elite cliques whose members had little influence and were often ephemeral to boot (Lewis 1996). Interest groups and corporatist institutions – other means of influence – were likewise weak (Ost 2000). Unions had been discredited by their association with communism and had suffered due to economic reforms and recessions (Crowley and Ost 2001, Kubicek 1999). Citizens in general were reluctant to join civil society organizations, much less engage in protests (Howard 2003). Few means were open to citizens to affect government besides voting (Greskovits 1998).

Moreover, protest voting was something of a tradition in communist countries (Greskovits 1998). Although communist-era elections featured only a single slate of candidates – the National Front – citizens did have the option of crossing names off the list or boycotting the vote altogether. Although such actions carried risks at different times and places, protest voting was one of the few acts of political dissent allowed at all and thus had considerable appeal. Postcommunist citizens looking to express their discontent thus found retrospective economic voting an attractive and feasible option for holding their rulers accountable.

3.11. CONCLUSION

This chapter paints a mixed picture. On the one hand, electoral accountability is working. Voters were not afraid to throw the bums out and punish them in accord with their performance in office. In fact, economic voting was even stronger and more consistent than that in established democracies. It existed at a reasonable level at the beginning of the transition – although it also grew somewhat stronger over time – and was applied to all types of governments and parties (although some indications existed that clarity of responsibility and party type have effects). Therefore, politicians should have a strong incentive to produce good performance lest they lose office.

Yet the universality of electoral punishment in the region should give observers pause. While governments could improve their electoral prospects by delivering better performance, they could at most avoid serious vote losses. The best they could hope for was to hold their ground, which, ideally, should have motivated them to produce the best outcomes they could in the hope of remaining in office. But the severity of punishment may have had one unintended consequence: If incumbents knew in advance that they were going to lose, they had little incentive to achieve good results. They might as well enrich themselves while they were at the trough because that opportunity would soon disappear. Instead of limiting rent-seeking, universal punishment may in fact encourage it. The relation between corruption and election results may be even stronger. Universal punishment could lead to corruption, but corruption in turn might spur punishment. One may posit a vicious circle of corruption, which leads to vote losses, which leads to more corruption, with little way out.

A similar vicious circle could explain one of the more peculiar phenomena of the postcommunist era – the growing size of the state (Grzymala-Busse 2003, O'Dwyer 2006). Whereas most observers expected government employment and spending to fall after communism, they in fact rose. It is possible that governments who saw the electoral writing on the wall decided to expand government while they could, placing their supporters in public service jobs.

In short, electoral accountability in the sense of a positive relation between vote shares and performance is not enough to produce strong incentives for good performance. Rather it is also necessary that incumbents have a reasonable chance of being reelected. Without this possibility, they have strong incentives to enrich themselves when they get into office instead of promoting the public good. The simple equation of accountability and good government is more complicated than commonly perceived.

4

Mandate Responsiveness

On 20 September 2006, the largest public protests since the fall of communism – perhaps even since the Revolution of 1956 – erupted in Budapest. The cause was a leaked videotape of a speech that Socialist Prime Minister Ferenc Gyurcsány had made to newly elected party MPs just after his party's victory in parliamentary elections. The tape showed the Prime Minister telling the MPs that "we have obviously been lying for the last one and a half, two years" and that "I had to pretend for 18 months that we were governing. Instead, we lied morning, noon, and night" (BBC 2006).

In particular, his party had repeatedly claimed during the campaign of the previous spring that the budget deficit was only 4.5% of gross domestic product (GDP) – a level that with minor reductions could qualify Hungary for entry into the Eurozone.[1] In fact, as he well knew, the actual level was 10% of GDP, which was high enough to scare away foreign investors and to require serious and painful cuts in public expenditures. He noted also in his speech that the party's policies of the previous four years, which had helped produce these deficits, were unsustainable and ill conceived.

To top things off, the bottom line of his speech was that party MPs would have to line up in favor of a harsh austerity package. These expenditure cuts were nowhere to be found in the party's campaign, which instead promised to maintain Hungary's generous welfare state and even to add new social programs. The video made it abundantly clear that the Socialists had misled voters during the campaign, covering over a crisis in public finances and promising programs that they knew could not be enacted. It was shock at these admissions – and the somewhat vulgar fashion in which they were delivered – which provoked public protests in Budapest calling for the prime minister's resignation.

The main opposition party, the Young Democrats (Fidesz) of Victor Orbán, who were now leading protests and calling for Gyurcsány's resignation, were

[1] To join the EU, deficits had to be below 3% of GDP.

not blameless in the matter. Their preelection rhetoric had promised even more to Hungarian voters. They had proposed to restore housing subsidies, to provide free medicine for children and the elderly, to introduce a fourteenth-month pension, and to halt privatization, all programs that their analysts must have known were infeasible given the country's yawning deficit. Of the two party programs, that of the Socialists was more in line with economic realities.

In fact, the election campaign, like the one four years before, could be characterized as a bidding war between the two parties over who could promise more social programs. As former Finance Minister Lajos Bokros put it, "In terms of economic policy and philosophy, the two large parties are almost identical, with very little choice between them.... Both are nepotist and profligate in fiscal policy terms, both are for more subsidies, for more government help and against allowing more freedom, market access and self-care" (Eddy 2006).

These events in Hungary nicely illustrate the theme of this chapter: the degree to which parties in Eastern Europe make clear and distinct election promises and then follow through on them – in short, the degree to which mandate responsiveness obtains. As I show, the Hungarian experience of major parties presenting similar or vague platforms and repudiating their promises after elections is not unique.

4.1. THE STUDY OF MANDATE RESPONSIVENESS

Mandate responsiveness is a three-step process (see Figure 2.2). The first step is a programmatic party system (Kitschelt 2000). A party system is programmatic if parties hold clear rather than diffuse positions on policy issues and on some salient issues diverge in their policy preferences. A programmatic party system can be compared with systems that are based on clientelism or charisma, where parties compete by offering citizens side payments or charismatic leaders rather than alternative policy appeals.

A programmatic party system is a necessary but not a sufficient condition for mandate responsiveness. For citizens to control policy through ex ante selection, they must at the least be able to choose from among distinctive programs. Likewise, for politicians to follow through on their campaign programs, they must have made clear promises whose fulfillment can be assessed. A party that promises nothing or only vague generalities is not constrained by its promises. This situation is exactly that of clientelist or charismatic party systems where politicians are free to pursue whatever policies they wish because they gain support through means other than policy commitments (specifically patronage and personality).

Until recently, the issue of programmatic party systems has received relatively little attention. Kitschelt and his collaborators (1999) were among the first to try to measure the clarity of party positions which they did by looking at the extent to which political actors and citizens agreed on the positions of political parties. Somewhat more study has been done of the diversity of party positions. Most of these studies, however, have focused less on the degree of choice citizens are offered than on the polarization of party systems (Sartori 1970) – whether they are dominated by extremes – and the extent of Downsian centripetal competition (Downs 1957) – whether parties move toward the center in an effort to win elections. Kitschelt et al. (1999) again made strides in this area by measuring the extent to which party systems offer voters distinctive choices.

The second step in mandate responsiveness directly involves citizens. For citizens to exercise control over politicians, they must choose among parties at least in part based on their programs, a phenomenon that is called issue voting (Kessel 1972, MacDonald et al. 1995). Voters should be cognizant of differences between the choices on offer and should vote based on those issues. If voters are unaware of the differences between parties or if they vote on some other basis, then they are exercising little control over policy through mandate resopnsiveness.

Numerous scholars have searched for issue voting in established democracies, usually correlating vote choices with policy preferences. Although not all studies have yielded positive results, many do find reasonable evidence of issue voting.[2] I do not pursue this issue because it would require more thorough and nuanced analyses than I can undertake here. Nevertheless, existing work by Tworzecki (2003) and Kitschelt et al. (1999) indicates both that postcommunist voters are aware of the divergent policy stances of parties and that at least some of them do practice issue voting.

The third step in the chain of mandate responsiveness is whether politicians follow through on their promises. Do the promises made in the first stage and chosen by citizens in the second stage ultimately become policy? Only if this is the case have citizens' choices made a difference. All of the programmaticness and issue voting in the world are for naught if politicians act purely as they see fit when they serve in office.

Political scientists have developed several methods to assess whether parties follow through on their promises. They have measured the relation between the emphases of party manifestos and changes in budgetary priorities (Klingemann et al. 1994), determined whether specific campaign promises were fulfilled (Fishel 1985, Kalogeropoulou 1989, Pomper and Lederman 1980, Rose 1984, Royed 1996, Thomson 2001), and evaluated the correlation between the main tenor of campaigns and subsequent policy (Stokes 2001a). These studies have typically found strong mandate responsiveness in advanced democracies but considerably weaker mandate responsiveness in new democracies. Particularly relevant for present purposes is Stokes's (2001a) study, which finds that a quarter of Latin American presidents violated their mandates within days of taking office.

[2] As Dalton (2005: 212) writes, "The impact of any one issue for the entire public is often modest because not all issues are salient to all voters. However, a more refined analysis of specific issue publics would find that individual voting decisions are heavily influenced by each voter's specific issue interests."

4.2. CLARITY OF PARTY POSITIONS

How programmatic are party systems in Eastern Europe? How well do they perform on the first stage of mandate responsiveness? Kitschelt and his collaborators (1999) pioneered the study of programmatic party systems and have done so by looking at four Eastern European countries. Their main finding is a high degree of programmatic appeals. Party systems in Bulgaria, the Czech Republic, Hungary, and Poland "display more or less clear programmatic divisions and competitive dimensions on which party rivals advertise alternative appeals" (Kitschelt et al. 1999: 260). This result particularly holds for the most salient issues in a country, where most parties represent clearly defined positions and packages of positions.

One of the shortcomings of their analysis, however, is their exclusive focus on postcommunist countries. As a result, it is difficult to say where these party systems lie on the entire scale of programmaticness. Programmaticness is not a causal relation like electoral accountability – which exists or does not – but rather a scale that requires comparative assessments. This section and the following one bring a comparative lens to the study of programmaticness by looking more widely at ten countries in Eastern Europe and comparing them with twenty established democracies, seven new democracies outside of the postcommunist sphere, and nine less democratic postcommunist countries.

I begin by looking at the clarity of party positions. Following Kitschelt et al. (1999), I measure clarity as the degree to which observers agree on the issue positions of individual parties. If multiple observers agree on where a party stands, that party has a clear position; conversely, if observers disagree – if some view it as liberal and others as conservative – its position is less clear.

The data come from a survey conducted by Benoit and Laver (2006). They asked experts on the politics of forty-eight countries to rate the position of all of the significant political parties in the countries they knew best on a twenty-point scale across a variety of issue dimensions.[3] They were asked to rate each party's position on such issues as attitudes toward taxation, government spending, privatization, and environmental protection. The issues were chosen because of their salience in the politics of each country.

I define the clarity of a party's position as the standard deviation of the experts' scores for that party on a particular issue dimension.[4] I limit the analysis to parties who received more than 4% of the national vote in the most recent elections to prevent obscure fringe parties from influencing the results.

[3] Kitschelt et al. (1999), by contrast, surveyed midlevel party functionaries.

[4] Although the standard deviation should represent the clarity of a party's policy position, it is also possible, as Benoit and Laver (2006) suggest, that it represents measurement error. For example, they hypothesize that the greater the length and complexity of the survey, the higher the standard deviations as experts suffer fatigue. They confirm that this is the case, though its substantive significance is very small. It is also possible that experts differ substantially in their knowledge of politics across countries. This may be the case in Eastern Europe, where political science is a brand-new profession. It is difficult to assess whether such systematic differences exist.

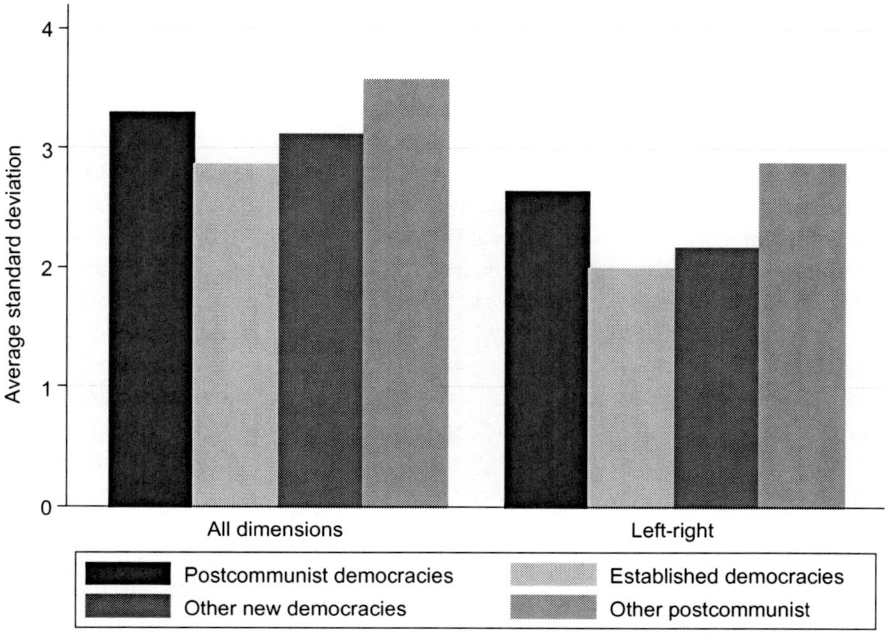

FIGURE 4.1. Clarity of party positions.

These parties are also the most relevant for voters trying to choose future policy directions.

How did the clarity of party programs in postcommunist democracies compare to those in other countries? Figure 4.1 presents the average standard deviations for all parties and dimensions in four groups of countries. Taller bars indicate higher standard deviations and, therefore, less agreement among raters and less clarity. The average standard deviation for the ten postcommunist democracies was 3.30 (s.e. .04) (again, positions were rated on twenty-point scales). This value is about 15% higher than the equivalent value of 2.87 (s.e. .03) for the established democracies – those countries that had democratized by 1945.[5] It is also slightly higher than the value of 3.13 (s.e. .08) for new democracies outside of the postcommunist region like Greece, Portugal, and Spain.[6] The only group of countries with less clear positions than the postcommunist democracies were the nondemocratic postcommunist countries (average standard deviation of 3.59, s.e. .06).[7] Party positions appear to be less clear in the postcommunist region than elsewhere.

These averages treat all issues equally, but a particularly important dimension in most democracies is the left–right one, which typically encompasses

[5] The established democracies are Australia, Austria, Belgium, Denmark, Finland, France, Germany, Iceland, Ireland, Italy, Japan, Luxembourg, Netherlands, New Zealand, Northern Ireland, Norway, Sweden, Switzerland, the United Kingdom, and the United States.

[6] The other new democracies are Cyprus, Greece, Israel, Malta, Portugal, Spain, and Turkey.

[7] The other postcommunist states are Albania, Belarus, Bosnia, Croatia, Macedonia, Moldova, Russia, Serbia, and Ukraine.

multiple issues and helps to structure vote choices. How do the postcommunist democracies compare on this dimension? Figure 4.1 shows even larger differences. The postcommunist parties have 33% higher standard deviations than parties in the established democracies (2.66, s.e. .13 vs. 2.00, s.e. .06). Again, the other new democracies do slightly better than the postcommunist democracies (average standard deviations of 2.18, s.e. .18) and the other postcommunist countries do worse (an average of 2.89, s.e. .24). Similar results obtain when isolating other salient issue dimensions.

This average measure of clarity is not without problems. First, electoral systems may systematically affect clarity. Where there are fewer parties, each party may have to cover more ground which results in an imprecision of position. Conversely, in multiparty systems, individual parties can carve out smaller, but more precise, niches. Second, clarity may depend on the salience of a particular policy dimension to politics. Parties are unlikely to present clear positions on dimensions that are relatively unimportant. Finally, the number of expert raters may further affect levels of agreement.

To correct for these possible biases, I regressed the standard deviations for each party dimension against dummy variables for the three country groups (the established democracies were the excluded category) in addition to controls for the number of parties, the size of each party (its vote share in the most recent election), the importance of a particular policy dimension to political competition in that country (assessed by raters in Benoit and Laver's survey), and the number of expert raters of that party dimension.

The results of these estimations (not shown) buttress and even strengthen the previous results. The difference between the standard deviations of the parties in the postcommunist democracies and the established democracies rises from 0.43 to 0.50 for all dimensions and from 0.66 to 0.70 for the left–right dimension. The postcommunist democracies continued to have significantly less clear programs than other new democracies. The control variables behaved mostly as expected. Parties had clearer positions on more salient dimensions and when they faced more competitors. Other robustness tests – for example, calculating country averages to control for the fact that countries with more parties have greater influence on the final results – do not alter these conclusions.

Are there any time trends in clarity? It is difficult to use these data to get a sense of trends because the survey was fielded at a single point in time. One way around this dilemma is to compare the clarity of parties of different ages. If clarity is increasing over time, older parties should have the clearest positions and younger parties the least clear. In the postcommunist region, one can distinguish four groups of parties: parties that existed before World War II (historical parties), successors to the communist ruling parties that ruled until 1989 (successor parties), parties founded in the immediate aftermath of the transition (standard parties), and parties founded after 1996 (second-generation parties).

Although the average levels of clarity across these groups do mostly fit expectations, the differences between them are extremely small and have average standard deviations ranging from 3.27 (s.e. .09) for the historical parties, to

3.25 (s.e. .09) for the successor parties, to 3.31 (s.e. .07) for the standard parties, to 3.35 (s.e. .07) for the second-generation parties. Differences between the groups are statistically insignificant and shrink even more when controls are added for party size, salience of the policy dimension, and number of raters. If an evolution in clarity occurs over time, it is likely not very large. In sum, the ideological positions of postcommunist parties are neither very clear nor becoming appreciably clearer.

4.3. DIVERSITY OF CHOICE

A second aspect of programmaticness is the diversity of choice. Do parties hold significantly different ideologies from each other on the main dimensions of political competition? Is there more than a dime's worth of difference between them? Only if this is the case can citizens hope that election choices would lead to different policies. If all parties hold the same positions, then elections are not a means for controlling policy.

I measure diversity of choice in two ways. The first is the standard deviation of the mean party positions of all of the parties on a particular policy dimension, not as in the previous analyses of raters' scores for each party. This measure takes into account the relative spread of all parties and may be termed the dispersion of party positions. An alternative measure is the range of ratings – the difference between the two most distant parties – for each policy dimension in each country. Although this measure may be affected by a single extreme party, such extremes do represent real choice in a party system.

Figure 4.2 presents the average dispersions and the average ranges for all policy dimensions for the four groups of countries described earlier. Taller bars indicate greater diversity of choice. The average standard deviation for the postcommunist democracies is 3.89 (s.e. .14), which is about 15% smaller than that for the established democracies (an average of 4.55, s.e. .11). The same result holds for ranges; postcommunist democracies have about 7% smaller ranges than the established democracies (10.24, s.e. .37 vs. 11.00, s.e. .26). The other new democracies have slightly more diversity than the postcommunist democracies on the first measure (an average standard deviation of 4.23, s.e. .31) and slightly less on the second (an average range of 9.32, s.e. .69). Not surprisingly, the other postcommunist states lag behind all three groups. These results are also robust to a focus on particular salient dimensions, including the general left-right dimension.

Again, extraneous factors may affect these ratings. Countries with more parties are likely to have more diversity as parties spread across the political spectrum, whereas two-party Downsian competition may push parties toward the center. Similarly, more diversity may exist on particularly salient dimensions. Regression analyses that control for these factors (not shown), however, do not alter the results. In fact, inclusion of these controls again increases the differences between the postcommunist democracies and the established democracies.

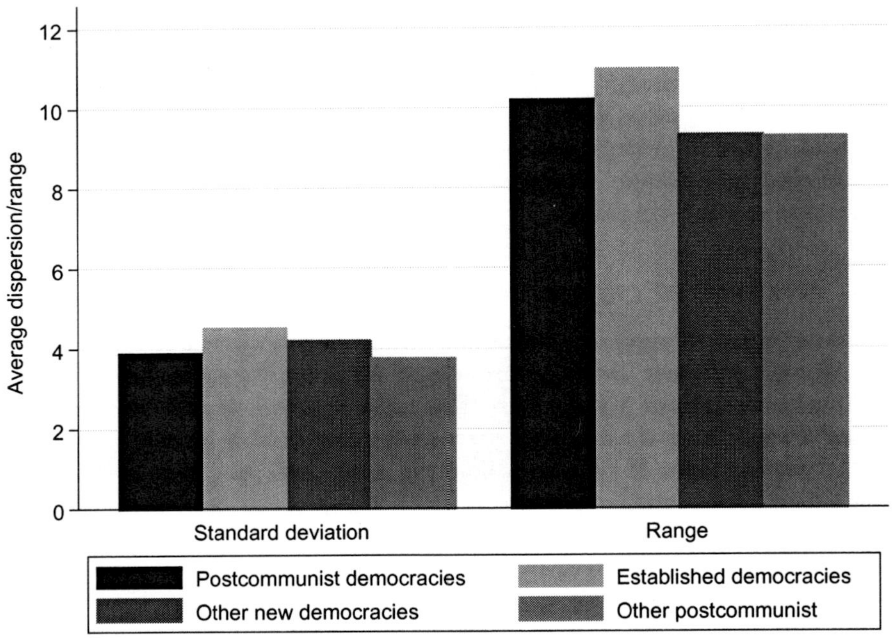

FIGURE 4.2. Diversity of party positions.

I can thus conclude that party systems in the postcommunist states offer not only less clear choices than those in the established democracies but also somewhat less variable choices. Indeed, these choices are less variable than those in other new democracies, though usually not by as wide a margin. The size of the difference from the established democracies is on the order of 10 to 20% even after controlling for contextual factors. Whether this is a lot or a little is a matter of judgment, but it is qualitatively noticeable.

4.4. ASSESSING CAMPAIGN PROMISES

I turn now to the third step in mandate responsiveness – promise fulfillment.[8] To assess promise fulfillment, I use a variant of Stokes's (2001a) methodology. She classifies every election campaign in Latin America as pro-reform, anti-reform, or ambiguous and then asks whether the elected government then introduced economic reforms. I focus on the same issue in Eastern Europe, but measure reform continuously rather than dichotomously. Did governments speed up reforms when they promised to speed them up and slow them down when they promised the same?

Economic reform refers to such policies as price and trade liberalization, enterprise privatization, and capital market opening. Not only is this issue salient to citizens because of its large effects on their lives, but as Kitschelt

[8] As mentioned earlier, I skip the second step – issue voting – due to a lack of data.

et al. (1999: 389) note, "the centrality of conflict over economic reform, the divide between social protectionists and market liberals, is common to all postcommunist democracies." Although few serious parties in Eastern Europe have rejected economic reforms altogether – an important difference from Latin America – many have argued for slowing them down or mitigating their distributional consequences.

How can one measure the campaign promises of governments? Although the measures of ideology used in the previous sections seem like an appropriate choice, in fact they are not. The reason is that they are ex post measures: they rate parties based not only on their campaigns but also on their behavior in office. Using such ratings biases an assessment of mandate responsiveness. Party ideologies would tend to correspond to policy choices because they are in part based on those choices. Moreover, these measures only capture a single moment in time. Parties who disappeared or merged are excluded and no measure of ideological change exists.

To escape from this bind, promises were measured as the stated stances of governing parties toward economic reform in electoral campaigns.[9] Did they promise to speed up or slow down market reforms? To determine these stances, I evaluated the descriptions of elections from journal articles and country-specific monographs. The aim was to produce an assessment of whether the parties who subsequently entered government ran on a pro- or anti-reform platform or did not take a clear position on the issue. I assigned a rating to each country-year based on the sitting government's campaign pledges toward reform. The appendix to this chapter lists the sources for these judgments.

A number of difficulties exist in creating this measure. Often multiple governments held power over the course of a particular year. In these cases, I used the position of the government who held power for the largest portion of the year. When governments consisted of multiple parties, as was typically the case, I focused on the dominant tenor of the government; in most cases, the governing parties agreed on their attitudes toward economic reform, though sometimes a minor partner dissented from this stance.

What sorts of promises about reform did Eastern European parties make? About 34% of the country-years from 1990 to 2004 are classified as featuring a government that promised to speed up reform while 38% featured one that promised to slow down reform. The remaining 28% of governments did not have clear positions on the issue. Countries seemed to alternate between governments committed to reform and those that wanted to slow down reform. One explanation for this pattern is that voters wished to produce socially friendly reforms. They did not trust anti-reformers to produce reform.and they did not trust reformers to limit the social fallout of reform. Therefore, they

9 Manifesto research might serve equally well but has been found to suffer from methodological problems (see Benoit and Laver 2006, King and Laver 1993). Manifesto scores for Eastern Europe did not exist when this manuscript was taking shape. They have since been published; see Klingemann et al. (2006).

elected reformers to pursue reform but then replaced them with anti-reformists to mitigate the social effects of the reforms.

The time trend favored reformists. Although parties in favor of slowing down reforms predominated in the early transition – 52% of country-years from 1990 to 1997 featured a government that had advocated slowing down reform – this percentage dropped to 26% in the 1998–2004 period. Opposition to reform became less electorally attractive over time, perhaps because reform was associated with accession to the EU, which was attractive particularly to left-wing parties. What changed in the later period was not governments promising to speed up reforms – up from 30 to 38% – but governments with ambiguous campaigns – up from 18 to 37% – which could be due to the declining salience of reform or to the fact that international integration required opponents of reform to hold their tongues. It should be noted that the 28% of country-years featuring governments that ran ambiguous campaigns constitute a clear failure of the mandate vision. Because incoming governments did not make clear promises, voters could not control policy by choosing among them, at least not in this policy domain.

These results are significant. Stokes finds in Latin America that candidates had to come out against reform to win elections. In Eastern Europe, by contrast, support for reform was by no means a losing proposition. Indeed, parties who presented themselves as for "capitalism without adjectives," like ODS in the Czech Republic or the Reform Party in Estonia, found themselves at the head of several governments. The relatively promarket orientation of the mass public that enabled this phenomenon is investigated in more depth in the next chapter.

Moreover, the anti-reformist governments that were elected usually did not reject reforms completely. Rather they argued for a more gradual pace of reform and greater social protections to help those hurt by reform. In this they differed from many parties in Latin America, who saw the entire reform project as misguided. Eastern European opposition to reforms, at least in its electorally successful guise, saw the problem of reform more in its implementation, which opponents to reform portrayed as corrupt, heavy-handed, and hard-hearted, than in its fundamental conception. Indeed, many left-wing parties became staunchly pro-European even as accession required market-friendly policies. For their relatively pro-reform attitudes, these countries could to some extent thank a communist regime that had so discredited a return to the status quo ante that all serious parties had to be for some reform.

4.5. ASSESSING PROMISE FULFILLMENT

Did governments who came to power pledging more reform actually produce more reform and did governments who came to power opposing reform actually produce less of it? Whereas Stokes portrays reform as a Manichaean choice, in Eastern Europe reform was more a matter of degree; virtually all governments engaged in some reform. To measure a government's progress in reform, I turn to the ratings of reform described briefly in the previous chapter. The

European Bank for Reconstruction and Development's (EBRD's) reform index rates each country's progress on a variety of different economic reforms from 1990 to the present (EBRD 1995–2009). The overall index of reform includes progress on eight policy areas: small-scale privatization, large-scale privatization, governance and enterprise restructuring, competition policy, banking reform, securities markets and nonbank financial institutions, price liberalization, and trade and foreign-exchange liberalization. In each policy area, countries are rated on a scale of 1 (the level of a centrally planned economy) to 4.33 (the level of an established market economy) with specific policies associated with one-third-point steps in between.[10] Scores on the eight policy areas are averaged to produce an overall reform score.

Combining these reform scores with data from the previous section produces a data set with annual measures of both progress in reform and the campaign promises of ruling parties for all ten countries from 1990 to 2004. The cross-national time-series nature of the data poses a number of problems for estimating the effects of campaign promises. To correct for autocorrelation, I used the change in levels of reform as the dependent variable and the lagged value of reform as an independent variable. I also included country fixed effects to account for unobserved differences in culture and history across countries.

Table 4.1 presents the results of pooled ordinary least squares (OLS) estimations of the determinants of reform. Model 1 includes only the two dummy variables for governments who pledged to speed up reform and governments with ambiguous positions (Reformist Promises and Ambiguous Promises). Although the reformist variable does have the correct sign – pro-reform governments are associated with faster reform – the effect is only imprecisely estimated and not significantly different from the reform rates of governments that promised to slow down reforms (the excluded category). Neither do governments who ran ambiguous campaigns produce faster or slower reform than anti-reformist governments. Campaign promises are not strongly associated with different reform trajectories.

These results may be criticized because they do not include controls for other influences on reform. Arguably the concept of mandate responsiveness does not require such controls; it implies that governments follow through on their promises, not that they do better or worse after controlling for context. The excuse that "we tried to follow through on our promises, but were not able to because conditions did not allow it," is not one that should necessarily affect assessments of mandate responsiveness. Indeed, governments in Stokes's (2001a) account typically made exactly these excuses. Parties should take these conditions into account in making their promises.

Nevertheless, one can ask whether contextual conditions affect the fulfillment of promises. One particularly salient circumstance is the macroeconomy. It may be easier to engage in reform in the midst of an economic crisis (Drazen

[10] There have been objections to this measure of reform as overly subjective, but few alternatives to it exist. See Kostadinova (N.D.) and Campos and Horvath (2006).

TABLE 4.1. *Promise Fulfillment*

	Model 1	Model 2	Model 3	Model 4	Model 5
Sample		**All Years**		**1990–1997**	**1998–2004**
Reform progress (lagged)	−0.260**	−0.279**	−0.263*	−0.299**	−0.055
	(0.019)	(0.028)	(0.020)	(0.046)	(0.057)
Reformist promises	0.038	0.031	0.032	0.081	0.021
	(0.026)	(0.024)	(0.027)	(0.061)	(0.017)
Ambiguous promises	0.010	0.020	0.007	−0.085	0.017
	(0.039)	(0.037)	(0.040)	(0.099)	(0.037)
Unemployment (lagged)		−0.002			
		(0.004)			
Growth (lagged)		−0.001			
		(0.002)			
Inflation (lagged)		0.000			
		(0.000)			
Coalition government			0.028		
			(0.033)		
Minority government			0.018		
			(0.030)		
Constant	0.916**	0.978**	0.897**	1.157**	0.198
	(0.076)	(0.084)	(0.079)	(0.207)	(0.183)
Observations	128	126	128	60	68
Adjusted R^2	0.59	0.64	0.58	0.45	0.07

** Significant at .01, * significant at .05.
Note: Standard errors in parentheses. All models include country fixed effects. Dependent variable is annual change in EBRD reform scores.

and Grilli 1993). Or poor economic performance may make reform more difficult because it is harder to compensate losers from reform. Moreover, different sorts of parties may come to power during different economic situations – for example, voters may prefer reformists when the economy is going well – which may in turn affect their success at reform.[11] Model 2 thus includes measures of the lagged levels of GDP growth, inflation, and unemployment to control for the economic determinants of reform. The inclusion of these variables does not alter the effect of reform promises. In fact, controlling for economic conditions slightly weakens the effect of campaign promises.

Institutions are another contextual factor that may affect reform. Where governments do not hold a majority of seats in parliament or share power among multiple parties, it may be more difficult for them to follow through on their promises because other parties can veto their choices. Model 3 thus adds controls for minority and coalition governments. Neither variable has a

[11] Stokes (2001a) uses a Heckman selection model to control for this effect. I found that economic conditions did not affect the likelihood that a pro-reformist or anti-reformist government held power.

significant effect on reform nor does their inclusion change the influence of the promises variables.[12]

A final question is whether mandate responsiveness changes over time. Mandate responsiveness may be weaker early in the transition as inexperience or external pressure prevents politicians from following through on their promises. Conversely, it may be weaker later in the transition as economic reform loses its salience and other issues come to the fore. Models 4 and 5 thus rerun model 1 for two separate periods: 1990 to 1997 and 1998 to 2004. In fact, the later possibility is closer to the truth. Pro-reform governments did have slightly more success in fulfilling their mandates early in the transition. Nevertheless, none of these results reaches conventional levels of significance. Mandate responsiveness was weak throughout the transition.

Other robustness tests support these results. Thus, panel-corrected standard error models (Prais-Winsten regressions) yielded similar results. Using subindices of the EBRD reform index, like privatization or liberalization, also yield negative results. Initial work with manifestoes data – isolating positive and negative mentions of reform – similarly showed no positive results.

In fact, these weak results comport with other work on the region. In assessing the behavior of leftist parties in five countries, Cook et al. (1999: 237) conclude that "after left parties achieved electoral success, the realization of their policy preferences was limited by a variety of domestic and international constraints that varied across the cases." Lipsmeyer's (2000, 2002) work relating party ideology to social policy choices also finds only scattered correspondence between left and right governments and policy changes. Scholars of economic reform in Eastern Europe meanwhile have argued that the key is not an ideologically committed right-wing government as other have presupposed but an alternation between right and left (Hellman 1996, Orenstein 2001). A focus on ideology has not been particularly fruitful in analyzing policy in Eastern Europe.[13]

4.6. ANECDOTAL EVIDENCE ON PROMISE FULFILLMENT

Looking at anecdotal evidence about the experience of individual governments introduces some subtlety into these results. In Latin America, Stokes (2001a) found that parties often vehemently promised to stop reforms but then introduced them within days or weeks of assuming office. Such a situation characterized the governments of presidents Fujimori in Peru and Menem in Argentina, among others.

Few such clear-cut mandate violations appeared in Eastern Europe. When opponents of reform came to power they generally did make an attempt to enact more labor-friendly policies before turning to market reforms. Consider

[12] Interactions between promises and government status or between promises and economic conditions are similarly insignificant.

[13] This is in marked contrast to work on Western Europe where ideology plays a major role (e.g., Boix 1998, Garrett 1998, Huber and Stephens 2001).

the Hungarian Socialist Party, which came to power in 1994 on a platform of reducing the pain of reform. Among its first acts in government was an attempt to negotiate a social pact with labor unions. Only when hit by a balance-of-payments crisis in 1995 did the Socialists turn around and adopt an austerity package. A similar situation played itself out in Poland after the Democratic Left Alliance was elected in 1993. Sudden dramatic reversals are difficult to pinpoint in the sample with the possible exception of the Lithuanian Democratic Labor Party in 1992, which in itself is somewhat of a success story for Eastern Europe, at least compared to Latin America.

Nor did there exist many cases of reform-favoring parties renouncing their commitments and embracing status quo policies immediately after elections. Supporters of reform usually did attempt to reform before backsliding and explained their failure to follow through on resistance from the bureaucracy, obstructionist opposition parties, or a fickle public. The vocally promarket prime minister of the Czech Republic, Václav Klaus, who arguably slowed reforms to ensure his party's political success (see Chapter 5), claimed that he would have pursued reforms more rapidly if not for the treason of his coalition partners. Although reversals occurred in both directions, they were not of the size and suddenness of those in Latin America.[14] Indeed, reform rarely went backward in Eastern Europe and improved at least marginally over every government in the sample.

4.7. EXPLAINING MANDATE RESPONSIVENESS

What explains the relative weakness of mandate responsiveness in Eastern Europe? The communist experience certainly played a role. Virtually all significant parties in the region emerged only after 1990 and thus carried virtually no baggage from the past. It is no surprise then that their programs were perceived as considerably less clear than those of parties with longer histories in other countries. Programmaticness was further hindered by the considerable flux of parties in Eastern Europe. Parties tended to be transient, entering and exiting the scene with regularity (Birch 2003, Rose and Munro 2003). As a result, their reputations were not based on a large number of campaigns or terms in government.

The governments that these parties formed also acted under tight constraints. In numerous policy areas, particularly the economic policies considered in the second half of the chapter, they were limited in the choices they could make (Greskovits 1998). International integration and loan agreements with the International Monetary Fund and World Bank often required countries to adopt specific policies. Although economic populism was not completely out of bounds – the actions of some Bulgarian and Romanian governments belie this view – it did entail a large cost in economic performance and international

[14] Part of the reason may be the frequency of consensus governments in Eastern Europe. In Latin America, presidents could often introduce reform by decree.

integration. Responsible governments therefore tended to avoid heterodox policies. But publicizing these constraints was not a particularly compelling campaign strategy. Instead parties tried to follow the public mood, which had become suspicious of reform. Upon taking power, many of these promises to slow reform turned inoperative as politicians found them to carry large costs. Meanwhile, parties that preferred faster reform often found that a public that had soured on reform put a brake on their ambitions (see Chapter 5).

The strong electoral accountability of the previous chapter may also have played a role in weakening mandate responsiveness. The fact that voters tended to punish incumbents severely made them desperate to find ways of attracting voters. Whereas improving their economic performance was one, albeit difficult, way for parties to avoid electoral retribution, campaign promises were another. Incumbent parties had a strong incentive to promise voters the moon and avoid mention of difficult choices to distract attention from performance failures. Such a dilemma confronts parties in all democracies, but the problem was more severe in Eastern Europe because few parties had assured bases of support. Their fate was on the line with every election, and so they had to use every tool at their disposal including unfulfillable promises.

A typical election in Eastern Europe thus featured several parties attempting to outbid one another on issues popular with voters. Just such a case was described in the introduction to this chapter, where the two main Hungarian parties competed in offering more social protections to the public. Ultimately, voters had little choice between the parties on the main social and economic issues (though they could choose between the parties on more symbolic issues or on their perceived competence and honesty). The upshot is that parties would either have difficulty fulfilling their promises or would have to mortgage the future to do so.

This behavior was short-sighted. Upon taking office, newly elected parties found that they could not fulfill their promises. Anecdotal evidence from campaigns in the region indicates that opposition parties did attack governing parties over their broken promises and may have managed to profit from such attacks (Roberts No date-b). Thus, the Czech Social Democrats delighted in replaying clips of Klaus's unfulfilled promise that reforms would lead to a doubling of incomes by the end of the millennium. But in the cutthroat electoral environment of Eastern Europe it was difficult for parties to take the responsible long-term view (Innes 2002).

4.8. CONCLUSION

This chapter has attempted to assess both the degree to which parties hold clear and distinct policy positions and the degree to which parties implement their promises in one important policy area. Although it is important to follow up these results with more detailed studies of campaigns and their realization using other measures of promises and outcomes, these results do suggest a fairly clear picture of mandate responsiveness in the region.

In particular, mandate responsiveness may be the weakest link in the quality of Eastern Europe democracies. Voters face a considerably cloudier picture in choosing among parties than in established democracies. Turning to actual policy making, there is only a weak connection between promises and fulfillment, at least on one prominent issue. A closer investigation of specific promises in the areas of pensions and housing in Chapters 6 and 7 yields the same conclusion. The weakness of these two elements of mandate responsiveness make ex ante control of politicians difficult.

This weakness may in turn shed light on the finding of electoral accountability in Chapter 3. Because it is difficult to control representatives ex ante, voters may turn to ex post sanctioning. Electoral accountability may be a necessary safety valve for weak mandate responsiveness. Such a combination may even be typical of new democracies. Stokes's finding of weak mandate responsiveness in Latin America occurs along with a high degree of electoral accountability (Remmer 1989). Conversely, in Western Europe, studies of mandate responsiveness have yielded positive results, whereas electoral accountability has been found to be weaker. I discuss this potential trade-off in the book's conclusion.

APPENDIX: SOURCES FOR JUDGMENTS OF CAMPAIGN PROMISES

Bulgaria: Barany (2002), Dimitrov (2001)
Czech Republic: Krause (2006), Orenstein (2001), Tworzecki (2003)
Estonia: Fitzmaurice (1993, 2001), Smith (2001), Taagepera (1997)
Hungary: Körösenyi (1999), Tworzecki (2003)
Latvia: Dreifelds (1996), Nørgaard (1996), Pabriks and Purs (2001)
Lithuania: Clark and Prekevičius (2003), Lane (2001)
Poland: Chan (1998), Millard (1999), Szczerbiak (2003), Tworzecki (1994)
Romania: Bacon (2004), Popescu (2003), Roper (2000)
Slovakia: Fitzmaurice (1995, 1999), Henderson (2002), Krause (2003, 2006)
Slovenia: Fink-Hafner (1997), Fitzmaurice (1997), Gow and Carmichael (2000)

5

Policy Responsiveness[1]

Václav Klaus was one of the most visible symbols of the transition in Eastern Europe.[2] By all accounts he was a committed and outspoken free marketeer, whose idols were Milton Friedman and Margaret Thatcher. But his uniqueness lay not just in these beliefs but also in the adeptness with which he used and discarded them in his rise to power.

The leaders of the Civic Forum, the umbrella party that was to sweep to power in the first free Czech elections, had little use for Klaus. Though by and large liberal, their mindset focused more on human rights and democracy than the economic freedom that Klaus advocated. Civic Forum's leaders did put Klaus on the party list for parliamentary elections, but placed him in the heavily industrialized Northern Moravian region, which had long been a bastion of the left and was to suffer severely from the transition. If there was a place where Klaus's neoliberal ideas were expected to fall flat, it was among the once-favored sons of the communist regime and soon-to-be-unemployed miners and factory workers.

Yet Klaus brought his neoliberal ideas to the region and won. He told miners that free-market reforms were both necessary and would bring results. When asked about the danger of foreigners buying up factories, he said that if they were willing to put down hard currency for clearly outdated factories, the country should gladly take their money. Fed up with forty years of repressive communist rule and holding positive memories of a successful market economy during the interwar era, Czechs lapped up Klaus's ideas. The optimism and persuasiveness of the message combined with the charisma and diligence of its messenger brought Klaus more preference votes than any candidate in the country and catapulted him to the head of the Ministry of Finance.[3]

[1] In collaboration with Byung-Yeon Kim.

[2] For more on Klaus, see Orenstein (1998, 2001), Saxonberg (1999), or, in Klaus's own words, Klaus (1997) or Blejer and Coricelli (1995).

[3] The country's electoral system allowed citizens to express a preference for particular candidates within party lists.

From that post, he engineered a series of reforms freeing virtually all consumer prices, opening the country's borders to trade, and undertaking one of the most daring privatization schemes the world had seen, which put most of the country's state-owned industries in the hands of its own citizens through a voucher auction.[4] And in following through on his neoliberal creed, he remained popular among citizens. In 1991, he helped to engineer the breakup of the Civic Forum and founded a new avowedly liberal party called the Civic Democratic Party (ODS). With Klaus at its head, ODS went on to win elections in 1992 – trouncing the far better known dissidents who joined other parties – even as the reforms that it championed produced dramatically higher prices and a severe recession.

As the country's prime minister, however, Klaus's behavior changed.[5] Instead of privatizing the country's banks and promoting the restructuring of industry – the orthodox next steps in the neoliberal reform program – Klaus used state-owned banks to funnel loans to the state's loss-making enterprises and keep them afloat (Brom and Orenstein 1994, Kenway and Klvačová 1996). Rather than deregulating rents and privatizing public housing, he kept both under tight state control (see Chapter 7). When the state's railroad employees demanded higher wages and an end to restructuring, Klaus blinked and gave in to their demands, a move that demoralized many of the true believers among his supporters (Husák 1997).

What was behind his change of heart, or at least behavior, on all of these issues? Although in his heart Klaus may have been a neoliberal, in his head he was a politician who wanted to build a dominant party that could govern the country for the long term (Orenstein 1998). In the early 1990s, Klaus could count on public support for his market-oriented philosophy and push ahead with his neoliberal project. But by the mid-1990s, the public had lost its stomach for market reforms and did not want to see its securities dismantled. A nationwide public opinion poll asking citizens whether they felt that a market economy was right or wrong for the country saw support drop monotonically – from 46% more citizens answering right than wrong in 1990 to 21% more answering wrong than right in 1997.[6]

Although he had adroitly taken advantage of a public eager to become European at the start of the 1990s, he now saw a public that preferred some of the social guarantees of the communist regime and had tired of belt tightening. It was no surprise then that this consummate politician adjusted his policies to

4 These reforms did coincide with more generous social policies – the social-liberal strategy described by Orenstein (2001). But these social policies were not under Klaus's control and he opposed them.

5 One reason for the change was that he was now responsible for all aspects of public policy. Earlier his portfolio had included only economic reform. Now, as prime minister, he was responsible for social policy as well.

6 See the discussion of the Central and Eastern Eurobarometer later in the chapter.

follow the public. And his moves paid off as his party managed to come out as the top vote getter again in elections in 1996.[7]

Klaus's shift to the left illustrates the theme of this chapter – the responsiveness of politicians to public preferences. Policy responsiveness is the hallmark trait of democratic quality because if the people are really ruling then policy should follow their preferences. It thus presents the toughest test of whether democracies in the region are functioning as democratic theory expects. This chapter attempts to determine whether politicians in the region do follow public preferences.

5.1. THE STUDY OF POLICY RESPONSIVENESS

Considerable difficulties exist in studying the responsiveness of politicians to the public. How can one recognize whether a public policy was adopted because citizens wanted it or because of a myriad of other factors? Even if a majority of the public is in favor of a particular policy, does that mean that public preferences caused it? It may be that politicians or the media convinced citizens that such a policy was necessary. Or perhaps both the policy choice and citizen preferences were caused by a third factor like an economic crisis.

To date, political scientists have used two methods to assess the relation between citizen preferences and public policy (Manza and Cook 2002). The older and more common method studies what is called dyadic or party representation. It looks for correlations between the ideologies of individual MPs and their constituencies – dyadic representation – or between entire parties and their electorates – party representation (Miller and Stokes 1963).[8] The idea behind this method is that correspondence means that MPs or parties are representing the views of their constituents and ultimately should produce the sort of policies that the majority of them desire.[9]

The study of dyadic/party representation, however, suffers from a number of methodological problems. It is difficult to parse out causality merely by looking at static measures (but see Hill and Hurley 1999). Does correspondence occur because voters influence representatives or because representatives influence voters?

[7] His coalition was the first incumbent government to be reelected in the region. Though the government lost its majority, this was mainly due to the poor performance of Klaus's coalition partners. His own party received a vote share almost identical to that four years prior despite numerous scandals.

[8] Dyadic representation refers to countries with single-member districts where representatives can be matched with a geographical constituency. In countries with proportional representation, the equivalent studies match parties and their supporters because multimember constituencies weaken the geographic linkage.

[9] For a survey of studies in this tradition, see Miller et al. (1999). Two recent advances are Kitschelt et al. (1999) and Luna and Zechmeister (2005). Attempts have also been made to assess collective representation – whether the position of the median or decisive legislator matches the position of the median voter. See Powell (2000) and Dalton (2005).

Another problem is the dependent variable in these studies. Most focus on roll call votes or the perceived or professed ideologies of representatives. The problem is that policy responsiveness implies that preferences are translated into public policy, not just legislative votes or party platforms. It is entirely possible that representatives or parties who are ideologically in tune with their electorates produce policy outcomes at variance with mass opinion. This could be because of a gap between words and deeds or social choice issues in the legislature. Although a finding of correspondence should be heartening for an assessment of democratic quality, it does not necessarily imply that politicians are delivering the polices that the public wants.

To overcome these problems, scholars have recently turned to time-series analysis and measures of policy outcomes (Erikson et al. 2002, Stimson et al. 1995), which allow them to estimate what has been called dynamic representation – the degree to which policy changes in response to opinion changes. Time-series analysis partially overcomes the problem of endogeneity. By looking at opinion prior to policy change, scholars gain some assurance that opinion is driving politicians rather than the other way around. And by considering actual policy outputs, one can get a better sense of whether politicians actually do as the public wills rather than merely appearing to support what the public wants. Most of the studies to take this approach have found good evidence of a relation between preferences and policy, but all of them have focused on the advanced industrial democracies, where such a finding is not surprising.[10]

This chapter extends these techniques to Eastern Europe, where few expected politicians to listen to the public. It analyzes whether actual policy outcomes follow public opinion in one of the key policy areas of the transition: basic economic reforms. But before doing so, it is worth describing a major study of party representation in Eastern Europe.

5.2. PARTY REPRESENTATION

While analyses of party representation cannot say whether public opinion causes policy, they do provide some assurance that politicians are listening to citizens. Kitschelt and his collaborators (1999) have produced a magisterial study of such connections in four Eastern European countries – part of their study was discussed in the previous chapter – and found that parties and their voters were on the same wavelength.

They conducted surveys of both midlevel party functionaries and the mass public and then calculated the correspondence between the average policy positions of party functionaries and the average positions of their electorates in a number of different policy areas. Their main finding was a high degree of

[10] Examples include Canes-Wrone and Shotts (2004), Wlezien (2004), Soroka and Wlezien (2004, 2005), Eichenberg and Stoll (2003), Franklin and Wlezien (1997). Earlier studies include Page and Shapiro (1983), Monroe (1979, 1995), and Brooks (1987, 1990). For challenges, see Bartels (2008) and Gilens (2005).

party representation in the region. In most countries and issue areas, the beliefs of party functionaries and party sympathizers were strongly correlated with each other. As Kitschelt et al. (1999: 340) put it, "Patterns of representation tend to be quite well structured on competitive political dimensions in the new postcommunist polities." This finding is even more powerful because it was obtained just three years after the transition, when politics was still in considerable flux.

Naturally, there were variations across issues.[11] As one would expect, representation was strongest on the general left–right dimension where the beliefs of functionaries and electorates about their positions largely corresponded. Parties were located at approximately the same position and in the same ordering as their electorates. The authors refer to this as absolute representation. Despite questions about the relevance of the left–right axis for postcommunist parties, voters and parties did agree on their positioning on this dimension even as its content differed by country.

Kitschelt et al., however, found that representation on specific issues tended not to be "absolute." Elites and their constituencies were not situated at the same place on the scale. More common was what they call relative representation where parties were ordered in the same way as their electorates but were not located at the exact same positions. Parties over- or understated differences between citizens or were shifted to the right or left.

This relative representation, particularly its overstating form that they call polarizing trusteeship, was common for salient issues. Parties exaggerated the positions of their electorates on the main economic issues that structured party competition in the Czech Republic and on the main social issues that structured competition in Hungary and Poland. The polarizing nature of representation makes sense. At this early stage in the transition, it was important for parties to draw attention to themselves and build up a reputation in a crowded field of parties (see Kedar 2005 for another explanation).[12] In any case, the main finding was of relatively strong party representation in Eastern Europe.

5.3. POLICY RESPONSIVENESS AND ECONOMIC REFORM

A shortcoming of Kitschelt's study is the lack of an actual policy component. Although it appears that the parties in Eastern European parliaments do share the opinions of their electorates, it is not clear that mass opinion was translated into the policies that citizens wanted. Indeed, all of the problems of preference aggregation and legislative voting put forward by social choice theorists suggest that policies may diverge from citizen preferences when they become the object of parliamentary politics (Riker 1982). A similar conclusion emerges from

[11] The only places where correspondence was weak were those where the public showed a wide consensus on the issue in question or an issue was not particularly salient.

[12] The opinions of functionaries may also be measured more precisely because they are better informed.

much of the new institutional literature, which argues that veto points may preserve the status quo even when preferences change (Tsebelis 2002).

Few studies have attempted to systematically compare public opinion and policy outcomes in Eastern Europe.[13] Indeed, public opinion has usually not figured as a cause of policy choices. Although some studies make gestures in its direction, most emphasize other factors like institutions (Stark and Bruszt 1998), parties (Cook et al. 1999), international constraints (Greskovits 1998), ideas (Appel 2004), or communist legacies (Linz and Stepan 1996). Where public opinion is mentioned, it is usually in normatively tinged analyses of why economic reforms are not proceeding as they should. The public is seen as potentially blocking actions but not producing them.

This chapter takes a step forward by using measures of public opinion and policy outcomes to produce direct measures of policy responsiveness in Eastern Europe. The analysis focuses on the issue of economic reform. Market-oriented economic reforms were perhaps the most salient issue during the 1990s as countries in the region moved to introduce the major institutions of a market economy. Economic reform again refers to such policies as privatization of state-owned industry, liberalization of prices, and the opening of borders to foreign trade. Debates occurred over all these reforms: whether they should be introduced quickly or gradually, to a greater or lesser extent, in a particular sequence, or accompanied by particular kinds of compensation. Because of their salience to citizens in the region, economic reforms present an important test of whether responsiveness pertains more generally.

In fact, they present a particularly difficult test of the responsiveness hypothesis. A general presumption exists that politicians are not responsive to citizens on the issue of economic reform (Przeworski 1991). Market reforms cause social pain. They lead to price increases, wage and job cuts, reductions in social guarantees, and foreign competition – all things citizens would prefer to avoid ex ante and that they tend to oppose ex post. As a result, politicians who wish to curry favor with citizens and win future elections are unlikely to undertake these reforms. Although reforms do bring benefits, they come at a temporal remove and thus do not help politicians who must win elections in the short run.

Yet all of the countries in the sample did ultimately introduce comprehensive reform programs to free prices, privatize industry, and dismantle social guarantees, although they differed in the pace, extent, and sequence of their programs. Given the assumption that reform is unpopular, it follows that politicians would have to ignore the public to introduce the sort of economic reforms that all of these countries ultimately did introduce.

Indeed, the major theories of economic reform see a very different set of factors as causing reform. They postulate that reforms occur when countries are hit by an economic crisis, when ideologically committed leaders come to power,

[13] The following analysis describes one of the few such studies and was undertaken in collaboration with Byung-Yeon Kim (Kim and Pirttila 2006).

or when leaders cannot be held accountable for their actions (Bates and Kreuger 1993, Drazen and Grilli 1993, Haggard and Kaufman 1995, Rodrik 1996, Williamson 1994). Few have argued that reforms are chosen when the public wants them and most have recommended that reformers insulate themselves from the public to pass reforms. Policy responsiveness and economic reform are considered an impossible combination. Given these doubts, is it possible that reform followed public opinion in Eastern Europe?

5.4. PUBLIC OPINION TOWARD ECONOMIC REFORM

What did the public in Eastern Europe think about reform? Is it true that citizens opposed economic reform as most accounts assume? The Central and Eastern Eurobarometer (CEEB), a cousin of the well-known Eurobarometer, can help answer this question. It was conducted in identical formats annually from 1990 to 1997 in seventeen Eastern European countries, including the ten postcommunist democracies.[14] The CEEB surveyed 1,000 nationally representative individuals in each country using a multistage random probability sample design.

The survey included one question that captured attitudes toward economic reforms. It read, "Do you personally feel that the creation of a free market economy, that is, one largely free from state control, is right or wrong for [your country's] future?" Although this question is not an exact match for the issue at hand – whether reforms should proceed more quickly or slowly – it does capture general opinions about the desirability of reforms.

A summary measure of public support for reform can be calculated as the difference between the percentage of respondents answering "right" and "wrong" (Public Support). Figure 5.1 shows the value of this measure in all ten countries for all the years where the question was asked. The level of support varies widely across countries and time from a maximum of +64% in Lithuania in 1991 to a minimum of −21% in the Czech Republic in 1997.

A number of facts about this measure are worthy of note. First, the average level of support for the free market across all countries and dates was +25% (s.e. 2.7). On average 63% of the sample supported the free market and 37% opposed it. Only eleven of the seventy-four country-years showed more citizens opposing the market than supporting it. A majority of citizens supported the free market in all ten countries and in each year the survey was conducted. It is in short far from obvious that citizens opposed reform in Eastern Europe.

A second question from this same survey confirms this impression.[15] This question asked, "The way things are going, do you feel that [your country's]

[14] The Central and Eastern Eurobarometer was discontinued in 1998 and revived in 2001 as the Candidate Countries Eurobarometer.

[15] Unlike the previous question, this question was asked in only a minority of countries and only for the years 1991 to 1995. For this reason it is not used in the analysis that follows. Changes in responses to the two questions are correlated at $r = .45$.

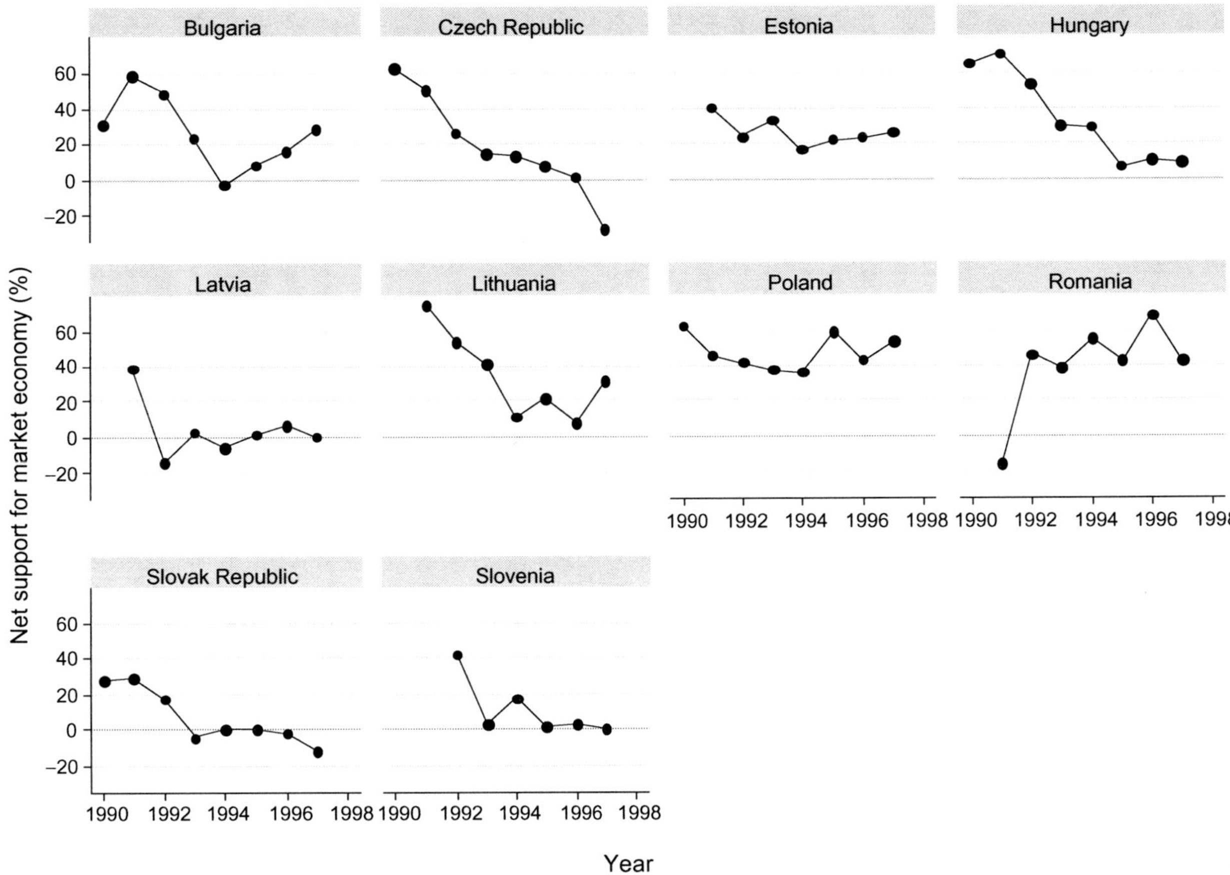

FIGURE 5.1. Public support for free-market economy.

economic reforms are going [too fast/about the right speed/too slow/there are no economic reforms]?" Across the region, 43% of respondents perceived the reform pace as too slow and only 15% as too fast, with 21% answering "about right."[16] In all ten countries, more citizens said too slow than too fast and in only two of the thirty-eight country-years did more respondents choose too fast. Citizens wanted a market economy and they wanted reform to go forward.

Others have confirmed this impression. Przeworski (1993), for example, has showed that Poles strongly supported Balcerowicz's shock therapy program at least until it began to cause high unemployment. Bunce (2001) has similarly argued that the distinctive fact about postcommunist political economy is the fact that the public desired market reforms. Finally, Stokes (2001b) has provided some evidence that rather than blaming politicians for reform, citizens viewed reforms as necessary or blamed the old regime for the pain they caused.

What explains these relatively positive attitudes toward reform (Bunce 2001)? Two factors stand out. One is the economic failures of the communist system. Although they produced growth in their early years, by the 1970s and 1980s communist economies were stagnating. Endemic shortages of basic consumer goods along with their shoddy quality and endless queues to obtain them convinced most citizens that the command economy did not work. Second, the prosperity of Western market economies showed citizens that there was another and better possibility. Indeed, the desire to join Western Europe – which from the start meant becoming market economies – only added force to this conclusion. If citizens knew one thing, it was that the old system had failed them and that they had better try something new.[17]

5.5. LINKING PUBLIC OPINION AND REFORM

Even this quick glance at public opinion gives some prima facie evidence for the idea of a link between opinion and economic reform. All ten countries did engage in major economic reforms so that, by 2004, all of them were viewed by the EU as "functioning market economies."[18] In the aggregate, citizens wanted a market economy and they got it.

A quick glance further to the East suggests that neither this desire nor its fulfillment was universal. The CEEB was conducted in identical forms in Armenia, Belarus, Georgia, Kazakhstan, Macedonia, Russia, and Ukraine. Support for a market economy in these countries averaged −9%, more than 30 points less than in the ten postcommunist democracies. Not surprisingly, these countries were all less consistent economic reformers and still have not created functioning market economies. At the macro level, there does appear to be a relationship between opinion and reform.

[16] Eight percent answered "there is no reform." It is unclear whether this response expressed a preference or a factual statement.

[17] Weyland (1998) likewise argues for Latin America that support for reform came from the belief that reform would rescue failing economies.

[18] Romania was the last country to achieve this designation.

What about at the micro level? Even though the public supported a market economy in the aggregate, significant differences existed in levels and trends in public opinion across the ten countries as Figure 5.1 shows. Significant differences also existed in reform trajectories. Some countries began with a big bang of reforms early in the transition, whereas others started slowly and picked up their reform pace only later. The question is whether changes in opinion explain changes in reform rates.

To make this inference, it is necessary to have more fine-grained measures of reform than whether a country introduced basic market institutions. Two indices of reform fit the bill. The EBRD reform index was introduced in the previous chapter. The World Bank has also created measures of reform progress in three categories: internal liberalization, external liberalization, and private sector entry (Berg et al. 1999, De Melo et al. 1996, Fischer et al. 1998). These ratings range from 0 to 1 and are averaged to produce a summary measure of reform. This measure was not used in the previous chapter because of its short time span, but it can be used here along with the European Bank for Reconstruction and Development (EBRD) index to generate more robust results. The EBRD and World Bank measures of reform are nevertheless highly correlated with each other (correlation coefficients are on the order of 0.7).

An initial test of the relation between public opinion and reform is the correlation between the change in reform rates and the net level of public support for a market economy in the previous year. The correlation is relatively strong and significant for both measures ($r = .40$, $p < .05$ for the World Bank measure, $r = .28$, $p < .05$ for the EBRD measure). When more citizens are in favor of a market economy, governments deliver faster economic reforms. By comparison, the same correlation coefficients for the six less democratic countries are substantively weaker and statistically insignificant ($r = .09$ and .06 for the World Bank and EBRD measures, respectively).

Simple correlations, however, do not establish causality. It may be that causality works in the opposite direction. Reforms may cause public opinion because they create a backlash against reform or produce winners who desire more reforms. Correlation analysis also ignores other causes of reform. For example, economic crises may force governments to reform and if a crisis simultaneously affects public opinion, the relation between opinion and reform may be spurious. Finally, because all of these changes were taking place over time, it is important to explicitly model the trend in economic reform. It is likely, for example, that countries undertake easier reforms at the start of the transition precisely because they are easy. Hence, reform rates should be higher early in the transition.

The key then is to model the relation between public opinion and reform, taking into account time trends, omitted variable bias, and reverse causality. As in the previous chapter, I accounted for time trends by estimating regression models with a lagged dependent variable on the right hand side. Similarly, to deal with omitted variable bias, I introduced controls for the economic factors that might tie a government's hands, expose it to international pressure, or limit the resources it has to compensate losers (additional political factors are introduced in later sections) (Falcetti et al. 2002, Fidrmuc 2000a, Heybey and Murrell 1999, Merlevede 2003). Thus, measures of growth, inflation, and unemployment were included. I also included country fixed effects in each model to capture differences between countries – history, culture, initial conditions – that are either unobserved or unmeasurable but may affect reform rates. Their inclusion means that the coefficients of public opinion capture differences over time within countries rather than differences in levels across countries.

Reverse causality or endogeneity presents the most difficult problem. Reforms may cause public opinion because they spur a backlash against reform or create winners in favor of more reform. If this is the case, then not only does public opinion not cause reform, but the regression estimates may show that it does. I took two different approaches to guard against reverse causality. First, I estimated models with lagged independent variables. This approach provides some assurance that the dependent variable is not affecting the independent variable. The future cannot influence the past. Second, I estimated two-stage least squares (2SLS) models, which utilized an instrument for public opinion that should be exogenous to reform. I describe the creation of this instrument in the next section.

5.6. ESTIMATING POLICY RESPONSIVENESS

Table 5.1 presents the results of these models using data on reform and opinion for the period from 1990 to 1997. The dependent variables are changes in the World Bank and EBRD measures of reform. The key independent variable is net support for a free-market economy, measured by the CEEB question on support for a market economy (Public Support). Models 1 and 2, using only lagged variables and fixed effects, show that public opinion has a strong and significant effect on reform progress for both measures of reform. Greater support for a free-market economy at time $t - 1$ leads to more reform at time t. Unemployment and to a lesser degree inflation also have significant effects – higher unemployment leads to less reform while higher inflation leads to more reform – but do not erase the effect of public opinion. The regressions also explain a large portion of the variance in reform increasing confidence that the relevant variables have been included.

As a stronger control for reverse causality, I estimated 2SLS models. This means first estimating the determinants of public opinion and using the predicted values of public opinion from these models to estimate reform rates. The idea is that these predicted values are instruments for public support. They are exogenous to reform but should still capture public support for reform.

To predict public support for reform, I included as independent variables a variety of economic conditions such as inflation, unemployment, and growth both contemporaneous with opinion and with a one-year lag. As an instrument, I added to these regressions a measure of income inequality (Gini coefficients), which should affect public opinion but is exogenous to reform (UNU-WIDER

TABLE 5.1. *Effect of Public Opinion on Economic Reform*

	Model 1	Model 2	Model 3	Model 4
Data	WB	EBRD	WB	EBRD
Estimation method	Pooled OLS	Pooled OLS	2SLS	2SLS
Reform progress (lagged)	0.001 (0.01)	−0.187 (1.64)	−0.088 (0.85)	−0.220* (1.86)
Public support (predicted)			0.40* (2.40)	−1.10* (2.24)
Public support (lagged)	0.20* (2.23)	0.50* (2.49)	0.00 (0.31)	0.90** (3.68)
Inflation (lagged)	0.029+ (1.91)	0.080+ (1.85)	0.037* (2.44)	0.081* (2.13)
Unemployment (lagged)	−0.030** (4.46)	0.001 (0.08)	−0.025** (3.95)	0.003 (0.26)
Growth (lagged)	0.004 (1.67)	−0.009 (1.52)	0.004 (1.61)	−0.012* (2.19)
Observations	62	59	62	59
R^2	0.68	0.52	0.71	0.57

** Significant at .01, * significant at .05, + significant at .10.
Note: t-values in parentheses. Results corrected for heteroskedasticity. Standard errors bootstrapped 1,000 times to correct for instrumental variable bias. Fixed effects coefficients not included.

2007). I expected that poor economic performance and high inequality would reduce support for the free market as ordinary citizens come to doubt whether market reforms are beneficial for them. Income inequality, however, should not directly affect reform choices since it does not affect the government's bottom line; it is in short exogenous to reform, but endogenous to public opinion.

The results (not shown) indicate that contemporaneous inflation, lagged unemployment, and income inequality all significantly affect support for reform. In situations where inflation, unemployment, and inequality are high, citizens turn against the free market. Most important, these variables collectively explain a substantial portion, but not all, of the variation in support for the market. The explained variance in these regressions is .45. I can thus reasonably use estimates of reform taken from these equations as an instrument for public support in the second stage of the 2SLS model.

These results are themselves significant. Some have argued that public opinion is too unstable and unpredictable to provide a reliable guide to politicians. The fact that a relatively small number of variables can provide good predictions of public opinion suggests that it is more stable and reasonable than the doubters argue. Indeed, a number of studies of opinion in the region have suggested a good deal of "rationality," at least in the sense that citizens' opinions on a large number of issues can be explained by a small number of underlying factors (Kitschelt et al. 1999, Shabad and Slomczynski 1999, Tworzecki 2003).

Models 3 and 4 present the results of the second-stage estimation, where the predicted values of public opinion are used to explain the causes of economic reform.[19] They confirm that public support is a strong and significant predictor of reform progress in all models. This outcome is most clear in the results for the World Bank measures of reform. Two slight differences are present in the estimations using the EBRD measure of reforms. The first is that lagged public support not contemporaneous support affects reform. This difference may be due to the fact that measurements were made for different time periods. Second, a significant negative effect of contemporaneous public support on reform appears, contrary to expectation. However, the mean and standard deviation of lagged public support is about two and a half times greater than that for predicted public support. Thus, the long-run effect of public support on reform progress is still positive.

Other variables behave mostly as expected. High unemployment has a breaking effect on reform, though this effect is weaker with EBRD reform scores. Higher inflation encourages reform, likely because economic reforms were seen as a cure for high inflation. In the EBRD sample, high growth leads to slower reform, probably because high growth indicated that reforms had run their course and were no longer necessary. None of these variables has as consistent effects as public support.

The effect of public support is substantively large. A 10% rise in reform support increases reform progress by 0.05, which is equal to the median of reform progress per year across countries. This implies that a country can achieve an increase equal to the median of reform progress with only a 10% increase in reform support without a change in any other factor. As an illustration, Latvia, whose annual average reform speed was 80% that of the Czech Republic over this period, could have achieved the same speed as the Czech Republic with an increase in public support from 3 to 16%. Comparing the effect of a one-standard-deviation change in the independent variables, the substantive effect of public support is second only to unemployment in affecting reform. In short, when support for reform rises, the speed of reform rises also, and to a substantively important degree.

5.7. RESPONSIVENESS TO WHOM?

But whose opinion does reform follow? The measure of public opinion used could be conceived as the opinion of the median voter. It was the average opinion in each country. Although strong normative reasons exist to favor responsiveness to the median voter, policy could in fact be more responsive to certain subgroups of the population than to the median (Bartels 2008,

[19] The results are corrected for heteroskedasticity and the standard errors are bootstrapped 1,000 times to correct for instrumental variable bias. I also estimated GMM models developed by Arellano and Bover (1995) and Blundell and Bond (1998) to control for biases in dynamic fixed effects. The results are substantively equivalent to those mentioned earlier.

Gilens 2005). A particular concern in Eastern Europe is that policy makers are beholden to the upper class. Wealthier voters may have an outsized influence on policy because they can buy influence directly through corruption or indirectly through campaign contributions. Although such effects exist in all countries, they may be stronger in the postcommunist region, where neither politicians nor parties possess much wealth and legal barriers against corruption are weak. On the other hand, public funding of campaigns is common in the region and levels of income inequality are still relatively low which equalize influence.

Does an upper-class bias in responsiveness exist in Eastern Europe? To answer this question, I recalculated levels of public support for the free market for different educational and income groups. The CEEB included questions about the respondent's highest educational attainment and their average monthly income. I focused in particular on the top and bottom educational categories and the top and bottom income quartiles.[20] Because the education question was asked in all surveys whereas the income question was often omitted and is subject to greater measurement error, the education measure should generate more reliable inferences.[21]

Figure 5.2 presents levels of support for the market among the top and bottom educational categories – university educated and a combination of primary and uncompleted secondary – in addition to the average.[22] Not surprisingly, poorer and less educated citizens are less in favor of a free-market economy than richer and more educated citizens. Indeed, these differences average 35% for the highest and lowest educational attainments and 41% for the top and bottom income quartiles. Yet, to explain changes in policy, what is important are changes in opinion, not levels.

A simple visual inspection reveals similar trends among the groups. The correlation coefficients between the highest and lowest groups are positive, large, and significant for six of the ten countries, positive but insignificant for three countries, and negative for one country. For all ten countries the correlation coefficient is 0.84. Correlating the high and low education categories with the average for each country yields correlation coefficients greater than 0.8 for all but four of the twenty coefficients. Similar results obtain for the income categories, where the highest and lowest quartiles are strongly and significantly correlated for five countries and weakly correlated for only two. In most cases, different demographic groups change their opinions in the same way. This first

[20] Because the income question presented respondents with preset categories (e.g., US$0–50, US$50–100, etc.), I could not calculate exact quartiles. Rather I aggregated the classes that most closely approximated the upper and lower 25% of the sample. The quartiles thus ranged in size from 20 to 30% of the sample.

[21] Citizens should have more difficulty recalling their monthly income than their educational career. It is worth adding that a relatively small percentage of the population – about 10% – was university educated. These included some of the best-connected citizens.

[22] I combine the lowest two educational categories because in several cases they were combined in the survey.

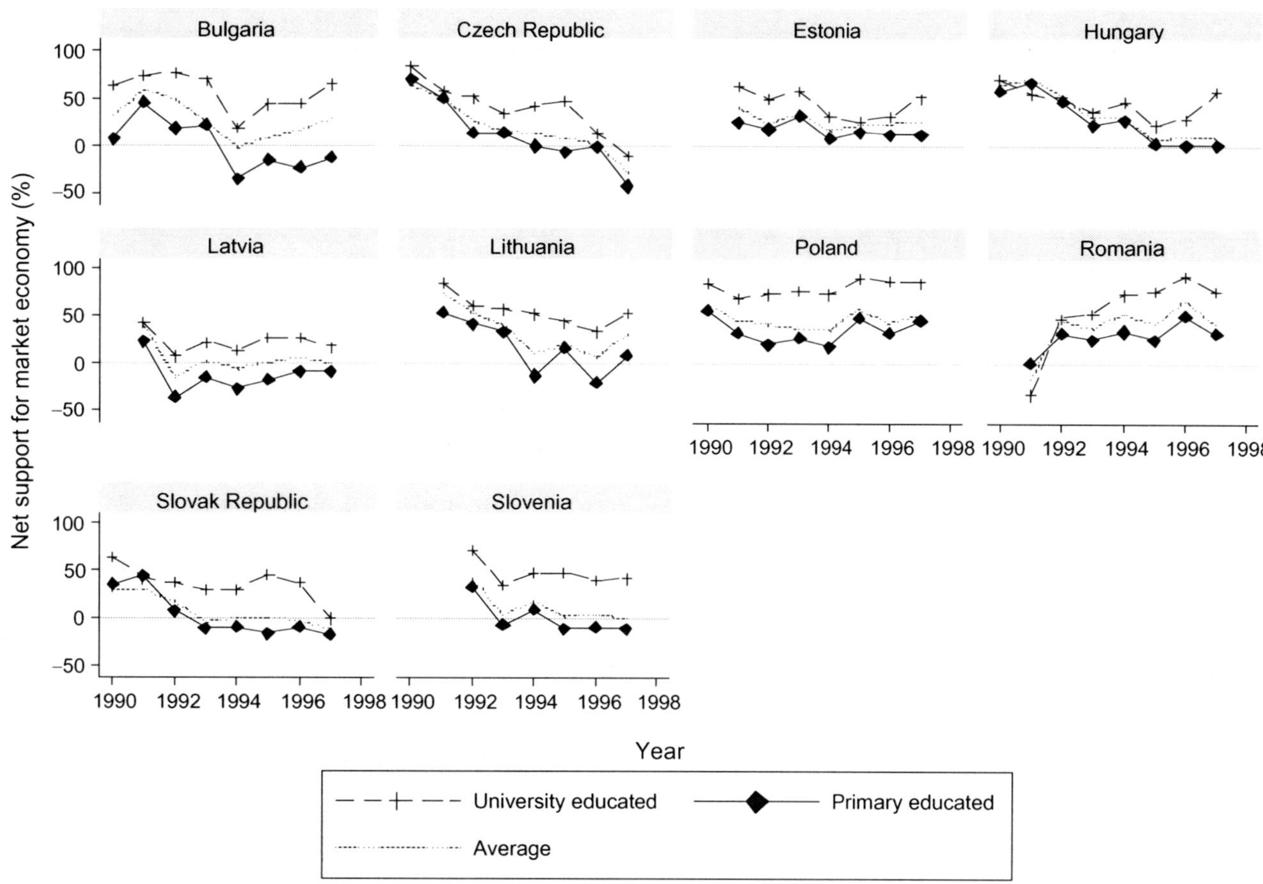

FIGURE 5.2. Public support for free-market economy by educational attainment.

cut, therefore, suggests that if policy is responsive to median opinion, then it is likely equally responsive to all groups.

To confirm this conclusion I entered the levels of public support for individual demographic groups into the regressions predicting reform outcomes. The results of these exercises (not shown) are nuanced but indicate that the worry about upper-class bias is exaggerated. With the World Bank measures, reform reacts more strongly to support from the poor and less educated than to the rich and more educated. The former variables have a significant effect whereas the latter do not. Results using the EBRD measures are less consistent with the rich having greater influence than the poor, but the less educated having more influence than the more educated.

In short, the suspicion that governments are responding to the better connected is not confirmed. There was no clear evidence that reform rates were more responsive to upper-class opinion. There is, however, one additional possibility that these regressions neglect. It is theoretically possible that the overall high rate of reform across the region indicates a greater responsiveness to the well off, who are more in favor of reform, even as changes in reform are responsive to the median voter. This connection, however, is difficult to test without data on the actual desired levels of reform among each group. It is likewise hard to explain why responsiveness to the median would characterize the one case and responsiveness to the elite the other.

5.8. ALTERNATIVE EXPLANATIONS: PARTIES, TIMING, AND INSTITUTIONS

Thus far the analysis has suggested that politicians respond directly to raw public opinion. They put their finger to the wind and follow its direction. But this mechanism ignores other political causes of reform. Three alternative paths may lead to a similar result without public opinion exerting direct effects.

In the first place, the impact of the public on policy is mediated by representatives. Policy may only change when the composition of parliament changes rather than continuously with public opinion. Although this is a form of policy responsiveness – policy does change with voter preferences – it is an indirect one. In fact, this form of responsiveness has more in common with the mandate conception because voters are sending a signal by choosing different parties at election time rather than controlling policy continuously.

The previous chapter showed that a measure of campaign promises had little effect on reform. Here I experiment with another measure of ideology, the party families of the parties represented in parliament (Mair and Mudde 1998). Like promises, party family is exogenous to policy. Parties typically associate with a party family – like Socialist, Communist, or Christian Democratic – at their origin. I hypothesize that parties who belong to the Liberal party family wish to speed up reform, whereas Social Democratic and Communist parties want to slow it down. Using Bugajski's (2002) assessments of party families in Eastern

TABLE 5.2. *Other Influences on Economic Reform*

Sample	Model 5 Party Families	Model 6 Election Years and One Year Prior	Model 7 Other Years	Model 8 Coalition	Model 9 Majority
Reform progress (lagged)	−0.264$^+$ (1.66)	−0.583 (1.65)	−0.075 (0.54)	−0.262$^+$ (1.66)	−0.270$^+$ (1.68)
Public support (predicted)	0.623$^+$ (1.93)	0.564 (0.95)	0.376* (2.07)	0.584* (1.98)	0.613* (2.13)
Public support (lagged)	0.039 (0.34)	0.135 (0.73)	−0.011 (0.09)	0.053 (0.45)	0.039 (0.37)
Inflation (lagged)	0.039* (2.10)	0.025 (0.82)	0.042$^+$ (1.91)	0.039* (2.14)	0.039* (2.14)
Unemployment (lagged)	−0.019* (2.31)	−0.030** (2.36)	−0.007 (1.05)	−0.020** (2.64)	−0.019** (2.50)
Growth (lagged)	0.002 (0.58)	0.001 (0.29)	0.001 (0.23)	0.002 (0.73)	0.002 (0.49)
Reformist parties	−0.000 (0.43)				
Coalition				−0.027 (0.68)	
Majority					0.020 (0.68)
Observations	62	32	32	62	62
R^2	0.56	0.64	0.55	0.56	0.56

** Significant at .01, * significant at .05, $^+$ significant at .10.

Notes: t-values in parentheses. Results corrected for heteroskedasticity. Standard errors bootstrapped with a repetition of 1,000 times to correct for instrumental variable bias. Constants not reported. Dependent variable is the World Bank measure of reform.

Europe, I thus created a measure of the difference in the percentage of seats held by Liberal parties and by Social Democratic or Communist parties.[23]

Table 5.2 presents an estimation of the determinants of reform progress with the inclusion of a variable indicating the composition of parliament (Reformist parties). Model 5 shows that this measure is itself insignificant and does not affect the significance of the public opinion variable. The same is true of an interaction between parliamentary composition and public support (not shown). Public opinion works directly on reform speed rather than indirectly through elections. This confirms the weak results for mandate responsiveness in the previous chapter. Politicians keep their finger to the wind regardless of their political affiliation.

[23] In other estimations I added the percentage of Christian Democratic parties to those of liberal parties with substantively similar results. I also experimented with ratios and differences, again with similar results.

Another possibility is that responsiveness changes with the electoral calendar. Politicians may be more responsive just before elections to gain favor with voters. Because voters tend to have short memories – recall from Chapter 3 that it was the state of the economy immediately before elections that affected results – politicians should be more sensitive to public opinion as elections approach (Achen and Bartels 2004). This logic underlies political business cycle theory: politicians pump up the economy when elections are around the corner. Canes-Wrone and Shotts (2004) have found that American politicians do become more responsive in the period prior to elections (though with a number of qualifications). A previous study of the political business cycle in Eastern Europe has found timing effects on macroeconomic policy (Hallerberg et al. 2002).

To test this idea, I divided the data set into two parts: preelection years (the election year and the year before) and other years. Models 6 and 7 present the basic model of reform for each period. Policy responsiveness does not rise in the preelectoral period. In fact, it is just the opposite. The public support variable is small and insignificant for the preelectoral period and positive and significant for the other period.

What explains this counterintuitive result? I would suggest that economic reforms have their own timing issues. In particular, reforms tend to have a negative short-run effect on the economy and a positive medium-run effect (Falcetti et al. 2002). As a result, politicians may be more sensitive to public opinion on reform earlier in the term, knowing that reforms only bear fruit by election time. Conversely, they may become less sensitive to public preferences later in the term, when they worry more about the short-term economic effects of reforms.

Finally, institutional factors may affect reforms. When a government faces numerous veto points, it should have difficulty responding to the public (Tsebelis 2002). Veto points ensure a degree of policy stability regardless of the preferences of the public or the government. Models 8 and 9 include controls for the two most prominent institutional veto points in these countries – whether a government consisted of multiple parties (Coalition) or whether it held only a minority of seats (Minority). In both cases, it should be more difficult for a government to follow the public because its powers to pass legislation by itself are limited. Although the signs on these variables fit expectations, neither is significantly different from zero. More to the point, their inclusion does not affect the responsiveness of politicians to public opinion.

5.9. EXPLAINING POLICY RESPONSIVENESS

These results leave the impression that it is public opinion itself that drives reform. But is this plausible? In the first place, one may doubt whether politicians in the region have access to good information about public opinion. Politicians in established democracies can rely on local party organizations, an activated citizenry, and a wide array of polling organizations to learn what citizens want. All of these links should be weaker in new democracies. Party organization is weak, citizens tend not to participate in politics, and opinion polling is relatively new.

Although I cannot offer direct evidence that politicians take advantage of accurate information of public opinion, I can offer some indirect evidence that sources of good information existed and that politicians were interested in them. By the 1980s, communist governments had begun to use opinion polling to gauge public dissatisfaction and wanted at least some unbiased information about what citizens were thinking (Henn 1999, Tworzecki 2003: 77–9). Soon after the transition, a large number of private, independent polling firms were founded. In Hungary, for example, "each newspaper has its own poll and nearly every day an opinion poll is reported, [conducted] by different companies. There are five companies producing polls for newspapers regularly and about 100 small ones" (Henn 1999: 140). A similar situation characterizes other countries. Although not all of these firms produced reliable data, each country did have a handful of firms with Western contacts and knowledge of up-to-date methodologies.

And evidence also exists that politicians use these polls. In a study of the polling industry in Eastern Europe, Henn (1999) finds that, as early as 1990, governments and larger political parties were commissioning polls on major public policy issues. Anecdotal evidence from pollsters and political leaders indicates that in Romania, perhaps the least likely case for such a result, the economic reform plan of the first government "drew heavily on the results of these polls" and that as early as 1991 opinion polls in Poland convinced parliament to reject an anti-abortion law despite strong pressure from church-related groups (Henn 1999: 131). A Romanian pollster likewise notes that "governments place significant emphasis on opinion polls in the more general area of policy development, including for instance the technical aspects of privatization policies, the development of social policies to soften the effects of national transition programmes on the elderly, and rural-urban migration policies" (Henn 1999: 131). Although this evidence is not proof that politicians consistently possess and use good information about citizens' preferences, it does suggest that it can happen.

Given that information is available, what impels politicians to listen to the public? I discuss this question in more depth in Section 9.3. However, I note here that the results from Chapter 3 indicate that politicians have good reason to listen. Electoral punishment is severe and often removes parties not only from government but from parliament altogether.[24] The fact that most parties in the region are new and lack established bases of support only strengthens this incentive. To survive elections, they need to do all they can to please voters. Given that economic performance is often beyond their control and economic

[24] Numerous examples exist of parties going from cabinet participation to losing representation in parliament. Consider Electoral Action Solidarity (AWS) in 2001 or Civic Democratic Alliance (ODA) in 1998.

reform was a highly salient issue, policy responsiveness in this area might have been their best bet.[25]

5.10. CONCLUSION

Policy responsiveness is in many respects the essence of democracy. It shows that the public is in fact ruling in the sense of determining policy choices. Although normative objections to policy responsiveness exist – citizens may be uninformed or inconstant and so responsiveness may lead to poor policy choices – it is difficult to retain faith in democracy while dismissing it. For this reason, the most heartening finding in this book may be the relatively high level of responsiveness in the region on the most salient issue of the transition. Although this responsiveness may come at the expense of substantive representation – politicians may not be producing the best policies for citizens – it is noteworthy that at least the essential linkage of democracy appears to be working.

One may object that this result is confined to a single policy area over a relatively short period of time. Yet, in some ways this policy area and time period provide one of the toughest tests of the responsiveness thesis. Most observers of economic reform have viewed it as a vote loser and therefore recommended that politicians insulate themselves from the public to engage in reform. The first eight years of the transition are also the time when links between the public and politicians should be weakest; citizens had little time to develop clear preferences and politicians had the fewest means to monitor them. These findings need to be supplemented by those on other policy areas and other times – as in the following chapters – but they do present a strong prima facie case that policy responsiveness exists.

Anecdotally, the finding of responsiveness is confirmed by economic reformers themselves. In a volume of conversations with "leading reformers," Mario Blejer and Fabrizio Corricelli (1995) found that the politicians responsible for basic economic reforms in the Czech Republic, Hungary, and Poland agreed with the present analysis. Thus, Václav Klaus stated that "Our strategy was to get the necessary support of as many citizens and as many interest groups as possible. We knew that social consensus was absolutely unavoidable" (Blejer and Corricelli 1995: 89). Leszek Balcerowicz, the Minister of Finance who launched shock therapy in Poland, noted that, even without a parliamentary majority, it was "still possible to get the acceptance of all parties" and stressed the importance of communicating with the public (Blejer and Corricelli 1995: 119, 124). Peter Bod, the Minister for Industry in Hungary, recalled that "political acceptability always plays a part in the timing of the measure" and pointed to the importance of "political acceptability" in almost all reforms (Blejer and

[25] This connection, however, is inconsistent with the weak connection between economic reforms and election outcomes in Chapter 3. The effect of reform on elections may be mediated by the effect of reform on economic conditions.

Corricelli 1995: 91, 122). These admissions are important because they come from politicians who were commonly perceived as thumbing their nose at the public.[26] Even they believed that responsiveness to society played a key role in reform.

[26] Reformers also had reasons to portray themselves in the opposite way. The brave economic reformer who does what is right over the protests of the masses is a powerful trope among the global elite.

PART III

CASE STUDY ANALYSIS

In Chapter 5 it was argued that economic reform in Eastern Europe was characterized by policy responsiveness. But doubts still remain. First, the statistical analysis only shows average effects across the region, not the relation between public opinion and individual policy choices. It is also limited to a single and possibly unique policy area. Most telling is that the statistical analysis treats responsiveness itself as a black box, where public opinion goes in one side and policy comes out of the other.

It is important then to open up this black box and see how, when, and why politicians follow public opinion. How did politicians perceive public opinion and the policy choices open to them? What induced them to favor one choice over another or package and sequence multiple choices? What sort of strategies did they use to introduce key policies and why did they choose those strategies? These questions are difficult to answer with aggregate statistical analysis but can probed with a qualitative, case study approach. That is the path taken in the following chapters. (I do not systematically consider electoral accountability and mandate responsiveness in the case studies because they are less amenable to case study analysis; they more closely resemble a black box connecting input and output.)

I follow Alexander George's (George and Bennett 2005: Chapter 3) method of structured, focused comparison, which has become the workhouse of qualitative methodology. I ask of each case a set of standardized questions about the research objective – the structured part – and look at specific elements of the cases that pertain to the objective – the focused part. The cases are the Czech Republic, Hungary, and Poland, which were chosen for their shared background conditions and divergent policy choices (see Section 1.4.2).

The difficulty is in choosing the set of issues about which to gather standardized data. Although there are many qualitative analyses of policy-making, and some do attempt to discern responsiveness (e.g., Jacobs 1993), no standard set of questions is available to determine whether responsiveness exists or not. I believe that six specific aspects of the policy process can throw light on the degree of responsiveness.

First, I search for evidence of public opinion about the issues in question. A quantitative analysis of this subject would consider time-series or cross-national comparisons of citizens' preferences over a variety of policy options as in the previous chapter. Such data do not exist in Eastern Europe for pension and housing policy, and particularly not for the multiple aspects of policy in play. Instead, I have to rely on polls conducted at a single point in time or at most a small number of points in time. I then ask if policy corresponds to the preferences of the majority in a method similar to that of Monroe (1979). Sometimes I did not find even these data and instead had to rely on objective measures of the public's interest or expert assessments of the public mood on a particular issue.

Second, I use the behavior of the public as a proxy for preferences. The existence of demonstrations or protests and their extent provides some indication of the breadth and depth of concern with a policy. However, it is important to consider the representativeness of such collective action. Did the groups in question represent the general public or only a minority of those affected by a particular policy?[1] In cases where citizens were given a choice to sign up for a policy or not – for example, opening a private pension account or buying a state-owned apartment – the degree to which they "voted with their feet" is another indirect indication of support or opposition.

Interest group behavior can also be used as an indicator of public support for a policy. If important interest groups give their assent to a policy or have formal veto powers but do not exercise them – for example, in a tripartite council – that provides some evidence of responsiveness. Again, there is a caveat. Interest groups are only a proxy for public opinion when they are particularly encompassing or diverse. Trade unions in particular sometimes play such a role.

Third, I consider the relation of important social groups to the policy process itself. Were major groups affected by the proposed changes invited to participate in discussions about the policy or help in drafting legislation? Was the government able to achieve a consensus on the new policy? If the answers to these questions are yes, it is more likely that policy making is responsive than if affected parties were excluded from the process and consensus was not achieved.

Fourth, I look at the relation between government ideology and policy choice. If policy shifts as the ideology of the government changes and in the same direction – for example, if the election of a left-wing government leads to more generous social policies – then this may count as evidence of policy responsiveness. A finding that the government's ideology and its policy choices do not correspond, however, does not rule out policy responsiveness. What is important is what the public wants for the particular policy in question rather than its general ideological mood. The two sometimes diverge. Indeed, in some cases mismatches between government ideology and policy may be

[1] On the determinants of contentious action see McAdam et al. (2001).

better evidence of responsiveness than matches. Matches may be the product of vociferous activists within a party who are not representative of the broader electorate. A responsive party may thus have to go against its ideology if it hopes to represent the median voter.

Fifth, I consider parliamentary behavior. The outcome of roll call votes may reflect the degree of responsiveness. Larger majorities are usually, but not always, indicative of greater public support for a policy. If most parties are persuaded to sign off on a bill, it is likely that a large portion of the public supports it. When major groups in society are dissatisfied with a certain course of action, parties representing those groups have every incentive to publicize their opposition, producing smaller or nonexistent majorities.

Sixth, politicians have at their disposal different legislative techniques for passing legislation that may indicate responsiveness or nonresponsiveness. One is the timing of policies. Voters typically have short memories; as a result, policies passed immediately before elections have a greater effect on election results. Knowing this, politicians should time the enactment of legislation to the electoral calendar. They should initiate less popular policies at the beginning of the term – in the hope that voters forget them – and more popular policies at the end of the term – in the hope that voters remember them (Canes-Wrone 2006). The timing of individual policies may thus say something about responsiveness.

Timing is just one of a number of what have been called blame avoidance techniques (Weaver 1986),[2] which are ways that politicians try to avoid being blamed for unpopular, but sometimes necessary, actions. They include such tactics as bundling unpopular with popular policies, enacting complicated and opaque changes, or postponing the effects of policies far into the future (Pierson 1994, Weaver 1986). What they have in common is that they make it very difficult for voters to connect political outcomes with the politicians responsible for them (Arnold 1990).

The question is what these techniques say about responsiveness. Most obviously they indicate that politicians are being nonresponsive – they are not choosing the policies that the public prefers. On the other hand, the use of blame avoidance techniques does indicate a concern with public opinion that has something in common with responsiveness. A truly nonresponsive government would simply introduce these policies without delay, dialogue, or compromise. It is also worth noting that such techniques are common in established democracies. Blame avoidance techniques represent a middle ground of responsiveness.

The structured, focused comparisons try to take all of these issues into account for each policy choice or nonchoice in these issue domains. I emphasize that most of these indicators are indirect. They are likely to be associated with responsiveness or nonresponsiveness, but they are not exactly that phenomenon itself. The hope is that enough of these indirect forms of evidence make up for the lack of direct evidence. A variety of different measures pointing in the same

[2] It may also be a credit-claiming technique (Mayhew 1974).

direction can provide more assurance in the validity of a conclusion than strong support from just a single measure.

All of these methods put these analyses squarely inside the methodology that has come to be called process-tracing (George and Bennett 2005: Chapter 10), which involves tracking down the events and actions taken between the proposed causes and effects. All of the indicators described in this section fall somewhere along these chains – protests, consultations, parliamentary debates, and legislative strategy are all part of the process that leads from opinion to policy.

In fact, the chain is even longer because I wish to rule out the possibility that public opinion is manipulated. An association between public preferences and policy outcomes might indicate that politicians are responding to the public. But, as I suggested in Chapter 1, it may also be a result of political manipulation. Even theories of public opinion based on rationality recognize the possibility that public opinion forms in response to elite discourse (Zaller 1992).

I thus try to unpack the causes of preferences. To what extent are public preferences formed independently of elite discourse, for example, as reactions to real events in the economy or society? And to what degree are elites consciously manipulating the information that citizens receive, for example, by conducting propaganda campaigns on issues or limiting alternative sources of information? Only if public preferences are formed largely free of manipulation by governments is it possible to conclude that policy responsiveness exists.

With all of this evidence, I rely on variation both over time and across countries to draw causal inferences. Each country introduced policies at different moments in time that did or did not correlate with contemporaneous levels of public support. Similarly, the three countries made dramatically different choices in these policy areas, which may correlate with different degrees of public support across countries.[3] All of these differences provide leverage on the central question of responsiveness.

[3] Readers may be disappointed that the opinions of policy makers themselves – whether they believed they were responding to the public or not – do not figure prominently in the following analyses. Although the author spoke with some policy makers, it was difficult to know whose opinions were trustworthy and whose were self-serving justifications. Most claimed that their decisions were the "correct" ones; they acted because it was the right thing to do given the circumstances. I decided, therefore, to focus more on relatively objective indicators of responsiveness than on actors' own assessments.

6

The Politics of Pension Reforms

Although pension reforms are not as salient or consequential as the economic reforms considered in the previous chapters, they likely place a close second. All communist countries ran universal pension schemes that were intended to cover the basic needs of retirees (Cook 1993). Because their societies were aging rapidly, a high percentage of citizens had a vested interest in the viability and generosity of these systems. Moreover, opinion polls showed that very large majorities of citizens believed that the state was responsible for the elderly and that pension benefits should be maintained if not increased.

At the same time, these schemes were quite expensive; often they constituted the largest single element of government budgets. Given the economic problems these countries faced, it was not clear whether governments could maintain the sort of commitments that citizens desired. And unlike economic reforms which were typically one-off decisions, pensions were an issue that had to be addressed year in and year out. The salience of pension politics and the dilemma of reconciling public support with fiscal austerity thus make it an important test of the responsiveness thesis.

How then did pension policy develop during the transition? Did politicians respond to public demands when altering the system? Or did economic and other pressures force them to engage in unpopular policy choices? More intriguing, what was behind the decision of two countries – Hungary and Poland – to partially privatize their pension systems, a reform widely believed to be out of bounds in established democracies? Could citizens have come to support the privatization of a system to which they believed they had an inherent right? Or were there other reasons that politicians embraced privatization? These questions are the focus of this chapter.

6.1. PENSION POLICY UNDER COMMUNISM

The communist countries of Eastern Europe ran pension systems in many respects similar to those in the industrialized democracies. After taking power

TABLE 6.1. *Pension System Parameters in 1989*

	Retirement Age	Replacement Rate	Expenditures (% GDP)
Czech Republic	M: 60; F:53–57	63.3	8.3
Hungary	M: 60; F: 55	63.8	9.1
Poland	M: 65; F: 60	53.3	6.6

Source: Schrooten et al. (1999).

in the aftermath of World War II, communist parties introduced new pension schemes in an effort to buy the support of workers and the aged.[1] They naturally turned to what is called pay-as-you-go (PAYG) financing, which means that current retirees received pensions mostly paid for by payroll taxes from current workers. Such a system allowed the communists to begin paying pensions immediately and win public support. These systems were gradually expanded through the 1950s and 1960s until they covered almost the entire population.[2]

As communist countries industrialized and grew, their pension systems became more generous. Replacement rates – the proportion of former wages covered by pensions – were raised and retirement ages lowered. Table 6.1 presents the status of these two variables along with spending on pensions as a percentage of GDP in 1989.[3] On all three variables, these countries had levels similar to the advanced industrial democracies. Increasing numbers of contributors – due to the postwar baby boom and expansions in coverage – and growing economies made this increasing generosity fiscally bearable at least for a time.

Communist pension systems, however, were distinctive in a number of ways. One was a weak link between contributions and benefits. In accord with communist ideology, citizens received nearly equal pensions regardless of their contributions to the system. The main exception to this trend was the institution of work categories. A number of occupations, including miners, police, and soldiers, were for political or economic reasons singled out for special benefits such as higher replacement rates, lower contribution rates, or lower retirement ages.[4] This institution was most pronounced in Poland, where perhaps a fifth of workers received privileges, but it was also significantly present

[1] Before the war, these countries had a variety of fully funded occupational pension schemes inspired by Bismarck's social policies. These systems were mostly bankrupted by the war. For more details on the history of pension provision in Eastern Europe, see Müller (1999).

[2] Farmers were typically the last group to be included in the system. Indeed, inclusion in the pension system was one inducement for them to join collective farms.

[3] Actual retirement ages were even lower due to a large number of exceptions and special privileges.

[4] Such programs are not unknown in the West. The uniqueness of communist systems was in using them to assert control over the labor force. Pensions were used as rewards for jobs seen as important by the state or as incentives to enter certain professions. For example, airplane pilots were given large pensions as an inducement not to defect.

in the Czech Republic and Hungary. Finally, pension monies were not isolated in ear-marked funds as is typical in advanced industrial economies, but were mixed in the general budget.

As economic growth slowed and even halted in the 1970s and 1980s, the costs of the pension system became more difficult to bear. Aging populations contributed to the problem as fewer workers had to support larger numbers of pensioners. Although explicit cuts in pensions were politically taboo – the communist welfare state traded social benefits for political quiescence (Cook 1993) – most countries did turn to less traceable cuts, mainly to incomplete indexation of pensions to inflation.

These problems were multiplied several times over by the transition. The large transformational recessions in these countries hit both the revenue and the expenditure sides of the pension system. As employment fell – due to the restructuring or bankruptcy of state-owned enterprises – the number of contributors fell in turn. Many new private firms operated outside of the formal economy or simply took advantage of undeveloped taxation systems and did not contribute to the pension system. At the same time, state provision of pensions remained popular: upwards of three-quarters of citizens in the three countries believed the state had an obligation to support the elderly (Lipsmeyer 2003). Transition recessions meanwhile threw many older workers out of their jobs and forced them to rely on the pension system for subsistence. Pensions were thus used as an important buffer to the difficult economic circumstances of the early transition.

6.2. RESPONSES TO THE TRANSITION

How did these countries negotiate these dilemmas? This chapter assesses policy responsiveness in three stages. This section details how countries initially responded to the transition. This period – extending from the first free elections to the end of the first electoral cycle around 1992 or 1993 – is bracketed because the type of reforms necessary and the changes taking place in the political economy gave policy making a distinctive cast. In the following two sections, I turn separately to parametric reforms later in the transition and to pension privatization.

The early transition is particularly worth investigating because the three countries responded to the transition in three different ways. Poland went on a spending spree through generous indexation and loosened early retirement conditions. The Czech Republic took the opposite path, allowing the value of pensions to decline relative to wages while spending remained flat. Hungary meanwhile followed Poland by raising spending, but not as much. These trends are illustrated graphically in Figures 6.1 and 6.2, which show the path of spending and replacement rates over the first five years of the transition. Milanović (1995) summarizes these paths by noting that the position of pensioners improved relative to the population in Poland, stayed constant in Hungary, and dropped in the Czech Republic. The task then is to determine

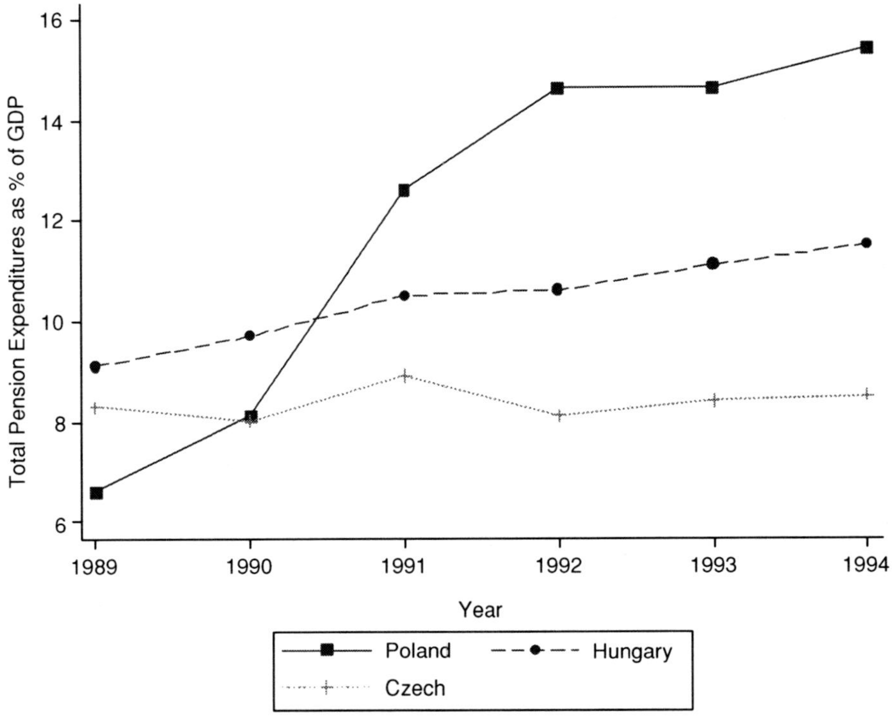

FIGURE 6.1. Pension expenditures.

whether these different trajectories are a consequence of responsive policy making. I treat each of the countries in turn.

6.2.1. Poland

Pension politics had come to the fore in Poland even before the transition. Throughout the 1970s and 1980s, workers took to the streets to protest against the government's economic policies. Their continued demands for higher wages translated into the same demands for pensions (Poznanski 1996). The communist regime was even somewhat responsive to these demands. As Golinowska (1999: 174) notes, the government raised pensions whenever it needed to rebuild support after a loss of legitimacy. Particularly common in Poland were special allowances for particular social groups. Farmers in fact had their own distinct pension system that was heavily subsidized by the state while miners and the uniformed services received generous advantages (Czepulis-Rutkowska 1999, Müller 1999). The government's strategy was to buy off these groups individually in the aftermath of sector-specific protests.

These policies led to large increases in spending during the 1980s, which the government tried to offset by manipulating indexation rules (Golinowska

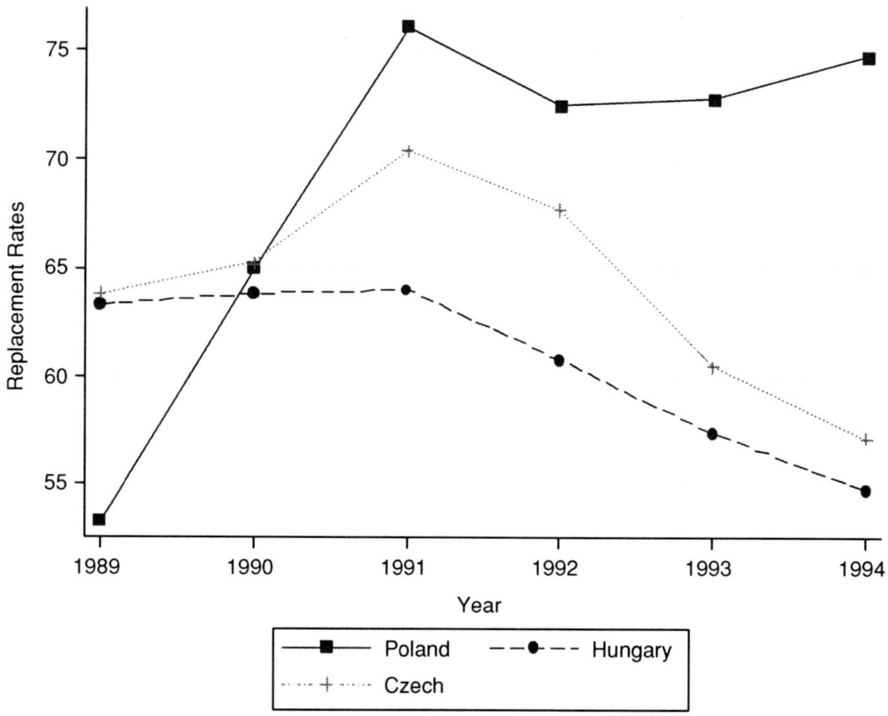

FIGURE 6.2. Pension replacement rates. *Source:* Schrooten et al. (1999).

1999: 175). This manipulation and the new specter of inflation in turn sensitized unions to the importance of those rules (Graham 1994). The result was increasing deficits in the pension system beginning in the 1980s. One action that the communist-era government took to rationalize the system, however, was to separate financing of pensions from the state budget.

Poland's first democratic governments were led by parties emerging from the Solidarity movement, which included both liberal and social democratic elements. Although these governments became known for their economic shock therapy programs, in fact they continued and often expanded the social policies of their predecessors. The first major policy, introduced in May 1990, was a generous indexation scheme – pensions were indexed to quarterly wage inflation – and an increase in the minimum pension to 35% of the average wage (Cain and Surdej 1999: 158). In Poland's high-inflation environment, this change helped to maintain the economic position of pensioners but at the cost of dramatically increasing spending.

The next step was a significant loosening of eligibility for early retirement and disability pensions. In 1991, the government allowed workers in companies threatened with bankruptcy to retire early with full benefits (Müller 1999). It also began to only laxly enforce the granting of disability pensions (Cain and Surdej 1999: 155–6). As a result, the number of retirees jumped by

34% between 1990 and 1994, despite the fact that Poland had the youngest population and the highest official retirement age of the three countries considered. Almost all of these new pensioners were below the official retirement age.

Together indexation, benefit increases, and early retirement produced galloping expenditures. By the mid-1990s they had risen to 15% of GDP, a level on par with Sweden. Although most Poles suffered during this period, pensioners did reasonably well. Due to generous indexation, the replacement rate – the average percentage of wages paid in pensions – rose from 53% in 1989 to 76% in 1991.

Attempts were made to restrain these trends. The architect of shock therapy and Minister of Finance Leszek Balcerowicz tried to reduce expenditures by switching from wage to price indexation, but he was unsuccessful. When Prime Minister Hanna Suchocka put forward a relatively modest proposal to reduce indexation from 100 to 91% of wages in December 1992, she was quickly beaten back with street protests, strikes, and defections in parliament (Cain and Surdej 1999). Half-hearted attempts to raise the retirement age for women met stiff public resistance and were withdrawn (Czepulis-Rutkowska 1999: 183). The government did use other means to keep spending under control. Ad hoc manipulations of the benefit formula and indexation were the most common, but they were largely ineffective (Czepulis-Rutkowska 1999: 150–1).

Policy makers also considered uniting Poland's large and fragmented system of work categories. In no case, however, were they able to completely abolish these privileges. Strikes, the threat of strikes, and demonstrations beat back all reform attempts (Inglot 1995). At one point a law ending all new privileges was rescinded after massive outcry (Graham 1994). Ultimately the Suchocka government fell in 1993 over a refusal to further increase wages and pensions.

It is worth adding that, just as expenditures were rising, revenues were falling. The many early retirees and newly unemployed were no longer contributing to the system, and state-owned firms, not to mention new private firms operating in the gray economy, often failed to pay their required payroll taxes. Unemployment alone rose from near 0% to 16% over the first four years of the transition. The government thus raised payroll taxes in 1989 and again in 1992, which put them at a hard-to-sustain 45% of wages (Inglot 1995). Deficits in the pension system rose to more than 4% of GDP even with these higher tax rates.

What explains these policy changes? Most scholars point to the pressure of hyperinflation and the need for rapid policy making, which led to poorly thought-out decisions (Cain and Surdej 1999: 159–60, Golinowska 1999: 176). Orenstein and Haas (2000), for example, refer to "time pressures, information shortage, and problem overload," an account confirmed by then Minister of Labor Jacek Kuroń, who expressed regret over decisions he did not well understand (also Golinowska 1999). Such problems, however, plagued all three countries and yet only in Poland did spending balloon.[5] Another explanation emphasizes the high unemployment rate in Poland, which necessitated offloading workers to the pension system. But many of the key policies predated the rise in unemployment and therefore cannot be explained by it (Vanhuysse 2006).

Yet, there is also a political explanation for these choices that better fits the facts. Payoffs for social pain were an established part of the policy repertoire in Poland. Just as pensions were raised under communism whenever the government felt itself under pressure, so did the first democratic governments respond in the same way to increasing public dissatisfaction. Indeed, in the process of making his mistakes, Kuroń became the country's most popular politician.[6]

The public for its part was used to such payoffs and actively demanded that pensions maintain their real value. Public opinion data for this period are not available, but all accounts stress that the public opposed cuts in pensions. Moreover, there was widespread sympathy for the plight of the elderly, who had to cope with rising prices (Inglot 1995). Many of the large number of strikes and protest events catalogued by Ekiert and Kubik (1999) featured demands for better pensions. Graham (1994) further emphasized how ad hoc indexation in the past made this issue a priority for citizens after the transition. Therefore, a reasonable correspondence exists between policies and public demands, a connection that becomes clearer by juxtaposing Poland to the Czech Republic and Hungary.

6.2.2. Czech Republic

Unlike Poland, Czechoslovakia maintained its social security system almost intact through the end of communism (De Deken 1994, Večerník 2002). Although reforms were contemplated in the late 1960s, the Soviet invasion put an end to even mention of reform. Because of harsh repression, public protest against relatively austere government policies was almost unknown. Whereas Poland and Hungary used cooptation to maintain social control – government spending and some political openness were traded for political quiescence – the Czech government turned to out-and-out repression to deal with discontent (Kitschelt et al. 1999). As a result, the government was able to keep a lid on government spending during the 1970s and 1980s.

As in Poland, the first democratic government of Czechoslovakia was a mix of liberals and social democrats united under the banner of the Civic Forum

[5] Kuroń was not the only minister of labor to suffer from lack of experience. The first Czechoslovak Minister of Labor, Petr Miller, was similarly at sea and initially refused the post because he considered himself unqualified. He only accepted after the president, Václav Havel, told him that they needed a union representative in the post. Like Kuroń, Miller became a talented defender of the Ministry's programs though only after he was taught what to say by his advisors. Although the two ministers were similar in this respect, their policies were very different.

[6] Kuroń was also quite a charismatic figure and an effective communicator.

party (OF). Unlike Poland, this government continued to keep pension spending under control. Eligibility for benefits was only slightly loosened, leading to a rise in the number of pensioners by 3.8% over the first six years of transition – a tenth of the equivalent number in Poland (Müller 1999: 129). The new government also introduced a relatively ungenerous indexation scheme. The Pension Act of 1991 indexed the minimum pension by a cost of living index (that is, prices rather than the more generous wages) and provided for ad hoc indexation of higher pensions when prices had increased by more than 5% (Poland's scheme was automatic and quarterly). In practice, the government often delayed these increases without suffering undue backlash. As a result, benefit growth lagged behind wages and replacement rates dropped from 64% of wages in 1989 to 57% in 1994.

The first government also managed to abolish the country's system of work categories. Labor unions agreed to this move in exchange for a promise to introduce a state-sponsored system of supplementary insurance run through large firms (Macha 1999: 249).[7] This deal was facilitated by the weak position of Czech unions – unlike Poland's heroic Solidarity, they had been discredited by their perceived collaboration with communism – and the somewhat lower percentage of workers in privileged occupations – 8 to 9% versus more than 20% in Poland (De Deken 1994). In the end, the government did not fulfill its end of the bargain and escaped without a strong reaction from unions. It ended up introducing a supplementary pension system but one that was voluntary and had no role for employers.

The Czechs also failed to separate the pension system from the state budget – a step that Hungary and Poland had undertaken under communism. Part of the reason was that, unlike in Hungary and Poland, the Czech pension system was running a surplus early in the transition which the government used to help bail out struggling industries. Surprisingly, little controversy emerged over the use of these monies until later in the 1990s.

In short, Czechoslovakia was considerably more tightfisted than Poland and Hungary. Expenditures remained constant at about 8% of GDP through most of the 1990s. This result may be partially because of its better macroeconomic situation. Unemployment in the Czech Republic only reached 4% by 1993. This meant that the government did not need to force workers out of the labor market by offering them early retirement.

But just as important was the willingness of society to accept this belt-tightening. Unaccustomed to payoffs in the face of social pain, society remained quiet in response to policies that would have activated Polish workers and retirees. Few indications of significant protest against these policies exist: labor did not strike and important legislation was passed without undue conflict. Relatively ungenerous pension policies did not become a serious political issue until later in the transition, when unions had recovered and the government pushed even more belt-tightening without any consultation.

[7] Personal communication with Ondřej Schneider, Patria Finance, Prague, 9 December 1999.

6.2.3. Hungary

Over the last years of communism, the Hungarian government struck an implicit deal with citizens where it promised generous social benefits in exchange for political quiescence (Seleny 2006, Tokes 1996). Like Poland, cooptation rather than repression was the name of the game. As a result, the pension system began accumulating deficits in the 1980s, which politicians dealt with through opaque adjustments to the benefit formula (Simonovits 1999). The regime also brought genuine social policy experts – rather than loyal communists – into government with the result that some reforms, like the separation of the pension system from the state budget, were undertaken in the late 1980s (Ferge 1999).[8]

The first democratically elected government, a conservative coalition led by the Hungarian Democratic Forum (MDF), continued these organizational reforms, splitting the new social insurance fund into a pension and a health fund and equipping both with self-governments that were popularly elected by citizens (Müller 1999: 64–6). This latter move already suggests some responsiveness to citizens.

In terms of policies that affected citizens more directly, the government used pensions to help alleviate social pain. Parliament adopted both an Early Retirement Program and a Pre-Pension Program that allowed redundant workers near retirement age to retire early with full benefits. Ferge (1999, also Inglot 1995) writes that both programs were adopted when it was decided that the financial burden on the pension system was more tolerable than high unemployment. The consequence, however, was a large increase in the number of retirees, from 109% of citizens over the retirement age in 1990 to 126% in 1994 (Gál 1999). As evidence of public support, both programs were approved by nearly unanimous majorities in parliament.

The two main attempts of the first government to cut costs involved the retirement age and the indexation system. When in 1991 parliament first tried to increase the country's relatively low retirement age – 60 for men and 55 for women – it met strong opposition from unions and the general public and was forced to back down (Müller 1999: 67). As costs continued to rise, the government returned to the issue in 1992 and did pass an increase, but then turned around and postponed the bill until after parliamentary elections amidst concerns over declining popularity (Müller 1999: 67). At this point, MDF was trailing the opposition badly in opinion polls.

Reforms of the indexation system took a similar course. Initially, the government used ad hoc indexation to control costs with the result that pensions became highly distorted; there was little relation between what citizens contributed and what they received (Müller 1999: 68, Simonovits 1999). By the fall of 1992, as its popularity declined, the government concluded a new social

[8] Despite this expertise, Hungary pursued similar policies to Poland, suggesting that responsiveness was more important than competence.

contract with unions that formalized biannual indexation of pensions to wage growth (Müller 1999: 68). This law especially favored the poor and further reduced incentives to contribute. The same social contract forced the government to back off from a higher retirement age and to instead raise benefits. After these concessions the government suspended all pension reforms until after elections scheduled for May 1994 (Inglot 1995).

One of the government's few successes was the elimination of work categories. This reform was aided by the fact that Hungary had largely standardized its pension system in 1975 and so faced fewer entrenched interests than in Poland (Inglot 1995). Uncontroversially – the vote was 208 to 3 – the first government also passed a law setting up a new voluntary funded pillar of the retirement scheme that would be subsidized with a tax credit on contributions (Müller 1999: 69, Vittas 1996). That is, citizens could open their own retirement accounts with a small bonus (a tax reduction) provided by the state.

The record of the first government was thus one of attempted austerity that gave way to expansions under pressure from unions and public protest. From an already high level of 9.1% of GDP in 1989, spending rose to 11.5% in 1994 (Gál 1999: 203). The pension system thus began running a deficit even with payroll taxes at 35.5% of wages. A high degree of tax evasion exacerbated deficits by reducing contributions just as expenditures were rising (Gál 1999). Attempts to keep spending under control introduced large distortions into the system – pensions differed drastically even among otherwise similar citizens depending on when they retired.

As in Poland, these changes can be characterized as responsive. A strong tradition of payoffs for social pain motivated the public and induced the government to postpone belt tightening. Gedeon (1995: 456–7) put it best when he concluded that the government "internalized welfare expectations created by the pre-89 regime."

6.2.4. Conclusion

Indeed, this last phrase nicely encapsulates the differences among the three countries early in the transition. Expectations of payoffs in response to social pain were highly entrenched in Poland and Hungary, leading to heavy public pressure on the government to avoid retrenchment and in fact to compensate citizens for the hardships of the transition. A public used to austerity in the Czech Republic, by contrast, did not actively demand such payoffs, leading to less generous policies. In this way, politicians were responsive to public preferences.

Can other explanations account for the same facts? Economic factors were often at the forefront of policy makers' minds. Poland and Hungary both suffered from higher unemployment than the Czech Republic, which induced them to use the pension system as a safety net for redundant workers. Although these economic differences help to explain divergent use of early retirement, economics does not explain the timing of these changes – often introduced before mass unemployment emerged – nor the more general differences between the countries in other areas like indexation or unification of the pension system.

Nor does policy overload explain why Poland and Hungary increased spending while the Czech Republic kept spending constant. Poland and particularly Hungary had far better trained bureaucrats than the Czech Republic as a result of their more open communist regimes. Czech ministries by contrast were staffed mostly with communist loyalists. One would have thought a priori that Poland and Hungary would introduce more sustainable pension policies; that they did not leads to other explanations. Inherited expectations and responsiveness to them best account for the full diversity of policies in the region.

6.3. PARAMETRIC REFORMS

In this section I turn to the second, third, and fourth electoral cycles after the transition. This phase may be called "normal" politics because new political institutions had stabilized and governments had to address the sort of distributional conflicts common in the established democracies.[9] I focus further on parametric reforms: changes in the parameters of existing pension systems like retirement ages, benefit and contribution levels, and special privileges.[10] The three countries did not differ greatly in these policy choices. All three countries tried with moderate success to cut spending. Hungary and Poland were marginally more successful than the Czech Republic, partially because they had been less successful at the start of the transition.

Not only were outcomes similar, but so was the style of policy making. The dominant style was the blame avoidance politics well described by Pierson (1994). Faced with fiscal pressures to cut pensions, governments typically sought ways to avoid responsibility for doing so. The reason was the popularity of pension provision. In the few cases where politicians did not take the public into account, they were punished for it. Although this should not be called responsive policy, it is a style of policy making that takes the public seriously (see Section 9.2).

6.3.1. Poland

During the election campaign of 1993, the Democratic Left Alliance (SLD) used Prime Minister Suchocka's ill-fated pension cuts to campaign against the government and promised to increase pensions even further. Upon taking power (in coalition with the smaller Polish Peasant Party), they did manage

9 For a comprehensive account of the course of these reforms, see Müller (1999).

10 There is an active literature on the politics of these parametric reforms. The general conclusion is that cuts are almost always unpopular. As Pierson and Weaver (1993: 110) put it, the costs of cuts are "concentrated, immediate, and highly visible, while the benefits are contingent, diffuse, and long-term." Politicians therefore avoid them or enact them using blame avoidance techniques. See Pierson (1994), Pierson and Weaver (1993), and Bonoli (2000).

to push through an increase in the minimum pension from 35 to 39% of the average wage and more generous indexation rules (Cain and Surdej 1999: 164–5). These changes, along with increasing tax evasion, only added to the system's deficit (Cain and Surdej 1999: 154).

As deficits grew, however, attention began to shift from the plight of retirees – the main focus of attention early in the transition – to the state of public finance. Golinowska (1999: 177) dates this shift to a 1994 conference held by the Polish Chamber of Commerce, which pointed to the deleterious effects of high payroll taxes on unemployment that had reached 16%. Pressures from the International Monetary Fund (IMF) and World Bank contributed to the sense of urgency. Trying to regain control of the budget, the Social Democratic government thus embarked on a two-track program of reform, with the Ministry of Welfare working on parametric changes and the Ministry of Finance preparing a privatization proposal (described separately in the following section).

Among the Ministry of Welfare's proposals were a change in the indexation formula to a less generous combination of wage and price increases, an increase in the retirement age of women to 65, and the elimination of most special privileges including those given to farmers under an institutionally separate and heavily subsidized scheme (Cook and Orenstein 1999: 88, Orenstein 2000). Most radically, the government prepared to convert the entire PAYG system into a notionally defined contribution (NDC) system (for details see Żukowski 1999: 99). This approach meant that benefits would be calculated as if each worker had his or her own personal account. Contributions would be recorded for each individual and a suitable rate of return applied to them. Upon retirement, contributors would receive the sum total of their contributions plus interest as if they had been investing them all the time even though the PAYG method of funding would remain intact. This system would introduce a tight relation between contributions and benefits.

Few of these reforms, however, came to fruition under the Social Democratic government. Public disapproval – particularly fierce in the case of special privileges[11] but also high for increases in the retirement age – cowed the government into postponing a discussion of reforms until after elections (Müller 1999: 113). In fact, by the time reforms were ready, the government was already within shouting distance of elections scheduled for September 1997, which they preferred not to jeopardize with unpopular policies. Instead, the government devoted its political capital to the partial privatization that is discussed in the next section. As far as the PAYG system went, third-rail politics prevailed. To keep the system in balance, the government again resorted to opaque manipulations of the benefit formula and indexation, which were ultimately ruled unconstitutional by the country's Constitutional Court (Hausner 2001).

[11] The case of privileges is particularly noteworthy. Farmers, for example, contributed only 10% of wages to the social security system versus 45% for others. Miners could retire early and receive higher benefits. See Cain and Surdej (1999: 162).

The right-wing coalition of Electoral Action Solidarity (AWS) and Freedom Union (UW) elected in 1997 returned to the reforms prepared by the Social Democrats in an effort to finally get control of spending. Indeed, the continuity in reform between two very different governments suggests a great deal of consensus about what had to be done (Cook and Orenstein 1999).[12] The government also conducted intensive negotiations with labor unions – principally the left-wing OPZZ and the right-wing Solidarity – in the tripartite council to achieve even greater consensus. These negotiations led to a number of compromises. On indexation, a 50/50 split between wage and price growth become a 75/25 split that was more favorable to retirees. Moves to increase the retirement age for women – shown in public opinion polls to be highly unpopular by a margin of 85 to 15 – were ditched altogether.[13] Protests by miners (who occupied the Ministry of Labor), farmers, railway workers, and even judges also led to the maintenance of many of their privileges (Cain and Surdej 1999, Orenstein 2000).[14]

Surprisingly, the government was able to go forward with the NDC reform, one of its most radical proposals. Yet, opinion polls indicate that NDC principles were broadly popular. Between 70 and 75% of those polled over the course of 1997 believed that lower contributions should lead to lower pensions and 80% were in favor of a system with individual accounts where benefits would exactly equal accumulated contributions (Chlon et al. 1999: 179–80). Only 20% of respondents thought that pensions should be basically equal for all.

There are understandable reasons for these opinions. Under the weight of decades of special privileges and manipulation of the benefit formula, benefits had become so detached from contributions that many citizens felt that they could do better without redistribution. Large majorities believed the system to be unfair (Chlon et al. 1999: 178–9). The same polls from 1997 found that 68 to 69% of respondents thought that the system was opaque and not understandable. Golinowska (1999: 181) notes that an earlier move to flatten pensions – that is, to weaken the link between contributions and benefits – was rejected by public opinion, which conversely wanted more differentiated benefits.

With this kind of support, it was no surprise that the government went forward with the NDC reform. On other reforms, however, the unanimous coalition that had supported privatization broke down. The Social Democrats who had prepared many of the reforms on indexation, privileges, and the retirement age now found it prudent to oppose most of these cuts. Disputes

12 Żukowski (1999: 169) refers to a "quite wide consensus on the pension reform."

13 Unless otherwise stated, all poll results for Poland refer to nationally representative surveys conducted by CBOS (Public Opinion Research Center) and available through www.cbos.pl. The poll referred to here was conducted in October 1999.

14 Privatization reduced the scope of these privileges because they were not included in the new funded pillar.

broke out not only between government and opposition but also within the government and even within individual parties (Orenstein 2000: 47–9). The timing of reforms also reflects their controversial nature. They were passed early in the government's term – in the hope that they would be forgotten by election time – but only after local elections in the fall of 1998 to avoid damaging the governing parties' prospects.

The summary message here is of governments that stepped carefully on the issue of pensions. The Social Democrats prepared proposals, but seeing their controversial nature and the necessity of passing them before elections, did little to alter existing policies. Although the AWS government was able to introduce cuts, it did so strategically at the beginning of its term, left out of the reform those issues that hurt concentrated groups, compromised on others, and in the case of NDC found public support for their reform. Spending ultimately remained high. This lack of severe retrenchment does provide some support for the responsiveness thesis. Pensioners would see few effects on their standard of living in the short term. According to Cain and Surdej (1999: 168), "democratic factors were probably the most important influence on policy outcomes."

6.3.2. Czech Republic

The right-wing government elected in the Czech Republic in 1992, particularly the Civic Democratic Party (ODS), boasted some of the strongest neoliberal rhetoric in the region, promising a market economy without adjectives.[15] It thus may have been expected to have enacted the most far-reaching cutbacks. Yet, for the first two years of its rule, the government showed little inclination to deal with the pension system. Only in 1994 did the government unveil a set of reforms that included a gradual increase in the retirement age (to 62 for men and 57–61 for women), a reduction in the replacement rate (with the remainder to be made up by voluntary supplementary insurance), and a tighter link between benefits and contributions. Importantly, the government did not vet these proposals with important civil society actors.

As a result, the draft law brought forth serious objections from the main trade union – the Czech-Moravian Confederation of Trade Unions (ČMKOS) – who wanted pension financing to be separated from the state budget, a postponement of changes to the retirement age, and clearer indexation conditions (Polívka 1998). When its concerns were not addressed, ČMKOS organized a protest in the center of Prague that drew 60,000 supporters (Müller 1999). This was the largest public protest since the revolution and the first time that the union flexed its political muscles. Meanwhile, 630,000 citizens signed a petition against various aspects of the bill (Macha 1999: 249).

Opinion polls showed that opposition was broad. A poll in June 1995 found that 67% of citizens opposed a retirement age increase for men (42%

[15] ODS's coalition partners were the smaller Christian Democratic Union (KDU-ČSL) and the liberal Civic Democratic Alliance (ODA).

strongly), 79% opposed an increase in the retirement age for women (55% strongly), and 65% wanted pensions separated from the state budget.[16] On the entire government proposal, a poll from March 1995 found that 51% rejected it, 27% wanted to postpone it, and only 12% supported it. And although the government could point to future demographic issues as reasons to engage in reform, it could not credibly claim that the system was in crisis. In fact, receipts from payroll taxes actually exceeded spending on pensions and the excess was used to prop up failing industries.

Tensions increased to such an extent that the Council on Economic and Social Agreement (RHSD) – a tripartite forum for negotiations among the government, business, and labor – was suspended for six months over the pension issue. The government itself was split with one of ODS's coalition partners, the Christian Democrats, whose electorate included many older people, backing away from the proposed law over the retirement age increase. The government ultimately softened some aspects of the bill, such as making all benefits earnings-related, and promised a separate pension account in the budget in the future. Even so, the Pension Insurance Act passed by a relatively narrow margin of 100 to 76 with the governing Christian Democrats abstaining and some coalition MPs voting against the proposal (Polívka 1998, Večerník 2002).

Though not particularly draconian, this law was the closest in the sample to a government confident enough in its own powers to ignore the public. Ultimately, forcing the reform on the public proved to be a poor strategic choice. The opposition Social Democratic Party improved its vote share by 20% in the 1996 election by harping on pension reform, among other issues, and by pledging to lower the retirement age and restore all funds "stolen" from the pension system.

This situation repeated itself when the ODS-led government was reelected in 1996, albeit now with only a minority of seats. Under heavy economic pressure from a run on the Czech crown, the government had to introduce two austerity packages that further reduced pension benefits. Again, the coalition Christian Democrats opposed the government on these cuts – ultimately leaving the government over them and forcing early elections – and again, the Social Democrats campaigned against the reforms and this time won the parliamentary elections. Indeed, public outcry over pensions was strong enough that preelection polls in 1998 consistently indicated that a party of retirees – the Party for Lifetime Security (SŽJ) – would cross the 5% threshold for entry into parliament, but these predictions were not fulfilled.[17]

[16] Unless otherwise stated, all poll results for the Czech Republic refer to nationally representative surveys conducted by Centrum pro výzkum veřejného mínění (Public Opinion Research Centre) and available through www.cvvm.cas.cz.

[17] This episode also produced one of the more curious incidents in Czech politics, when the eccentric chairman of SŽJ promised to eat a bug if his party did not make it into parliament and then followed through on his promise. Mandate responsiveness indeed!

The Social Democrats had well learned the dangers of crossing the public on social guarantees and for the next eight years of their rule avoided any substantial change in the pension system. Various minor changes in fact increased the system's generosity. By 1999 the deficit in the system had reached 1% of GDP and the government was receiving stern warnings from the World Bank and IMF about the necessity for reform (Lasagabaster et al. 2002). The Social Democrats did, however, back away from their earlier promises to rescind the reforms introduced by ODS. Only in 2004, their sixth year in power, were they willing to support an all-party commission to study the issue of reform. Although some agreement was reached in the commission on the need for greater austerity – particularly a higher retirement age and some benefit cuts – the commission's report appeared just before elections and was thus a dead letter for the ruling coalition, which neither prepared nor introduced any reform legislation. The public largely supported the government's inaction.

In sum, right-wing governments pushed reform in the face of strong public opposition. Although these governments were strong enough to carry the day, they suffered politically for their nonresponsiveness. Their successor, the left-wing Social Democrats, learned this lesson and halted all reform despite its increasing urgency.

6.3.3. Hungary

The Hungarian Socialist Party (MSZP) won elections in 1994 with promises to soften the social impact of the transition and negotiate a socioeconomic pact with the main labor unions.[18] In fact, the new socialist government was soon overwhelmed by economic difficulties. Mounting debts – the budget deficit reached 7.5% of GDP in 1994 – frightened foreign investors who had played a large role in Hungary's recovery and spurred a run on the forint (Cook and Orenstein 1999: 92–3). The new Minister of Finance, Lajos Bokros, took advantage of this situation to embark on a major reform of public finances. Because the pension system was suffering from rising spending and declining contributions, it became a focus for his plans (Simonovits 1999: 213–4).

As in Poland, these reforms had two tracks. The Ministry of Finance worked on privatization while the Ministry of Labor focused on parametric reforms. On the parametric side, policy makers returned to the reforms of indexation and the retirement age over which the previous government had stumbled. This time, however, greater economic pressure ensured that some reform would be passed.

Nevertheless, the government had to deal with strong public disapproval and repeatedly compromised to get its reforms passed. Polls from 1995 showed that upward of 90% of Hungarians opposed a proposed increase in the retirement

[18] Although they won a majority of seats, they formed a coalition government with the liberal Alliance of Free Democrats.

age to 65 for men and 60 for women.[19] There was even organized opposition led by the Association of Large Families that Ferge (1999: 233) calls "extremely strong." Other polls found that even when told that a higher retirement age would lead to higher pensions, only 16% of respondents approved of an increase – the same percentage who wanted the retirement age to be decreased (TÁRKI 1996). This pressure led the government to water down the increase to an age of only 62, phased in gradually until 2009 (Gál 1999: 203).

Proposals for a conversion to less expensive price indexation also occasioned protests that the government was "not brave enough" to ignore (Simonovits 1999: 217). The Socialists only saved this part of the reform by agreeing to the Swiss formula that splits indexation equally between price and wage growth (Simonovits 1999: 211). Even this vital cost-saving measure was postponed until 2001. The same fate met plans for a closer link between contributions and benefits, which was postponed until 2013 (Simonovits 1999: 211).[20] Reforms of the disability pension system – which like early retirement had been overused – were also postponed (Orenstein 2000: 36). Other reforms included penalties for early retirement and incentives to work longer. As one would expect, opposition MPs voted against these proposals although the government's large majority – it held two-thirds of seats – guaranteed that they would pass.

These postponements and gradual phase-ins closely fit the politics of blame avoidance described by Pierson and Weaver (1993). At the end of their term, the Socialists even instituted pension increases as an election present to make up for the future cuts (Orenstein 2000: 36). It should be mentioned that all of these policies were negotiated with trade unions in the context of the country's tripartite institution, the Interest Reconciliation Council (ÉT). The Hungarian Socialists were committed to achieving consensus on these changes. As a sop to the major unions, elections to the pension self-government were ended and unions were given entitlements to seats.

All of these reforms took place in the context of a simultaneous discussion over privatization. Indeed, some claim that the headline issue of privatization helped to distract public attention from the more unpopular parametric reforms. A similar tactic was said to characterize Bokros's earlier austerity packages, where cuts in small but visible programs like family allowances were said to distract attention from a more consequential currency devaluation. The relative popularity of privatization enabled the government to bundle that program with the less popular parametric reforms – another well-known blame avoidance technique.

[19] All Hungarian poll results refer to nationally representative surveys conducted by TÁRKI (Social Research Center) and available through www.tarki.hu.

[20] Polls by TÁRKI (1996) found evidence that, over the first six years of transition, there was an increase in support for insurance principles (in other words, closer links between contributions and benefits) as opposed to equal pensions.

Subsequent governments did little to alter the fundamental shape of the pension system. The right-wing Fidesz government elected in 1998 ran its campaign against the austerity programs of the Socialists and was thus ill positioned to engage in rationalization. Upon achieving power, they did little to push reforms forward.[21] Both the Fidesz government and the Socialists who succeeded them in 2002 managed to provide additional benefits even as the budget deficit grew once again to unsustainable proportions. By the end of the Socialists' term in 2006, they were putting forward a plan for five years of pension increases while Fidesz was promising a fourteenth-month pension if elected. Although these increases were presumably responsive to public desires, they were far from sustainable as shown in the introduction to Chapter 4.

Hungary then initially witnessed opposition to pension cuts and an economic environment that seemed to require them. The Socialist government squared this circle through a variety of well-known blame avoidance techniques. Compromise, gradual phase-ins, postponements, and bundling were their means to enact reforms without provoking the public. After these austerity programs, parties returned to a more generous and increasingly unsustainable pension policy, which was nevertheless popular with the public.

6.3.4. Conclusion

Does responsiveness characterize parametric reforms? On the surface, no. All three countries were forced to engage in some unpopular pension cuts, whether by reducing the generosity of indexation or by raising the retirement age. It was largely economic constraints, whether real or perceived, that forced them into these decisions.

But evidence also exists that governments did worry about public responses. In most cases politicians did compromise, postpone, and bundle to make these cuts more palatable. In all but the Czech reforms of 1995–1997, policymakers consulted with key societal actors. Furthermore, the size of retrenchment was limited. All three countries spent considerably more on pensions after 1989 than they did before 1989. Although aging populations were responsible for some of this increase, more important was the expansion of early retirement and increases in benefits. Even cuts in the mid-1990s did not alter this dynamic. Finally, some of these reforms did actually achieve public acceptance. As a result of frequent manipulations that distorted benefits, citizens often desired stronger links between benefits and contributions, which all countries did introduce. Although it is a mistake to characterize parametric pension reforms as responsive, they do follow the same style of blame avoidance common in established democracies.

[21] The government did eliminate the pension fund self-governments, which were controlled by unions affiliated with the opposition Socialists.

6.4. PRIVATIZATION

My goal in this section is to explain why Hungary and Poland partially privatized their pension systems whereas the Czech Republic did not.[22] Privatization (also known as the creation of a funded or fully funded pillar) means the introduction of private investment accounts to which current workers are required to contribute a certain percentage of their income. These monies are then invested and the accumulated returns are paid out to the contributor upon his or her retirement. Instead of the young paying for the old, as in a PAYG scheme, each individual supports him- or herself through mandatory savings and investment. Such a privatization can be full – if this system entirely replaces the PAYG system – or partial – if the PAYG system continues to operate side by side with private accounts, though perhaps on a smaller scale.

Privatization gained salience as a possible reform of the pension system when the World Bank (1994) recommended it in its influential study, *Averting the Old Age Crisis*. The idea was that a privatized system could deal well with an aging society because it always has the funds to pay benefits. A PAYG system, by contrast, may not be able to sustain itself when the number of retirees rises relative to the working population. Privatization is also reputed to have desirable macroeconomic effects (Feldstein 1997, but see Orszag and Stiglitz 1999). For example, it is said to increase savings and deepen capital markets, which should help long-term growth. It should also discourage tax evasion because benefits and contributions are closely linked.

On the other hand, privatization faces a number of economic and political obstacles.[23] First, it is extremely expensive. Countries cannot just shut down their PAYG schemes; they have to rely on younger workers to pay the pensions for older citizens who do not have time to build up enough savings to support themselves. This is known as the double payment problem: younger workers have to support two pension systems in the process of privatization. Second, the switch to private accounts breaks the existing social contract of young supporting old and in turn being supported by a future generation; younger voters may find it unjust to be denied a benefit that others have received. Privatization likewise makes redistribution from rich to poor more difficult because citizens now "own" their own pension accounts. Redistribution can be more easily hidden when money is transferred from young to old. Finally, private accounts transfer considerable risk to workers; although they may earn returns through investment, they may also make losses. In all these ways, the

[22] For the definitive account of privatization in Hungary and Poland, see Orenstein (2000).

[23] There is a rapidly growing literature on the politics of privatization. Its main conclusion is that economic and international forces are the main causes of privatization. Countries introduce privatization when they are compelled to by low savings rates and international pressure (Brooks 2002, Madrid 2003, Müller 1999). By contrast, privatization may be impeded by a high number of veto points and large commitments to the existing pension system (Bonoli 2000, Kay 1999, Orenstein 2000).

majority of voters can be expected to view privatization as the loss of an existing benefit and oppose it. (Privatization, however, may have supporters including the financial services industry and wealthier individuals who clearly benefit from it.)

For all these reasons, privatization is typically considered a "difficult" reform. It is considered particularly difficult in countries with large PAYG systems both because of the expense and because most of the population has a stake in the existing social contract. The question then is whether Hungary and Poland were able to overcome these difficulties and introduce privatization in a responsive way.

6.4.1. Poland

The Course of Reform. Although the possibility of privatization had been mentioned in Poland as early as 1991, serious discussion of the issue only began after the Social Democratic government took power in 1993. In fact, the idea was part of the future Minister of Finance Grzegorz Kołodko's (1993) "Strategy for Poland." According to Hausner (2001), the idea of privatization rose on the agenda when decisions by the Constitutional Court blocked the government's ad hoc attempts to keep spending in check.[24] The Court, however, did leave open the possibility of fundamental change in the system. Policy makers for their part were beginning to realize the enormous burden that a pension system eating up 15% of GDP was putting on the economy and the labor market in particular. As noted earlier, a series of conferences in 1994 began to turn opinion away from the plight of the elderly and toward fiscal matters and the problem of unemployment.

Initial reform proposals came out of the Ministry of Labor and focused on the rationalization of the existing system. The Ministry of Finance, now led by Kołodko, criticized these plans as insufficient and, with technical help from the World Bank, put forward its own proposal for a funded pillar. Although the initial plan to direct three-quarters of contributions to the private pillar was not submitted to government, it did, according to Müller (1999), help to focus debate. For a year and a half, however, the Ministry of Labor, under the powerful party leader and future Prime Minister Leszek Miller, prevented the privatization proposal from going forward. Indeed, the Minister of Finance Kołodko was a nonpartisan without a strong political base.

The deadlock was broken only in early 1996 when a government shakeup moved Miller up to the Ministry of Interior. The new Prime Minister, Wlodzimierz Cimoszewicz, and Miller's successor at Labor, Andrej Bączkowski, were more centrist and open to cooperation with the opposition Solidarity movement, of which Bączkowski was in fact a member (Orenstein 2000). The shakeup was prompted by increasingly successful criticism of the government as

24 It is worth adding that, even without the Court decision, ad hoc cuts were not a sustainable strategy in the long term.

weakly committed to reform and living off the fruits of earlier painful reforms. Tellingly, Cook and Orenstein (1999: 88) write that "the left government was guided heavily by public opinion polls that showed that the Polish population wanted more radical reform than that proposed by Miller in 1995."

These changes moved reform into a new phase. It was now supported by the Prime Minister and the Minister of Labor. Jerzy Hausner, who was soon to take over the reform job, recalls the prime minister telling him that he wanted a major reform before elections to restore the party's reformist credentials.[25] To speed the process, Bączkowski successfully lobbied for a special office for pension reform, independent of any ministry. The newly created Office of the Plenipotentiary for Social Security Reform could bypass hostile bureaucrats in the Ministry of Labor while freeing reformers from the burden of running the current system (Müller 1999, Orenstein 2000). Bączkowski's unexpected death and the appointment of a new minister of labor opposed to privatization seemed to threaten the reform, but the Plenipotentiary was then made directly subordinate to the prime minister, who was committed to privatization (Müller 1999: 111).

The Plenipotentiary took its proposals for reform – which included both parametric changes and a new funded pillar – to numerous consultations with labor unions and pensioners' organizations (Müller 1999: 114). Surprisingly, both major unions, the right-wing Solidarity and the left-wing OPZZ, supported privatization in tripartite discussions in April 1997 and allowed it to go forward (Orenstein 2000). Hausner (2001) calls this the key moment in reform because unions became involved in creating the system rather than criticizing it. The final proposal had approximately a quarter of the payroll tax entering the new private pillar.

In the end, privatization sailed through parliament. When it came to a vote in the summer of 1997, more than 90% of MPs voted in favor (Hausner 2001). As Żukowski (1999: 169) notes, "There has, in fact, been no major political party or social group that has opposed reform entirely." The main debate over reform ultimately concerned how it would be funded – Solidarity pushed for state-owned firms to be included in the assets of the new pension funds (Gesell et al. 1999) – rather than its existence. The new system began operations in April 1998 with participants choosing from among a variety of private pension funds and contributing 7.3% of their wages to those accounts.

Analysis. Was privatization characterized by responsive policy making? Although there is little evidence that the public demanded reform on its own initiative, there is considerable evidence that once the government proposed privatization it could count on considerable public support. In the first place, public dissatisfaction with the existing system was rising. By April 1997, two-thirds of poll respondents believed that the current system was in bad shape and only 9% that it was in good shape (Chlon 2000: 8–9, Żukowski 1999: 169).

[25] Personal communication from Jerzy Hausner, Cracow, 15 May 2001.

TABLE 6.2. *Opinions on the Pension System in Poland*

	Response			
	April 1997		October 1997	
Question	Positive/ Yes	Negative/ No	Positive/ Yes	Negative/ No
General evaluation of pension system	10	67	8	66
System is transparent and understandable	13	69	11	68
Know basis on which pension is calculated	24	62	18	66
Feel security that pension will provide for one's old age	10	78	10	78
Current pension assures good quality of life	6	84	4	85
Pension benefits a subject of political wrangling	63	15	61	13

Note: Percentage of respondents agreeing or disagreeing, including "don't know" responses. Polls conducted by CBOS.

Fifty percent more believed it to be in very bad shape than two years earlier. Citizens had numerous gripes about the existing system. As Table 6.2 shows, two-thirds or more of poll respondents saw it as nontransparent, unsustainable, not providing sufficient benefits, and the object of political wrangling. By the summer of 1997, 66% of respondents believed that pension reforms were both "necessary and urgent" versus 24% who believed that they were "necessary but could be delayed" and just 2% that they were not necessary.

The same opinion polls, conducted as the reform effort came to a head, showed that the public was overwhelmingly in favor of the principles of privatization (Chlon 2000). More than 80% of citizens believed that pensions should accumulate in private accounts (52% strongly) and 68% agreed with the principle that pensions should be funded (vs. 16% opposed). These opinions were remarkably consistent across gender, age, educational, and income groups. Even citizens over 65, those with only a primary education, and those in the lowest income groups supported both funding and individual accounts.[26]

Poles also had faith that the new system would work better. Among those who chose to participate in the new system – those aged between 30 and 50 had a choice between remaining in the old system and joining the new one – the two most cited reasons for joining were a belief that it would produce higher (49%) and more secure pensions (48%) (Chlon 2000: 42–3). Conversely, of those who chose not to switch, only 10% mentioned lack of trust in pension funds (Golinowska 1999). When asked independently about their attitudes

[26] Regression analyses confirm that attitudes toward the existing system were the key determinant of support for privatization and demographic variables had only a small effect. See Roberts (2008).

toward investment types, majorities had positive views toward banks, stocks, and bonds (Chlon 2000: 19). Golinowska (1999: 180) emphasizes the positive image of the country's first mutual fund, the Pioneer Fund.

One may discount these opinions because many citizens were not well informed about the reforms and the survey questions were sometimes vague (Chlon 2000: 60). But other factors support this picture of public permissiveness. The consent of labor unions and other social groups for the reform is another indicator of approval. One analysis notes that the largest left-wing union, OPZZ, who would be expected to oppose privatization, conducted polls among its members and found that many supported reform (VÚPSV 2002). The Solidarity union put together its own proposal for privatization. Similarly, the fact that the reform was proposed by a left-wing government suggests that it was not ideologically motivated. The very large percentage of MPs who voted in favor of privatization gives the same impression (only a small number of far-right parliamentarians voted against it).

Other circumstantial evidence in favor of privatization comes from the timing and implementation of reform. The funded pillar was passed in July 1997, just before parliamentary elections in September 1997. In short, the government did not fear electoral retribution from reform and in fact hoped to gain from it. Although it cannot be shown that the privatization helped its prospects, SLD did increase its vote share between 1993 and 1997, but it ultimately lost the elections to a newly unified right. Finally, when the reform was ultimately implemented in April 1998, Poles voted for it with their feet. Of those with a choice of whether to join the new system or remain in the old one, 80% of 30–40-year-olds entered the new scheme (Chlon 2000).[27] As Cook and Orenstein (1999: 88) sum up, "Extensively public opinion tested, negotiated, and legislated by disparate political forces, pension reform in Poland became the keystone of a new centrist consensus on social policy."

6.4.2. Czech Republic

The Course of Nonreform. One would expect a priori the Czech Republic to be a more likely site for privatization than Poland. From 1992 to 1997, the country's prime minister, Václav Klaus, was a strong supporter of Thatcherite reforms and trumpeted the importance of individual responsibility. The country's pension system also remained in surplus, making it easier to cope with the double payment problem.

Yet, the only move toward privatization was the institution in 1994 of a voluntary system of supplementary pension insurance with a small state subsidy to encourage participation. Although Prime Minister Klaus hoped that supplementary insurance would reduce dependence on the public system, its

[27] The system was designed to be most advantageous for this group. Among 40- to 50-year-olds for whom the new system was less advantageous because of the brevity of their remaining working years, 30% joined.

voluntary nature and the low level of the state subsidy made this impossible. A large number of citizens did open accounts, but most of them were over 50 years old, contributed small amounts, and used the system for short-term savings (Jelínek and Schneider 1999).

With that reform, most talk of privatization ended. In the mid-1990s only one small party, the Civic Democratic Alliance (ODA), publicly advocated privatization. More telling is that no serious proposals for privatization were put forward. The Czech Social Democratic Party (CSSD), the dominant party in government from 1998 to 2006, repeatedly stated that it had no interest in privatization and viewed it as unnecessary and potentially destructive.

Although the right-wing parties began to support privatization in the late 1990s – it appeared in the electoral manifesto of Klaus's ODS in 1998 – they neither emphasized the issue nor put forward concrete proposals.[28] Interest groups were similarly silent. Although some economists associated with investment banks touted the idea in the press, their influence on policy was minimal. Pension funds were also lukewarm in their support (Večerník 2002).[29] When an all-party commission convened in 2004 to consider how to reform the pension system, privatization could not achieve consensus due to opposition from the left-wing parties and was not included in the commission's final recommendations.

Analysis. What explains the relatively low prominence of privatization in the Czech Republic compared to that in Poland despite more favorable initial conditions? In the first place, public attitudes toward the pension system were very different. According to public opinion polls, Czechs had considerable confidence in the existing system. A majority surveyed in 1998 believed that the average pension was sufficient to cover the basic needs of pensioners (Haberlová and Hartl 1998: 68). A similar majority reported that it did not use the voluntary pension system because it believed that the state pension would be sufficient (Jelínek and Schneider 1999).

Some grounds for this optimism existed because the pension system remained in surplus through 1998 and spending did not rise as precipitously as in Hungary and Poland. By the late 1990s, however, indicators began to turn negative, leading the World Bank and IMF to criticize the country for its lack of attention to the pension system (Lasagabaster et al. 2002). Nevertheless, citizens did not see the need to reform the system. Whereas polls in 1998 showed that 59% of citizens believed that cuts needed to be made, this percentage dropped to 51% in 2002.

As for privatization itself, only 14% of respondents supported a shift to private accounts, although 54% agreed that substantial changes in the system

[28] Večerník (2001) notes that a proposal for a compulsory funded pillar was discussed in the Council of Economic Ministers in 1997 but was not submitted to the government.

[29] Personal communication from Eva Vitková, Association of Pension Funds, Prague, 3 February 2000.

were required (Haberlová and Hartl 1998: 111). When asked about the ideal shape of the pension system, the most popular option was the status quo, with nearly 50% in favor versus 35% supporting a privatized system and 15% a minimal state pension (Haberlová and Hartl 1998: 111). Opinions of the existing system were highly correlated with opinions of changes. Those who had the most faith in the old system were least supportive of a shift to private accounts (Haberlová and Hartl 1998: 115). These opinions did not change greatly in subsequent years. In the fall of 2001, citizens favored the current system by a margin of 69 to 31 and opposed a proposal of private accounts combined with a higher retirement age by 39 to 61.[30]

Equally telling were suspicions about investing. When asked whether citizens should be required to start a retirement savings account at a bank, 80% answered in the negative, while 61% said the same about mandatory pension funds (Haberlová and Hartl 1998: 127). This suspicion of investing had its roots in the numerous scandals of the country's voucher privatization program that allowed citizens to invest their vouchers in private mutual funds (Orenstein 2001). Many of these funds went bankrupt or found their assets stripped by management, leaving investors high and dry. The Czech stock market also lacked regulation and was believed to be dominated by inside traders. Independent ratings of financial markets in the three countries indicate that on measures of disclosure and reporting requirements, protection of small shareholders, and degree of insider trading the Czechs lagged behind the Poles and Hungarians (EBRD 1995–2009).

The voluntary private pension system also provoked doubts. Little regulation of these funds resulted in many going bankrupt (Jelínek and Schneider 1999: 282). The number of funds declined from forty-four in 1994 to only fourteen in 1999 (Jelínek and Schneider 1999). Because of weak reporting requirements, return rates were anyone's guess. These weak regulations and poor performance led to an "alarmingly high suspicion that pension funds might behave improperly" (Jelínek and Schneider 1999: 269).[31]

A survey from 1997 in fact indicated that the second largest reason for not using the supplementary pension system – cited by 59% of respondents and exceeded only by lack of finances – was "lack of confidence" in investment funds (Haberlová and Hartl 1998: 99, Jelínek and Schneider 1999: 270). The same survey found that 63% of respondents with an opinion believed that pension funds were irresponsible (Haberlová and Hartl 1998: 97, Jelínek and Schneider 1999: 268). Tellingly, 54% of respondents did not invest because they believed that the state pension would be sufficient. The funds themselves seemed to share this distrust and remained uninterested in privatization. Jelínek and Schneider (1999) suggest that they feared the increased state regulation and oversight that a mandatory system would bring.

[30] The poll did not separate the latter two options.

[31] Večerník (2001) writes that "Supplementary pension insurance is less popular than had been expected owing to a lack of confidence in financial institutions."

Independent economists concurred with the public's suspicion of investment funds. A study by the Czech Business Bank (ČSOB) at the end of 1997 to assess the readiness of Czech capital markets for a mandatory funded pillar gave a poor evaluation of the Czech situation (Dvořák 1997). It noted that the pension system would first have to be separated from the state budget – a step that has still not been taken – and that a further two and a half years would be necessary to fully prepare capital markets for the inflow of funds.

6.4.3. Hungary

The Course of Reform. Although privatization had been floated as an option in Hungary as early as 1992, it was not taken seriously (Ferge 1999: 235). The seating of a Socialist-Liberal government in 1994 was expected to set that possibility back even further. However, thinking changed during the country's financial crisis in 1995, when the government began to take seriously the necessity of cutting social expenditures and appeasing financial markets. High budget deficits combined with rising pension spending and the difficulty of parametric reforms pushed the government toward new solutions.

The job of preparing reforms was delegated in the summer of 1995 to a newly formed Committee for the Reform of the Treasury subordinate to the Ministry of Finance. Its initial recommendations were for parametric changes in the existing system. Not satisfied with the depth of the proposal, the Minister of Finance Lajos Bokros had his ministry put forward an alternative plan for full privatization that was prepared with the help of the World Bank (Orenstein 2000). Although the move would worsen public finances in the short run, Bokros believed that it would reassure foreign investors and help the economy in the long run.

As in Poland, differences over the advisability of privatization led to a conflict between the Ministry of Finance and the Ministry of Welfare. This standoff lasted from the summer of 1995 to the spring of 1996 (Müller 1999, Orenstein 2000). The key moment in reform came when the two ministries agreed on a joint proposal in April 1996. The agreement included a funded pillar – reduced from 100 to 30% of contributions – and the parametric reforms described in the previous section. The Ministry of Finance would prepare the new funded pillar with a mandate to complete the reform by elections in June 1998 (Müller 1999, Orenstein 2000).

Although it is not clear why the Ministry of Welfare dropped its opposition to reform, most sources believe that Prime Minister Gyula Horn put his weight behind privatization (Danics 1998, Müller 1999). Not coincidentally, the prime minister, as head of the Socialist Party, was the official most responsible for the electoral prospects of the government. Also possible is that bundling parametric reforms with privatization increased the attractiveness of privatization (Müller 1999: 78). But this strategy implies that privatization itself was popular.

After this agreement, the government created an interministerial committee that would prepare the technical details of the reform. The government also committed itself to securing the agreement of the major labor unions. In fact, it endowed the country's tripartite institution, which typically could only advise on legislation, with a veto over the reform. Numerous meetings followed between the government and a wide variety of public organizations including labor unions and pensioners' organizations (for a list of the twenty-two meetings, see Orenstein 2000). Cook and Orenstein (1999: 98) write that "A major effort was made to include as wide a range of pension experts as possible in the discussions of the working group."

The country's largest union, the left-wing National Association of Trade Unions (MSZOSZ), was initially opposed to privatization, but most of its objections were over the parametric reforms and its bureaucratic fiefdoms within the pension system (Orenstein 2000: 36). The government was willing to compromise on these issues, as shown in the previous section. The size of the private pillar was also reduced from 30 to 25% of contributions. Once the tripartite council had given its blessing to the reform, passage was almost assured.

Debate over the bill in parliament lasted six weeks. Although a large number of amendments were proposed, few were accepted (Ferge 1999). In July 1997, parliament approved the reform, mainly on government versus opposition lines, with 78% of MPs present and 55 to 58% of all MPs voting for the various laws and only 16 to 18% against. Though most members of the main opposition party, Fidesz, voted against the reform, Orenstein (2000: 34) notes that a significant portion in fact favored privatization. In January 1998, the system began operations with participants choosing pension funds and contributing 6% of their earnings to those funds.

Analysis. Was privatization a matter of responsive policy making? The law's adoption was certainly more conflict-ridden than that in Poland. Opposition parties did vote against the reform and unions were reluctant to accept privatization, at one point even threatening strikes. Some observers also point to pressure from the World Bank and a lack of dialogue. Ferge (1999: 242), for example, refers to it as a "reform from above" and mentions government scaremongering, although Orenstein (2000) and Simonovits (1999: 227) dispute this description. A strong consensus was not achieved as both policy experts and the pension fund self-government refused to sign off on the reform (Müller 1999: 79).

As in Poland, the public had soured on the pension system. Several commentators mention a sharp loss of faith in the existing system in the mid-1990s. Müller (1999: 126) cites a poll which found that 65% of respondents considered the state of the current system either rather or decidedly poor. Similarly, 89% of nonpensioners believed that, if the situation remained unchanged, they could not expect the system to cover their needs in the future and 71% of pensioners believed that their pension was going to lose most of its value (Danics 1998). Scandals in the self-government of the insurance funds – albeit mainly on the healthcare side – shook public confidence in state oversight. Indeed, the subsequent government eliminated these self-governments altogether. These doubts appear to be reasonable responses to the government's inability to control expenditures and the ad hoc changes that had produced a manifestly unfair system.

There was considerable albeit not overwhelming enthusiasm for the new system. A poll commissioned by the government in October 1996 found that 56% of those surveyed supported adding a funded pillar and another 17% wanted a purely private scheme versus only 22% in favor of the status quo (TÁRKI 1996). As in Poland, these opinions were remarkably similar across demographic groups.

Some of this enthusiasm was probably connected with the relative success of Hungary's voluntary pension scheme, which was set up in November 1993. This system gave citizens tax deductions for contributions. Although it was less subscribed than the Czech system – it boasted one million members in 1999 – its operations were more transparent.[32] Financial returns were good and the regulatory system was better constructed (Vittas 1996). Public opinion polls indicated that those who had invested were more likely to support a new private pillar than those who did not (TÁRKI 1996).

As in Poland, there were a variety of indirect indicators of responsiveness. It was a leftist government who introduced the reform, suggesting that it was not ideologically motivated. Indeed, the Hungarian Socialist Party had come to power by pledging to reduce the social costs of the transition. The reform was also passed just ten months before parliamentary elections and was scheduled to be implemented with a large information campaign just five months before elections. Again, the government appeared to believe that privatization would not hurt and likely would help its election prospects. In fact, the Socialists performed well in the subsequent elections – winning the most votes and seats – though their performance cannot be linked directly to these reforms.

Major interest groups signed on to the reform, although opposition parties did not. Indeed, the new Fidesz government elected in 1998 chose not to expand the second pillar as had been agreed and in fact considered revoking it altogether (Rocha and Vittas 2002). Enrollment rates in the new pillar were high. Because all current workers had a choice of whether to enter the new system, it was uncertain how many would switch. Government estimates of enrollment figures were quickly exceeded and were the cause of some financial difficulties. The government expected 1.3 to 1.5 million people to switch and ended up with 2 million (Ferge 1999: 239). Ultimately, 80% of those in their twenties and thirties and 50% of all workers joined the new system (Rocha and Vittas 2002: 379). Orenstein (2000: 37) remarks that the reform "has gained the confidence of a wide cross-section of the population." Even a skeptic of the reform writes that it was a "huge success among citizens" (Ferge 1999: 239).

[32] The cited poll found that 13% of respondents had a voluntary pension account and 23% planned to open one. The higher enrollments in the Czech system, however, consisted mainly of older people who used the scheme for short-term savings (Jelínek and Schneider 1999).

6.4.4. Conclusion

In sum, a good deal of responsiveness characterizes privatization. It occurred where public opinion was in favor of it and did not occur where citizens were against it. Evidence for this conclusion comes from both public opinion and the policy process. Many of the circumstances surrounding the passage of these laws indicate that politicians saw them as exercises in credit claiming and responsiveness. Indeed, it is hard to explain such facts as the timing of these reforms, their association with left-wing governments, the large majorities they attracted in parliaments, and the assent of social partners without postulating a supportive public. Although it may be true, as Nelson (2001) argues, that the public was not "driving" the reform in the sense of actively demanding it, the public did accept it.

Two conditions appear to be necessary for privatization to become popular. First, citizens had to lose confidence in the existing system. This occurred where they believed it was in crisis and therefore could not guarantee benefits in the future or where benefits were perceived to be unfair. Second, citizens had to have confidence in financial markets so that they would not fear losing their contributions in a private system. Where these two conditions were met, citizens supported privatization; they saw it as a new benefit that could make up for the failures of the old system. The prospect of earning high returns through investment and making up for past losses added to this perception. Thus, in Poland and Hungary, citizens saw the old system as unsustainable and capital markets as trustworthy, leading them to embrace privatization. In the Czech Republic, by contrast, the old system was perceived as functional and capital markets as risky and corrupt; privatization looked like a bad bet.

Alternative explanations do not account for all of the facts of privatization.[33] One may argue that it was introduced under pressure from the World Bank. But little evidence exists that the World Bank provided anything other than technical assistance and small loans to governments already determined to privatize.[34] As Nelson (2001) writes, "The specific designs of the reforms were overwhelmingly the result of domestic rather than international goals and pressures."

General economic conditions do not explain decisions either. Although Poland and Hungary did suffer from larger internal and external deficits than the Czech Republic, this should have delayed privatization rather than encouraged it. Privatization was an expensive proposition that would worsen public finances in the short and medium terms. What Poland and Hungary needed was cuts in expenditures, not a large increase in taxes and debt.

Similarly, Müller's (1999) conclusion that ideologically committed Ministries of Finance controlled the reform is belied by two facts. In the first place,

[33] I do not consider Brooks's (2005) diffusion argument because these countries were similarly situated with regard to diffusion effects.

[34] Poland received loans of US$2.6 million and Hungary of US$124 million to support privatization (Andrews 2006).

the pension reforms contradicted the purported goal of these Ministries to reduce budget deficits. If finance ministers were determined to reduce deficits, they would have concentrated on parametric reforms. In the second place, prime ministers intervened at key points to push the reforms forward. It was not just economists who pushed privatization, but party leaders who had to consider the electoral effects of these policies.

One may also object that public opinion had been manipulated to favor reform. Although Ferge (1999: 237, 239–42) has made this argument, others have seen the debate around privatization as open and fair (Orenstein 2000, Simonovits 1999: 227). It is also not clear why left-wing governments would be so determined to privatize that they would take it upon themselves to massage public opinion.

I have tried instead to put forward an argument that public opinion toward privatization had a reasonable basis in actual circumstances. In Poland and Hungary, the pension system suffered serious problems that led citizens to lose confidence in it. Both countries' pension systems were marked by high spending and large deficits that imperiled their sustainability, not to mention unfair benefit structures. Conversely, the financial system in the Czech Republic had been so mismanaged that it gave citizens cause for doubts about privatization. Where the public lost confidence in the existing pension system and maintained confidence in capital markets, privatization could proceed in a responsive way.

6.5. CONCLUSIONS

In line with theories of the third rail, policy makers stepped carefully on pension policy. Legacies from communism, particularly inherited public attitudes, shaped initial responses, indicating a degree of responsiveness to the public. Much of this responsiveness disappeared when economic circumstances forced politicians to engage in cuts, although even here policymakers typically attempted to allay the public through blame avoidance techniques. Most surprising is that pension privatization occurred only where public opinion was permissive. Rather than a product of autonomous politicians as most would expect, privatization was enabled by public support.

Did mandate responsiveness also function in pension policy? Did parties follow through on clear campaign promises? The answer is a clear no. Most early governments were vague about their plans for the pension system, which is perhaps understandable given the problems they faced and the uncertainty of the transition. Even later, however, correspondence did not improve. Promises of cuts were rare in campaigns, but they quickly emerged on policy agendas. Most conspicuous was the absence of privatization from the manifestos of parties introducing it in Hungary and Poland but its presence in the manifestos of some Czech governing parties that did not introduce it. In fact, the left-wing parties in Hungary and Poland supported a more generous public scheme, leading Cook and Orenstein (1999: 100) to write that the Hungarian Socialists "engaged in a major policy reversal." In short, citizens exercised little ex ante control of policy through mandates even as they did influence day-to-day decisions.

The reason for this style of policy making is fairly clear. Politicians recognized that citizens were in favor of a generous and functioning pension system and worried about the opinions of elderly voters. Večerník (2001) writes that there is an "emerging regard for pensioners as voters," which meant that "no political party failed to stress its commitment to pensioners in its electioneering." Inglot (2003: 227) quotes Polish Minister of Labor Leszek Miller as saying that "nine million pensioners who vote could not be ignored and any government coalition that does not want to provoke a large social conflict must take this into consideration." More precisely, Vanhuysse (2006) estimated that 40% of voters in these countries were at or near retirement age. To win elections and to remain in office, politicians needed to produce pension policies that would satisfy voters.

At the same time, governments were under considerable fiscal pressure to make some cuts to the pension system. They squared this circle in a number of ways. One was to be responsive and increase the generosity of pensions. But this course was not sustainable in the long run. Another solution was to promise generosity and then conveniently forget these promises. Similarly, politicians could hide cuts through blame avoidance techniques. A final technique can be seen in privatization, where governments could plausibly "save" the pension system and offer a new benefit even while engaging in fiscal rationalization. What does come through in all these ways is of politicians thinking of voters as they make policy.

7

The Politics of Housing Reforms

Housing was probably the feature that most distinguished communist welfare states from their Western counterparts. Indeed, the differences were great enough that some scholars have spoken of an East European Housing Model (Hegedüs and Tosics 1996). The main characteristics of the model were a high degree of state ownership, centralized allocation of dwellings, strict limits on housing exchanges, extremely low and undifferentiated rents, strong tenant rights, and a dominant role for the state in new construction.

Housing reforms after the transition may not have been as salient as economic reforms or pension policy, but they present an interesting test of the responsiveness thesis for several reasons. In the first place there is the depth of the change: whereas communist regimes had proclaimed housing a human right and to a large extent decommodified it, the new democratic regimes had to adapt the housing sector to a market economy. Could governments turn a right into a market commodity and do so without angering the public? Housing policy is likewise worthy of study because of its differential effects. Unlike economic or pension reforms, housing policy had large effects on certain groups of citizens – residents of public housing – and small effects on others – homeowners. Responsiveness to the median voter may be more difficult where different groups have very different preferences.

This chapter looks at the changes introduced in housing policy after the transition. It focuses on three different areas. The first is how the state dealt with the large public housing stock – did it keep the apartments in state hands or privatize them to tenants? The second is rent regulation – did the state allow rents to rise to market levels or maintain the low rents from the communist era? The third is construction subsidies – did states maintain their large building programs from communism or introduce cuts? As in the previous chapter, I ask whether policy choices in these areas reflected public preferences and, to a lesser extent, campaign promises.

TABLE 7.1. *Housing Indicators in Eastern Europe and Other Regions*

	Eastern Europe	Middle-Income States	Western Europe
Share of state-owned housing	28%	–	18%
Rent-to-income ratio	5.7%	20.5%	15.9%

Note: Figures reflect status in 1990.
Source: Hegedüs et al. (1996).

7.1. HOUSING POLICY UNDER COMMUNISM

A number of unique factors made up what has been called the East European Housing Model (Hegedüs and Tosics 1996). Because communist regimes classified housing as a basic human need, ideology dictated that it be decommodified as much as possible. To prevent landlords from "exploiting" tenants, the vast majority of private apartment buildings were nationalized. As Table 7.1 shows, this approach led to some of the highest levels of state ownership in the world. Almost all citizens who did not own their own homes became tenants of the state.

Decommodification also dictated that housing be affordable, which led governments to fix monthly rents at very low levels. As Table 7.1 shows, citizens usually paid less than 10% of their incomes on housing. Making up for their lack of property rights, citizens were given strong occupancy rights that they could pass on to relatives. Eviction was almost unheard of. The free exchange of apartments, however, was restricted to keep better control over the labor force and to prevent the accumulation of capital or property.[1] The result was that citizens were more or less tied to the flat they lived in. Those who did not have occupancy rights to a flat had to petition the local government for a newly built or vacated flat.[2]

As part of the drive to squeeze out private enterprise and any form of independent power, all construction firms were nationalized. In their place, governments created large conglomerates that were charged with building housing for the newly urbanized working class and did so by erecting inexpensive concrete housing projects on the outskirts of major cities. In short, the housing sector served both communist ideology and the power monopoly of the ruling communists.

Despite increasing attention to the sector in the 1970s and 1980s, construction rates lagged behind that of Western states (Renaud 1991). Without incentives for efficient production or distribution, communist states produced

[1] Citizens nevertheless found clever ways to circumvent these rules by entering into fictitious exchanges.

[2] One could move up the waiting list by getting married or having children. The result of this allocation system was that young people typically lived with their parents until they married, marriages and child births occurred at young ages, and divorced couples often had to share the same flat.

less housing at greater cost than countries with market-based housing sectors. Because housing was not a priority sector of the economy – unlike coal, steel, or weapons – it was starved of resources in the general plans. As a result, supply lagged behind demand.

These strict regulations produced a high degree of dissatisfaction.[3] Citizens faced long waiting lists before being allocated housing and even then had little say in the size, quality, or location of their flat. Having received a flat that was typically small, poorly constructed, and located in large colonies of concrete towers, tenants found it all but impossible to move or even to arrange repairs. Although low rents provided some solace, most citizens wanted a system that gave them more choice and greater quality. At the same time, large majorities believed that the state bore responsibility for ensuring decent housing (Lipsmeyer 2003). Though on aggregate measures the countries of Eastern Europe were better off than other countries at similar income levels, expectations far exceeded achievements. Citizens looked to Western Europe as their model and saw how their states fell short on quality, accessibility, and choice.

7.2. PRIVATIZATION

One of the first policies that the new democratic governments considered was privatization. Low rents meant that states were providing a large subsidy to tenants. Privatization was one way to reduce the burden on already tight budgets. Privatization also held out the hope of kickstarting a housing market; state ownership dominated in urban areas, which inhibited the development of market exchange and limited citizens' mobility and choice. Privatization could also be popular if it transferred a valuable asset to citizens at a low price. On the other hand, the public sector did serve as an important social safety net. Most Western European countries supported substantial public housing sectors for less-well-off citizens, a precedent that these countries might heed.

Interestingly, the three countries took vastly different approaches to privatization. The key fact to be explained is the distinction between Hungary, on the one hand, which privatized more than 90% of its public housing stock, and the Czech Republic and Poland, on the other, who limited privatization and maintained a significant state-owned rental sector. In a survey of housing policies in Eastern Europe, Lux (2003) refers to Hungary as an exemplar of the Home Ownership Model and the Czech Republic and Poland as exemplars of the Rental Model. Are these differences a consequence of responsiveness or another factor?[4]

[3] For a literary description of the problems, see Voinovich (1977).

[4] Relatively little has been written on the politics of housing reforms. Doling (1997: 82) writes of a widespread belief among housing scholars that politics plays only a minor role in housing policy.

7.2.1. Hungary

Under communism, Hungary's economy was more market-oriented than other states in the communist bloc and its housing sector was no exception (Seleny 2006). By 1988, more than 60% of housing investment was made by individual families compared to only 30% in Czechoslovakia and Poland (Struyk 1996: 32). Consequently, by the fall of communism more than three-quarters of the housing stock was in private hands and the public sector made up only 22% of the stock.[5] Hungary also raised rents in public housing so that by 1990 citizens were paying 10% of their incomes on housing expenses. Although low by Western standards, rents were higher than in other communist countries.

Furthermore, privatization of state-owned apartments officially began in Hungary in 1969 as part of the government's more general move toward a market-based economy. The option to privatize initially applied only to smaller buildings, but by the 1980s larger buildings also became eligible. Hegedüs, Mark, and Tosics (1996: 114) argue that this was due to pressure from occupants of the better flats – usually members of the nomenklatura, the communist elite – who wanted the security of ownership and from local governments who were under economic pressure from the subsidy burden. Despite discounts on purchase, privatization remained at a low level until the transition, mainly because municipalities exercised their power to block sales or to require a certain proportion of tenants to buy before selling. By most indications, demand for privatization was substantial even in the 1980s.

After the transition to democracy, the first move of the newly elected conservative government was the 1991 Act on the Transfer of Property, which transferred ownership of public housing to municipalities. Such a transfer occurred in virtually every Eastern European country and was intended to improve efficiency because municipal governments could best react to local conditions. Municipalities would now be responsible not only for the financial upkeep of these loss-making apartments, but would also have power over privatization terms – including the volume of sales and discounts – and rent levels.

Hegedüs, Mark, Struyk, and Tosics (1993) note that this transfer gave municipalities two choices. They could create a viable public rental sector by gradually raising rents, introducing housing allowances for the poorest tenants, and limiting privatization. Or they could sell off most of their stock at give-away prices. Using simulations, they found that only the first option would have a positive effect on municipal finances, whereas the second would lead to even larger losses as the public sector was residualized. It would contain apartments in the worst condition requiring the highest maintenance costs and housing the poorest citizens with the least ability to pay. Nevertheless, virtually all towns chose this second path despite the success of an experimental project that demonstrated the first option in the town of Szolnok (Hegedüs et al. 1993).

[5] Unless otherwise stated, all pre-1996 housing statistics are from Hegedüs et al. (1996).

There were a number of reasons for this choice. The precedent of large discounts on privatization under communism meant that current policy would have to respect those same conditions because of public expectations of fairness. It would be hard to deny citizens the benefits formerly granted to the nomenklatura. Second, there was a classic time-inconsistency problem. Creating a viable state sector would involve political costs today – higher rents and limited privatization – with benefits – a functioning social rental sector and improved municipal finances – later. By contrast, privatization would bring political benefits in the present with costs to be paid later. Finally, local officials were worried more about the direct budgetary costs of a housing allowance than the indirect costs of a residualized sector.

Local governments did, however, find ways to restrict privatization. They placed buildings on prohibition lists or required a minimum percentage of purchasers before selling. Observers attribute this behavior to the fact that public housing gave local politicians considerable power.[6] Leases on vacant apartments and the contracts for maintenance could be distributed to build political support. As a result, a significant but not overwhelming percentage of the public housing stock – about 20% – was privatized between 1990 and 1992 (Hegedüs, Mark, and Tosics 1996). Because prices were so low for those allowed to buy – buyers often paid 10% of the assessed value of their flat – those who were denied this option expressed considerable dissatisfaction.

The delaying tactics of municipalities ultimately led to the Rental Housing Act of 1993. This Act gave tenants a right to buy at a minimum discount of 50% off the value of the apartment with a five-year deadline to purchase.[7] The law thus ended prohibition lists, minimum thresholds, and high prices. Although Hungary's Constitutional Court later limited the deadline – with tenants retaining the right of first purchase – the Act essentially forced local governments to choose giveaway privatization (Bodnar 2001). The right to buy limited the discretion of municipalities and the deadlines encouraged even waverers to buy. The consequences were predictable. By 1997 three-quarters of the public housing stock had been privatized and by 2000 more than 90% had been liquidated, leaving Hungary with one of the smallest public sectors in Europe (Hegedüs and Somogyi 2005).

What was behind this law? For the government, political motivations were foremost. At the time of passage, about a year prior to elections, the Hungarian Democratic Forum government was trailing badly in opinion polls and hoped that voters would view privatization as an "election present" (Hegedüs, Mark, and Tosics 1996: 127). Despite the government's narrow majority in parliament, the bill passed easily – by a vote of 137 to 69 – indicating fairly

6 Personal communications with Iván Tosics, Metropolitan Research Institute, Budapest, 17 March 2000.

7 These discounts were actually lower than those granted before, but citizens were now guaranteed a right to buy and, as Bodnar (2001: 45) notes, the market prices used for calculations were typically large underestimates. Hegedüs, Mark, and Tosics (1996) call the discounts so high as to be "giveaway privatization."

widespread support.[8] One prominent observer in fact saw no political opposition to right-to-buy policies, whereas another emphasized lobbying at the local level from tenants who wished to buy.[9]

Evidence on public attitudes confirms this account. A survey of tenants found that demand-side pressures for privatization were strong (Hegedüs, Mark and Tosics 1996: 119). Seventy percent of all tenants surveyed wanted to privatize their flat. Their motives were to acquire the value of the flat and to have a secure position against future rent increases. Reasons for not buying included the poor condition of the property in question or lack of resources. Tenants had good economic reasons for taking this position. Although rents had stagnated after the transition, utility prices had skyrocketed; by 1994 the average citizen was paying 23.5% of his or her income in housing expenditures. Tenants in public housing were thus not gaining a large advantage by remaining in the state sector. If they were already paying most of the costs of housing, then they might as well own their apartment.

Although not apparent from the survey, I would also suggest that a home-ownership culture had developed in Hungary, which further encouraged citizens to purchase their apartments (Kemeny 1981). The high degree of home-ownership under communism is one indication that citizens preferred owning their housing rather than renting and may have its roots in the relatively recent migration of citizens from farms to cities. As late as the 1950s, Hungary's economy was primarily agricultural (Berend 1996).

The activities of interest groups likewise indicate support for privatization. Because of its relatively open political environment, Hungarians were able to form a broadly popular Association of Tenants even before the transition (Györi and Matern 1997, Pickvance 1994). Although its initial goals were to demand better service from the state apartment management companies, after the transition the association had to choose between its original mission and helping tenants who faced bureaucratic hurdles in privatizing their flats. It ultimately decided to pursue the latter course, putting most of its resources into promoting privatization. This decision appears to be a concession to the strong desire of most tenants to privatize. The association's influence was felt in government. According to Hegedüs, Mark, and Tosics (1996: 117), "The legislature made basic changes to the original proposals prepared by the Minister of the Interior in response to the successful lobbying of the Association of Tenants."

7.2.2. Czech Republic

In contrast to Hungary, the East European Housing Model remained almost entirely intact in Czechoslovakia until the transition. In 1989, 70% of the country lived in state rentals or cooperatives versus only 30% in privately

[8] The two main opposition parties at the time, the Socialists and Fidesz, voted against the final bill.

[9] Personal communications from Joszef Hegedüs on 14 April 2000 and Iván Tosics on 17 March 2000, both of Metropolitan Research Institute, Budapest.

owned homes or flats. Rents were maintained at very low levels and in fact were unchanged from 1964 to 1989 (De Deken 1994). In 1990, citizens were paying on average 2.7% of income in rent (or 6.6% of income for rent and utilities combined). Privatization was unheard of before 1989. Indeed, the communists trumpeted their apartment building program as one of their greatest achievements.

As in other Eastern European countries, the first democratically elected government, led by the diverse Civic Forum (OF), moved quickly to transfer publicly owned housing to municipalities. But instead of passing a law to encourage privatization, it let municipalities set their own policies. Although the major political forces were not against privatization, they saw no compelling need to artificially encourage it.

The only area where privatization became an issue was the restitution of apartments or buildings seized by the communists after their coup in 1948. Of the three countries, only the Czech Republic engaged in substantial restitution, returning about 7% of the housing stock, mainly in the historic center of large cities, to its original owners.[10] On the surface one would expect restitution to be unpopular because its main beneficiaries were mainly the prewar elite rather than ordinary citizens who had suffered under communism.

Yet, the public voiced few objections. The reason is the strong sense that those harmed by communism deserved justice. Because of the regime's harsh repression up until 1989 – a contrast to the more cooptive approach in Hungary and Poland – and the memory of a rich and successful prewar state, many believed that justice required some sort of compensation to those hurt by the regime. Indeed, the Czech Republic was the only country in the sample to adopt a strong lustration law prohibiting former communist officials from holding state positions. In explaining differences in restitution, Appel (2005: 390) thus writes, "Each country adopted its own version of restitution, depending on the normative concerns of the people, constrained importantly, however, by the local political and social context."

Returning to standard methods of privatization, Czech municipalities were reluctant privatizers. They typically chose to privatize only entire buildings, usually after a fixed quota (often half) of tenants agreed to privatize and often refused tenants' requests to privatize. Towns that did privatize most of their stock, for example the North Bohemian town of Teplice, were known more as ideological zealots than as responsive politicians.

Only in 1994 did the Czech parliament, now dominated by right-wing parties, pass a law on privatization procedures. Even this law, however, did not give citizens a right to buy or set deadlines for purchase – the two most effective means for speeding up privatization. Rather it allowed the sale of individual flats to tenants. But because this method created administrative headaches for

[10] Only 1% of the public housing stock was restituted in Poland and none in Hungary. Hungary, however, did offer former owners compensation for their property in the form of privatization bonds.

municipalities – buildings would be in the joint ownership of the towns and those tenants who privatized – it was not often used. For these reasons, the law itself was not particularly controversial.

As a result of these policies, privatization remained lower in the Czech Republic than in other postcommunist countries. Up to 1998, only 19% of the state-owned stock was privatized and though privatization picked up after then – to about 50% by 2003 – nearly a quarter of the country's housing stock still remains in public hands in 2005, down from about one-third at the time of the transition (Sýkora 2003).

Were these actions a consequence of responsive policy making? There is little evidence of strong support for giveaway privatization in the Czech Republic. A nationally representative poll conducted in March 1995 found that 52% of respondents were in favor of the possibility of purchasing their flat, but most of these respondents lived in cooperative flats to which they had already made significant financial contributions.[11] Of those who lived in state-owned flats, only 21% actually wished to purchase their flat, and of those who lived in communally owned flats, only 13% wished to privatize (see also Michalovic 1996: 145). For these more relevant groups, privatization was not a popular choice.

This tepid support for privatization is likely because of low rents – which made renting cheaper than owning – and a long-standing culture of renting. Over the first four years of transition, rents rose from only 2.7 to 3.1% of income whereas utility costs rose from 3.9 to 7.8%. Rents remained low even later in the transition. Public housing was a good deal for tenants throughout the transition. Czechs were also used to renting. The Czech Republic was the earliest industrializer in the region and so citizens had experienced rental housing for a long time. Privatization became more popular only as condominium prices rose in the late 1990s, which made owning a more favorable financial proposition for tenants who could sell their privatized flats for a large profit.

Political factors confirm this account. The Association for the Protection of Tenants, which was founded in 1991, evinced little interest in privatization and did not support tenants seeking to privatize.[12] In fact, its main fear, after rent deregulation and a strengthening of landlord rights, was that privatization would be forced on people who could not afford it. Even as late as 2000, when privatization began to gain steam, the leader of the Association claimed in a newspaper op-ed that "privatization is the pathway to hell" (Krečková and Procházková 2000). The organization was also politically influential, supplying important MPs to the Czech Social Democratic Party and appearing frequently in the media.

[11] As before, all poll results for the Czech Republic refer to nationally representative surveys conducted by the CVVM organization, which are available through www.cvvm.cz.

[12] Personal communication, Milan Tarabal, Association for the Protection of Tenants, Prague, 24 November 1999.

The weakness of support for privatization in the Czech Republic is somewhat surprising given that the country was ruled for six years by a prime minister, Václav Klaus, vocally committed to neoliberal policies and the legacy of Margaret Thatcher, one of whose major achievements was the privatization of public housing. Yet, this same prime minister never put forward a program for giveaway privatization and, as Section 7.3.2 shows, instead expressed sympathy for tenants in public housing. He seems to have realized that the public rental sector was a sensitive issue for the public.[13] Indeed, no prominent group proposed giveaway privatization in the Czech Republic.

7.2.3. Poland

Poland's housing experience under communism fits somewhere in between that of Hungary and the Czech Republic. Its housing structure more closely resembled that of Czechoslovakia with only 40% of housing in private ownership, 30% in the public rental sector, and most of the rest in cooperatives. Poland did, however, introduce some market reforms in the 1980s. A law passed in 1985 allowed some privatization, albeit at the full assessed value of the apartment and only with the approval of the municipality. The upshot was that sales were meager. Rents were raised somewhat under communism, but because of high inflation, their level remained low, falling to about 1% of income (or 6% including the cost of utilities) in 1990 (Muzioł-Węclawowicz 1996).

After the transition, Poland followed other countries in transferring state-owned housing to municipalities. It was nearer to the Czech Republic, however, in letting privatization take its own course. Municipalities were free to set their own policies with little advice from the central government and as a result the general level of privatization remained low. Flats that were privatized, however, were sold at large discounts, usually 50 to 80% off the assessed value (Uchman and Adamski 2003: 132). Giveaway privatization was proposed by some parties connected with Solidarity, who saw it as a way to correct past injustices and break away from communism, but it was opposed by both Social Democrats and Liberals, whose positions found more resonance in society.

Only in 1995 did a new left-wing government led by the Democratic Left Alliance (SLD) pass a law regulating privatization (Kozlowski 1996). The Act on Housing Ownership allowed greater discounts on privatization and freed municipalities of maintenance responsibilities in mixed ownership buildings – an administrative and fiscal headache for them in the past. The Constitutional Court meanwhile countenanced other price rebates. In other respects, the 1985 law remained in force and privatization procedures did not change substantially. There was no right to buy or deadline for privatization. An Act on Rents (see Section 7.3.3) did allow municipalities to increase rents, which provided a spur to privatization. Nevertheless, by 1997 privatization had only reached

[13] Politicians liked to trumpet the fact that they lived in large housing estates along with the rest of the population.

about 16% of the publicly owned stock despite large discounts, and by 2000 it had only risen to 49% (Hegedüs and Struyk 2005).

Privatization returned as an issue in the run-up to presidential elections in 2000 when parties connected to Solidarity proposed to transfer all remaining state-owned apartments to sitting tenants free of charge. The right-wing Solidarity-dominated government managed to pass this proposal, albeit without the support of its liberal coalition partner, but could not override a presidential veto (Radio Free Europe–Radio Liberty 2000). Observers argue that the bill was more an attempt to associate the president, a former communist official, with the old regime than to appease public demands. It did him no harm, however; he won reelection in a landslide.

The responsiveness of privatization policy is less clear-cut in Poland than in the other two countries. Although direct evidence on public opinion is lacking, there are few indications of strong public support for privatization. A nationwide poll from 1995 found that 36% of citizens viewed their housing circumstances as good or very good, 48% as adequate, and only 16% as poor or very poor.[14] The Polish Association of Tenants, the main interest group representing tenants, was almost entirely concerned with rent increases and had little interest in privatization, which, like their Czech counterparts, they viewed as counterproductive.

As in the Czech Republic, these attitudes have their roots in a rational evaluation of the benefits of privatization. Low rents and a large rental sector dampened incentives for privatization. Over the first four years of transition, rents increased only marginally (from 1 to 1.8% of income) and utility prices remained under reasonable control. Even after rent deregulation was allowed, most municipalities kept rents fairly low.

A difference between the two countries was that the Solidarity parties were more vocally in favor of mass privatization than their liberal counterparts in the Czech Republic. This difference is a consequence of the electoral base of the two groups. Whereas Czech liberals drew their support from the young and upwardly mobile, Solidarity drew more on emotional anticommunism. The precedent of privatization to the communist nomenklatura in Poland inspired feelings of injustice about continued state ownership as did the fact that communists had been allocated the best flats. Indeed, one of the major electoral draws of the Solidarity-connected parties has been such injustices and the benefits enjoyed by the former communists. However, the failure of these proposals to help Solidarity's election prospects or to hurt those of the postcommunists indicates that such feelings may not have been widespread.

7.2.4. Conclusion

Privatization in these three countries appears to correspond with the desires of their citizens. Where they were satisfied with public housing, privatization

[14] Unless otherwise stated, all poll results from Poland refer to nationally representative surveys conducted by CBOS and available through www.cbos.pl.

was limited; where there was dissatisfaction or a sense of injustice, privatization moved forward. The most acute observers of housing politics in the region concur with this finding of responsiveness. Hegedüs and Struyk (2005: 8) argue that privatization was "the result of short-term political interests" and Struyk (1996: 23) adds that it was "clearly popular." The fact that flats were sold at high discounts reflects this desire to meet the public halfway – if citizens desired to buy their flats, they certainly desired to buy them for a low price.[15]

Public preferences moreover did not arise out of thin air. They were rooted in both a rational assessment of the benefits of renting and owning and cultural attitudes toward homeownership and renting. Countries that maintained low rents and a viable rental sector gave citizens reason to believe in public housing. Countries that increased the price of public housing and encouraged homeownership gave citizens reasons to desire privatization. A further impetus to these preferences was the existence of privatization under the old regime, which produced a belief that justice required similar benefits in the present.

Other factors do not play an important role. There is little evidence that economic factors drove the decision of whether to privatize. All three states suffered losses from public housing, but these losses were arguably higher in the low-privatizing Czech Republic and Poland due to their larger public sectors and lower rents. Poland's government was also under the greatest budgetary pressure of the three and yet it did not give away its public housing. In any case, large discounts on sales in all three states meant that they earned comparatively little revenue from privatization. Nor does political ideology account for these differences. Although a conservative government in Hungary did privatize, the government was not committed to neoliberalism and pursued a gradual program of economic reform. Conversely, a committed neoliberal government in the Czech Republic did little to encourage privatization, and privatization's main supporters in Poland were Christian nationalists.

7.3. RENT DEREGULATION

Simultaneously with decisions about privatization, governments had to set rents for the flats that remained in the public sector. The extremely low levels of rent inherited from the communist era meant that countries were paying large implicit subsidies to the housing sector. Moreover, creating a housing market and encouraging labor mobility required more flexible rents.

However, these low rents were popular with tenants. It is conventional wisdom that rent deregulation is difficult to introduce. It inflicts considerable pain on an identifiable, concentrated group – tenants of rent-controlled apartments – and provides diffuse benefits to a larger, unorganized group – future purchasers or renters of housing (Arnold 1990, Wilson and DiIulio 1998). The question this section addresses is how policy makers dealt with this dilemma. Could

[15] For large-N evidence supporting this conclusion, see Roberts (2003).

they deregulate rents and still listen to the public or was this an impossible combination?

7.3.1. Hungary

Hungary had already raised rents significantly before the transition. Rent increases had been enacted over public protests in 1983 and 1989 (Hegedüs, Mark, and Tosics 1996). Although rent did not cover maintenance costs even after these increases, Hungary still exited communism with citizens paying 10% of their income in rent and utilities – a higher rate than in most other communist countries. As in other areas of the economy, Hungary was the most market-oriented country in the communist camp.

Fearing public backlash against further increases, the first democratic government transferred the setting of rents to municipalities in 1991. This transfer would not only move blame for increases away from the government but also force blame on the opposition Socialists who won the first local elections and controlled many local governments. Understandably, few municipalities took advantage of their power to raise rents, and the ratio of rent to income dropped in the early 1990s from 5 to 2.8% of income, though utility prices rose dramatically at the same time. Only the city of Szolnok, which cooperated closely with international advisors from the Urban Institute, tried to produce a sustainable public housing sector by raising rents and introducing a housing allowance (Hegedüs, Mark, and Tosics 1993). For reasons already suggested, their example was not widely imitated.

Even the possibility of rent increases, however, was worrisome to the central government. In need of support for the coming election, the ruling Hungarian Democratic Forum passed a one-year moratorium on increases in June 1993 that would last until just after the next elections (Hegedüs, Mark, and Tosics 1996: 121). As with privatization, this moratorium was widely seen as an election present to voters and had little economic justification. Short-run responsiveness came at the cost of long-run representation.

Even after the moratorium ended, little changed. By 1995, only one of Budapest's twenty-two districts had raised rents, despite the fact that these districts contained most of the country's rental housing (Hegedüs, Mark, and Tosics 1996: 122). A survey of five provincial cities found that all of them had raised rents in the 1993–1995 period; however, four of the five experienced protests (Pickvance 1997). The difference between Budapest and the provinces may have been the more difficult financial situation in the provinces. Because most of the country's public housing was in Budapest, its experience was the more typical.

After 1995, however, rent policy had become irrelevant. Massive privatization meant that almost all flats were in the private sector, where market rents prevailed, and the public sector housed only the very poor. Rent regulation thus persisted – as late as 2003 rents only covered 30 to 40% of costs and tenants still protested against rent increases – but was a marginal phenomenon

(Hegedüs and Somogyi 2005). Hungary's path in rental policy was thus marked by initially high rents, short-run populist efforts to shift blame and keep rents low, and a long-term solution through massive privatization. Although not responsiveness per se, public attitudes did play a role in policy choices.

7.3.2. The Czech Republic

The maintenance of a large public rental sector in the Czech Republic produced much more conflict over deregulation. Rents in Czechoslovakia had remained virtually unchanged since the introduction of communism and were in fact frozen from 1964 to 1989. Tenants were thus used to paying a very small percentage of their income – less than 2% in 1990 (De Deken 1994).

Rent increases were thus a fiscal necessity in the Czech Republic. A 100% increase was passed by parliament in July 1992; however, in line with the blame avoidance thesis, this increase was timed for one month after parliamentary elections, giving tenants four years to forget it (Kingsley and Mikelsons 1996: 195–7). As in Hungary analysts found that substantially larger rent increases could be combined with a housing benefit without unduly burdening tenants or the state budget, but the government still felt that such increases were too politically risky (Telgarsky et al. 1992).

Unlike Hungary and Poland, rent-setting remained in the hands of the central government – in particular the Ministry of Finance – and was not transferred to municipalities (Michalovic 1996). This meant the central government would receive full blame for unpopular increases. It is unclear whether the right-wing governing parties elected in 1992 thought that central control would allow them to deregulate more quickly, as they promised in their programs, or if it would conversely allow them to avoid painful increases.

Subsequent policy, however, showed that central control would produce neither deregulation nor popularity. A 40% rent increase in January 1994 was widely unpopular and showed the dangers of an ad hoc approach.[16] The government then enacted an automatic system of annual rent increases based on the inflation rate, the size of the municipality, and a discretionary coefficient initially set to 1 but raised after elections in 1996. By making rent increases automatic, the government could thus keep them out of the public eye – they no longer required public parliamentary action – and avoid some blame for deregulation. Governments also timed increases above the inflation rate to the electoral calendar so that rents usually stagnated in election years (Sýkora 2003).

Most telling is that the neoliberal Prime Minister Václav Klaus spoke publicly about the plight of public tenants – prominently mentioning his own elderly mother, who lived in public housing – and pledged to protect vulnerable

[16] Because of the low inherited rents, however, 51% of respondents in a public opinion poll from January 1994 said that they would cope with higher rents "easily" or only "with small problems" whereas 38% said that they would cause "large" or "irresolvable" problems.

tenants. One government official, in fact, noted that the Ministry of Finance had proposed much faster rent increases than those enacted but was personally overruled by the prime minister.[17]

Because of the large public sector, deregulation remained a prominent issue. Increasing its visibility was the policy of restitution that had put a significant number of apartment buildings with regulated rents in the hands of private owners. Because these buildings were mainly in very attractive locations in Prague and other large cities, tenants feared that an end to regulation would cause their rents to rise dramatically. The plight of the many elderly dwellers in these apartments and the fact that some buildings were now owned by foreigners increased public sympathy for regulation. In reality the situation was not so dire, because only 7% of flats with regulated rents were privately owned. Most flats with regulated rents were owned by municipalities who had good political reasons not to raise rents excessively.

Nevertheless, the Association for the Protection of Tenants lobbied hard to protect tenants and highlighted abuses by new private owners who tried to force out their inherited tenants. Legally, the regulated rents only applied to those with occupancy rights to the flat. If they left, then new tenants could be charged market rents.

On the wave of public oppposition to these practices, the Social Democrats campaigned for a moratorium on rent increases, an issue that helped them to finish second in the 1996 elections and to triumph in 1998. For the subsequent eight years of Social Democratic rule, rents increased very slowly if at all. The discretionary coefficient was unchanged, meaning that rents rose mainly in line with inflation. The Social Democrats in fact worked closely with the Association for the Protection of Tenants – members of the Association served as Social Democratic MPs – which was adamantly opposed to rent increases. This stagnation led to very wide disparities between regulated and market rents (Sýkora 2003: 86–7).

Throughout this period, public opinion remained in favor of rent regulation; 71% of citizens supported it in 1994 and 68% in 2001. A poll in October 1996 revealed that three-quarters of citizens with an opinion believed that rent increases were unnecessary, and another poll in April 1997 found that 67% of citizens with an opinion and a whopping 88% of tenants in state-owned flats opposed a rent increase.

Strong external pressures were necessary for the Social Democrats to consider increasing rents at all. To remain in power from 1998 to 2002, the Social Democrats depended on tacit support from the right-wing ODS. In exchange for this support, ODS demanded an end to regulated rents, which the Social Democrats agreed to but did not enact (Roberts 2003). It is worth noting that ODS did not pursue this policy when it was in power.

[17] Personal communication with official from the Czech Ministry of Finance, Prague, 21 November 2000.

The next spur to action was a decision of the Constitutional Court in 2000 that the current rent regulation scheme was unconstitutional because it interfered with private property rights. Rather than fixing the regulation, the government instead voided the unconstitutional law and promised to come up with a new scheme. Successive attempts at a new law failed to clear parliament – opposed from the right for not going far enough and from the left for hurting tenants. During this time, rents remained fixed at their regulated levels. At the same time owners continued winning lawsuits against the government and began to bring cases to the European Court of Human Rights in Strasbourg. These latter cases were expected to be decided in favor of the owners – an important precedent from Poland is discussed in the next section – and would likely require considerable compensation to be paid to the owners for the many years of restrictive regulations.

These circumstances forced the government's hand. A new law allowing rent increases was passed after heated debate at the end of the Social Democrats' second term. The issue was controversial enough that it passed with only one vote to spare.[18] Again, the bill attracted criticism from both the left and the right. The law mandated gradual rent increases – an average of 14% per year differentiated by locality – from 2007 to 2010, after which rents would be set by market agreements (Alda 2006). Significantly, the first increases would only come into effect in January 2007 – six months after parliamentary elections. The Social Democrats could thus claim some credit for protecting tenants from other parties who advocated faster increases and could avoid blame because increases would only take effect after they had left office.

7.3.3. Poland

Like Hungary, Poland tried to raise rents under communism, but high inflation and public protests meant that rent-to-income ratios remained fairly low, ultimately settling at 1% in 1990 – a number closer to the Czech Republic than the more market-oriented Hungary. Only in 1992 did a newly seated liberal/Christian Democratic government pass a 100% increase in rents, although because of even higher inflation, the rent-to-income ratio remained low (Muzioł-Węclawowicz 1996: 243). This move was followed by two years of nonaction, which caused the rent-to-income ratio to drop from a low 4.4% in 1992 to an even lower 2.4% in 1994 (Merill et al. 1998). This limited action was not a surprise given the difficult economic circumstances of this period and the fragile nature of government coalitions.

Change had to wait for the election of the social democratic Democratic Left Alliance in September 1993. Among its achievements was a law on rents and housing allowances (Hejduk 1996). As in Hungary, this Act gave power over rent regulation to municipalities but capped total annual rents at 3% of the replacement cost of the apartment. Municipalities were also required to set up

[18] The governing coalition at the time had a one-vote majority.

a housing allowance program for tenants unable to afford higher rents (Merill et al. 1998). The government could thus claim credit for a new housing benefit while placing blame for rent increases on municipalities. The bill did, however, engender enough controversy that it was initially rejected by the Senate, which was then overridden. Muzioł-Węclawowicz (1996: 244) referred to its passage as an "intense struggle" requiring compromise on both sides.

Municipalities, however, were cautious in using their new freedom. No municipality raised rents to the centrally mandated limit, though most did institute some increase. The largest rent increases occurred immediately after the law came into force, and rents continued to rise slightly through 1995 and 1996 (Merill et al. 1998). By the end of 1996 and into 1997, however, rents actually decreased. This pattern closely maps the electoral cycle because national elections were held in the fall of 1997 and local elections in the fall of 1998.

Even after elections, the situation did not change drastically. A survey of municipalities in 2002 found that, in more than three-quarters of towns, rents did not cover maintenance costs and this trend was even more pronounced in large cities – the site of most public flats – where rents did not cover costs in 92% of cities (Uchman and Adamski 2003: 158). Only two cities managed to raise rents above the level of 2% of replacement costs – still considerably below the maximum set in the Act[19] – and did so only after significant consultation with tenants (Merill et al. 1998).

What moved Poland's rent policy forward was the same sort of external pressure as in the Czech Republic. Private owners of apartment buildings began to seek redress for their losses under the rent regulation scheme. In contrast to the Czech Republic, these owners were not typically the beneficiaries of restitution but rather were individuals who had remained owners under communism. Poland did not legally nationalize all apartment buildings under communism, but it did act as the de facto owner. After the transition, the legal owners found themselves subject to the same rent regulations as municipal owners. In turn, they began to bring lawsuits arguing that they were impeded in their free use of private property.

The most significant turn in their situation came in 2006 when the European Court of Human Rights ruled in favor of Countess Marie Hutten-Czapska, the owner of an apartment building in Poland, who argued that the country's rent regulations had interfered with her right to private property (Bouc 2006). The Court ruled that the parties had to negotiate a just settlement for her injuries, a process that is currently taking place. More important is that the case set a precedent for both Polish and Czech landlords. Although neither country has resolved the problem, the prospect of paying compensation to all private landlords hurt by regulation is likely to lead the Polish government to speed up rent deregulation as a way to avoid penalties.

19 By contrast, many Czech municipalities used the maximum allowable rent, although their maximum was lower than in Poland.

7.3.4. Conclusion

The dilemma of rent policy in all three countries was the necessity of raising rents combined with the unpopularity of doing so. Only insofar as they kept rents low were governments policy-responsive. But large subsidies and the other negative effects of rent control compelled states to do something. Several solutions offered themselves. One was mass privatization, which simply eliminated the public rental sector. Although this strategy could have negative effects on the poor – by eliminating most social housing and putting flats in the hands of those who could not afford them – it would carry many of the political benefits described in the previous section. This was the solution that Hungary chose.[20]

For states that retained a large rent sector, something else had to be done. Blame avoidance was the surest response. Rents were increased but in ways that made them difficult to trace to politicians. Rent policy was transferred to municipalities (in Hungary and Poland) or made automatic (in the Czech Republic) and was usually timed to avoid increases close to elections. In the Czech Republic and Poland, it was only external pressures in the form of court decisions that compelled them to draw up faster plans for deregulation. Although it would be a stretch to call these policies responsive, they do indicate that politicians worried about the public acceptability of their actions.[21]

7.4. SUBSIDIES FOR CONSTRUCTION

The last policy under consideration is subsidies for housing construction. The Czech Republic, Hungary, and Poland pursued quite similar policies in this area and so they are considered in tandem in this section. Although the state dominated housing construction during most of the communist era, by the 1970s, and more so the 1980s, fiscal difficulties forced all three countries to scale down direct support. Instead, governments attempted to involve citizens in financing construction through self-building or cooperatives. Not only were building materials made available, but citizens could obtain long-term, low-interest housing loans from the state bank. In line with its other market-oriented policies, Hungary took this development the farthest, but it was significantly present in Poland and less so in Czechoslovakia.

The new democratic governments had to decide what to do with these programs. The decision was the same in all three cases. State-sponsored construction was phased out and low-interest loans discontinued. In the first case,

[20] Another stop-gap solution that was pursued mainly in less-developed states was to skimp on maintenance and upkeep. This approach would reduce the costs of rent control, but at the price of worsening living standards, and would come back to bite these countries later.

[21] Another sign of responsiveness can be found in the maintenance of strong occupancy rights for public tenants. In all three countries, relatives could still inherit the right to a public flat and evictions were difficult and usually required the landlord to find a replacement flat. For more general evidence that is consistent with this account, see Hegedüs and Tosics (1998).

governments committed themselves to completing projects already in the pipeline, but they ended almost all new projects. Between 1990 and 1994, the percentage of total new construction financed by the state fell from 42 to 28% in the Czech Republic, 52 to 3% in Hungary, and 46 to 10% in Poland (Hegedüs et al. 1996). And these declines underestimated the drop in state support because at the same time total housing construction declined by almost half. Altogether state spending on housing fell from 4 to 6% of GDP to around 1% (Hegedüs and Struyk 2005).

It would be difficult to say that the cuts enjoyed public support. Most citizens believed that the government should be responsible for providing decent housing: a 1997 poll found that 80% of Czechs, 76% of Hungarians, and 90% of Poles agreed with this proposition (Lipsmeyer 2002). Moreover, there was a widespread perception that these countries suffered from a large housing shortage even though they were fairly typical of countries at their income level (Struyk 2000). Because of deep recessions and high interest rates, most who desired housing would have to choose between state-built housing and no housing at all. In short, citizens had few objections to state-sponsored construction if it would increase the availability and affordability of housing.

Yet, there is a political logic to the decision to curtail state construction. All three states were under large fiscal pressures early in the transition. Looking for ways to cut spending, it is no surprise that they chose housing construction rather than, say, pensions. The difference is in the character of public support. Whereas the public generally supported construction, there was no organized demand for new construction. The beneficiaries of state construction were future tenants in public housing. They had no natural means of organizing, were not losing a benefit they already possessed, and would see the fruits of continued state construction only in the future (Pierson 1994). Politicians and presumably citizens also expected private markets to pick up some of the slack in construction. There was a viable market alternative.[22] Again, cuts were not a responsive policy, but they were a policy that took the public into account.

Governments were far more cautious in dealing with the loans they had granted under communism. As interest rates rose dramatically after the transition, these loans became a large burden on their holders. All three states managed to find ways to help home or apartment owners deal with these new costs. The problem was most severe in Hungary, where the loans were most widespread. After experimenting with market interest rates, the government ultimately gave loanholders the option to either write off half of the loan and pay half at the market rate or pay the entire loan at 12% (Hegedüs et al. 1996: 88–90). Poland recalculated payments as a percentage of the borrowers' income rather than requiring them to pay market rates. This required a large amount of public resources: as late as 2000, 40% of the housing budget went to paying off these loans (Struyk 2000). The problem was less widespread in

[22] Pierson (1994) finds much the same dynamic in established democracies, where state support for construction varies with economic circumstances rather than public demand.

the Czech Republic, but even there the interest rate was maintained at a low level and the government compensated banks for their losses (Sýkora 1998).

The political logic of these policies is again clear. Governments were responsive to a concentrated group of citizens with clear preferences. The change in the terms of these loans hurt their holders, who demanded redress and received it. Although it is not clear that these policies were responsive to society as a whole, assessments of the general mood at the time suggest that those hurt by the transition through no fault of their own were viewed quite sympathetically.

After these responses to the transition, subsidy policy becomes more complicated. In the mid-1990s, governments introduced a variety of new policies to support housing construction and affordability.[23] Three main types were widely adopted: interest-rate buydowns on mortgages, lump-sum grants for new housing construction paid to either municipalities or individuals, and contract savings schemes. This last type refers to a banking institution common in Austria and Germany (in German, Bausparkassen). Members regularly deposit money in a designated bank account for a set number of years, often with an added state subsidy. At the end of this time, the bank offers them a low-interest housing loan. The idea is that the savers prove their creditworthiness through the regular deposits and thus receive favored treatment.

Were these subsidy policies responsive? Although little tracking of public opinion has been performed, considerable evidence exists that publics did want an increase in subsidies for construction and the purchase of new housing. Indeed, in all three countries, virtually every party running for office proposed increasing subsidies for housing beginning in the mid-1990s and lasting until the current day. Parties clearly felt that such promises would help them to win elections, presumably because they were popular. Hegedüs and Somogyi (2005) argued that by the late 1990s housing had become a hot issue as citizens shook off transitional recessions and wished to improve their living conditions. The parliamentary majorities in favor of these policies were also typically large – most parties voted for the expansion of subsidies or the introduction of new programs. Another indirect indicator of the public mood is that takeup on these policies was high. Citizens did take advantage of the subsidies on offer, which often resulted in cost overruns.

On the other hand, doubts exist about whether governments were providing the extent of subsidies that citizens desired. It is likely that they were falling short. The total size of subsidy programs (excluding indirect subsidies through rent regulations) was on the order of 1% of GDP (Hegedüs and Struyk 2005). These expenditures were considerably lower than the 2 to 3% common in Western European countries, where the housing sector was in far better shape. It is reasonable to conclude that citizens desired a higher level of subsidies but that governments were constrained by economic pressures from enacting them. The large number of programs in each country, however, allowed many

[23] Describing the full range of programs would require a chapter of its own. For more detailed summaries, see Diamond (1999), Hegedüs and Struyk (2005), Lux (2003), and Struyk (2000).

citizens to benefit in some way from subsidies even if to a small extent, which may have been the intent of policy makers.

A better explanation for subsidy policy is, therefore, economics. Spending dropped early in the transition, when economic circumstances were particularly tight, and rose later as economies began to grow. Governments could sometimes fight against these constraints, but in the end they would surrender to them. The right-wing Fidesz party in Hungary, for example, introduced a massive loan subsidy program in 2000 that burst the budget – spending was set to rise to 3 to 4% of GDP – and forced the subsequent Socialist government to cut it back, despite its popularity (Hegedüs and Somogyi 2005).

7.5. CONCLUSIONS

How strongly did linkages function in housing policy? Policy responsiveness was strong in privatization policy: where citizens wanted privatization, they received it. Moreover, citizen preferences were largely exogenous to the political process – they arose from reasonable assessments of the benefits of privatization, traditions of ownership or renting, and beliefs about fairness. Policy responsiveness was considerably weaker in rental policy because rent increases were almost always unpopular. Nevertheless, there is some evidence that politicians did worry about public reactions to rent increases and modulated them to take public opinion into account. Subsidy policy is difficult to evaluate because of a lack of information on public preferences. Drops in state construction were likely undesired by the public, but neither did the public voice strong opposition to them. There does appear to be a growing desire for state subsidies for housing investment, and most governments have tried to come up with new policies to meet these demands. Economic pressures, however, have limited the degree to which they could provide these subsidies.

What about mandate responsiveness? Were governments following through on their campaign promises in taking these actions? Solely based on programs, an observer would not have been able to predict which governments engaged in mass privatization and which did not. Ideologically, ODS was probably the most likely candidate for privatization, but it avoided the issue altogether. Most campaigns were similarly ambiguous regarding rent policy, likely because parties realized it was a touchy subject. Nevertheless, parties that promised stable rents could sometimes fulfill their promises. For subsidies, most parties promised large increases in subsidies and construction that they could not deliver. Altogether citizens could not exercise much control by choosing among alternative policy packages.

What explains these results? Privatization and rent deregulation interact in interesting ways. States with higher rent-to-income ratios under communism, like Hungary, entered democratic politics with a high pent-up demand for privatization. Not coincidentally, these were also states that experimented with privatization under the old regime and thus were marked by some concerns over justice in sales. Democratic governments responded to these demands by enacting pro-privatization policies. A consequence of this was difficulty in raising rents further as the public sector became home mostly to poor tenants. Moreover, initially high rent-to-income ratios under communism put a limit on further rent increases.

The second group of states includes those with lower rent-to-income ratios under communism – in this sample the Czech Republic and Poland. These states featured weaker demand for privatization because of more emphasis on public housing and lower rents, and they were not as zealous in enacting pro-privatization policies. Consequently, they were left with larger and more mixed public sectors, which allowed them to gradually increase rents. The initially lower rents also made these increases somewhat less painful and the object of less opposition. In short, communist-era housing policies set the stage for the postcommunist interplay between privatization and rent policy.

What distinguished housing subsidies from pensions? Why was housing spending cut, while pension spending increased? Like pensions, all citizens consume housing and so subsidies might be expected to rise once democracy took hold. Two factors prevented this from happening. First, an alternative form of market provision existed for housing and in fact a large number of people already owned their own housing. Such a private alternative did not exist for most pensioners. Second, although a large group was already receiving benefits in pension policy, many beneficiaries of housing subsidies were only potential recipients. This fact limited their ability to organize and generate public sympathy for their plight and, due to negativity bias, lessened the pain they felt from cuts. The different structures of the two policy areas thus led to different political imperatives.

PART IV

IMPLICATIONS

8

Explaining Democratic Quality

The previous five chapters have sought to investigate the degree to which citizens control their rulers in Eastern Europe. The results are cause for both optimism and concern. On the positive side, citizens are not loathe to throw governments out of office and they usually do so for cause. Similarly, there is good evidence that, even between elections, politicians pay attention to public opinion when making policy choices. On the other hand, voters may punish governments too consistently, thereby removing their incentives to perform well. More problematic is the failure of parties to present clear and distinctive programs in campaigns and to follow through on them.

It remains to ask what is behind these results. What explains the type and strength of popular control in Eastern Europe? Why does democratic quality take the forms that it does? These questions are important if one cares about producing high-quality democracies. Although improving mass–elite linkages is not the only or necessarily even the most important goal in these countries, there are good reasons for desiring greater popular rule (see Section 1.3). Even if strong linkages produce bad policies, as some have argued, it is important to know what causes strong linkages in order to get better outcomes.

This chapter puts forward five explanations for quality. They attribute the strength of linkages to socioeconomic modernization, civil society, political institutions, authoritarian legacies, and transition constraints. The chapter then considers evidence for these theories from the types of linkages and changes in the strength of linkages within Eastern Europe and the relative strength of linkages in Eastern Europe compared to other regions.

The inferences in this chapter are less than fully rigorous. The comparisons across regions rely on studies using different methodologies and data sources whereas those within the region depend on very small numbers of observations. Nevertheless, to the extent that a series of weak tests converges on a single explanation, the results may possess validity. The aim of this chapter is less to deliver the final word than to launch an opening salvo in the study of the causes of quality.

8.1. EXPLANATIONS OF DEMOCRATIC QUALITY

Because the study of democratic quality is relatively new, most studies have concentrated on refining concepts and developing measures rather than explaining outcomes. The former tasks have also been the main contributions of this book. Yet the novelty of the field should not prevent scholars from considering the causes of quality. In this spirit, this section presents five explanations for democratic quality and the mechanisms through which they work.

8.1.1. Socioeconomic Modernization

Socioeconomic modernization has been put forward as one of the major causes of democratization and democratic consolidation (Boix and Stokes 2003, Lipset 1959, 1994, Przeworski et al. 2000), but it can also help to explain democratic quality. Modernization is defined as the transformation of a traditional, rural, agriculture society into an industrialized, urbanized, educated one. These changes are presumed to encourage democracy because they create a citizenry with the motivation and resources to demand accountability from its rulers.

Modernization can presumably have the same effects on democratic quality. Demanding accountability through free and fair elections – the essence of democratization – is not so far from democratic quality, where elections not only take place but they are also effective tools of popular control. For many of the same reasons that modernization theory suggests, educated, middle-class citizens should have the will along with the resources and organizational skills necessary to choose the sort of politicians they desire, to hold them accountable for their past performance, and to monitor and petition them even in between elections.

Specifically, education and media savvy give citizens the ability to understand political arguments and to separate good ones from manipulative ones. A level of material security gives citizens the ability to resist clientelist appeals based on vote-buying and provides them with the leisure time to devote to politics. Urbanization offers fertile ground for the formation of interest associations and independent thinking. The distribution of wealth within a society also matters. An equitable distribution of wealth means that few citizens are excluded from political influence due to their penury or are able to buy policies with their great wealth.

I would emphasize that this version of modernization theory puts primary causal emphasis not on high incomes per se but on the capabilities of citizens (Nussbaum and Sen 1993). Modernization is therefore something of a misnomer. Capabilities would be a better term. It is the existence of citizens with the skills and desire to participate effectively in politics that matters. What is important is the level of human development and agency emphasized so eloquently by O'Donnell (2004). Thus, a country with a high income but with a large class living in abject poverty without education and existential security would be poor soil for citizen control, precisely because many citizens would lack the ability to participate effectively in politics and would be systematically underrepresented in politics.

8.1.2. Civil Society

A recent addition to theories of democratic development is civil society. The foremost exponent of this idea is Robert Putnam (1992, 2000) who has argued that a strong and vibrant civil society helps democracy to work better. Civil society refers to "that arena of the polity where self-organizing groups, movements, and individuals, relatively autonomous from the state, attempt to articulate values, create associations, and solidarities, and advance their interests" (Linz and Stepan 1996: 7). According to Putnam, where civil society is dense, and where citizens join more of these voluntary groups, democracy should function better.

How is it that these nonpolitical organizations can have such important political consequences? Putnam argues that joining associations has both internal effects on individual citizens and external effects on the polity (Putnam 1993: 89). The internal effects are in the creation of citizens willing to cooperate with each other and make sacrifices for the good of their community. The idea is that, by associating with others in these organizations, individuals become more tolerant and public-spirited. The external effects are in improving interest articulation and interest aggregation. Atomized citizens cannot expect to influence politics, but as part of a group they are a force to be reckoned with. When citizens join groups they are better able to communicate their opinions to politicians, monitor their actions, and take them to task for nonresponsiveness. In this sense, they function something like parties but at a level closer to citizens' interests. Strong civil society, therefore, should promote strong linkages.

8.1.3. Political Institutions

As Chapter 2 mentioned, different varieties of democratic institutions should promote different sorts of connections between citizens and politicians. Scholars have distinguished two major forms of democratic political institutions: majoritarian and consensus/proportional (Lijphart 1999, Powell 2000). As the name indicates, majoritarian systems allow bare majorities to rule as they wish. They feature two parties competing for complete control of the government. Consensus/proportional systems, by contrast, try to give a share of power to all segments of the public. They do this by encouraging multiparty systems and coalition governments and granting veto power to opposition parties in parliamentary committees, upper houses, and strong judiciaries.

These institutions can affect the relation between citizens and politicians (Powell 2000). Majoritarian institutions should help electoral accountability because they make it easy for voters to identify who is responsible for policy outcomes – the single party that holds the reins of power. This party should also be able to fulfill its campaign promises because it does not need to share power.

Majoritarian systems fall short on programmaticness because, with only two large parties, voters have few choices and parties are compelled to take centrist positions. Conversely, consensus/proportional institutions should encourage programmatic party systems because voters can choose between a variety of parties offering different programs. The multiplicity of veto points, however, may limit the ability of parties to fulfill their promises and impede electoral accountability because voters have difficult assigning responsibility.

It is unclear which institutions produce stronger policy responsiveness (Powell 2000). Majoritarian institutions should promote policy responsiveness because, in two-party competition, parties need to stay close to the median voter to win elections and, therefore, both parties try to please the median voter. Proportional institutions should achieve responsiveness but through a different pathway. By giving all parties a proportionate say in legislation, policy should be an average of the positions of all the parties in the assembly and again reflect the median voter.[1]

8.1.4. Authoritarian Legacies

Although the previous three explanations have general applicability, there are some factors specific to countries transiting to democracy that may affect democratic quality. In fact, it is precisely these countries that have occasioned the greatest doubts about quality.

Scholars have been particularly interested in the impact of authoritarian legacies. Linz and Stepan (1996) pioneered the study of the relation between prior regime type and democratic consolidation. They identified five aspects of authoritarian regimes that might affect democratic consolidation and, by extension, democratic quality. One of these – civil society – has been considered already and another – economic society – is considered in the following section. Two others – stateness and rule of law – are less relevant to linkages.[2]

I focus instead on the legacy referred to by Linz and Stepan as political society. It is defined as "the arena in which the polity specifically arranges itself to contest the legitimate right to exercise control over public power and the state apparatus" and includes such core institutions as "political parties, elections, electoral rules, political leadership, interparty alliances, and legislatures" (Linz and Stepan 1996: 8).

The way that political society was constituted under the ancien regime has important implications for the way citizens interact with their government in the new democracy. The presence of well-known political parties with clear ideologies at the inception of democracy is an important element in establishing representational links between citizens and leaders. Where parties have to be

[1] Powell (2000) finds empirically that consensus/proportional institutions produce closer correspondence. In majoritarian systems, parties often stray from the median and represent only a minority of the electorate.

[2] One could draw connections between these variables and linkages, but they would be far from direct.

created from scratch, they are likely to have weaker representational capacities. Similarly, the presence of experienced political leaders and traditions of cooperation should allow an easier conversion of public preferences into policy. Where political elites are not used to bargaining and compromising, policy making may tend toward immobilism or strong man rule. The same goes for the functioning of formal political institutions. In places where an authoritarian regime featured parliaments with at least some power and elections with some competition, it should be easier to establish a degree of popular control because these institutions are used to processing public preferences. If institutions were merely ciphers under the old regime, it may be more difficult to refashion them as functioning vessels of representation.

One could also include the inherited political dispositions of citizens here. To the degree that the authoritarian regime engaged in forced mobilization or ideological indoctrination campaigns, citizens are more likely to exit these regimes either skeptical of political participation or with an "us versus them" mentality, neither of which is conducive to democratic politics. More liberal authoritarian regimes, by contrast, may leave less of a negative stamp on citizens' political dispositions.

8.1.5. Transition and Economic Constraints

Just as the legacies of authoritarian rule could have important effects on quality, so could the unique constraints that derived from the transition. Most transitions to democracy do not take place under auspicious circumstances. Rather new democracies often find themselves constructing not just new political institutions but also new economic institutions (Haggard and Kaufman 1995). They are forced to engage in major economic reforms, which are themselves impelled by poor economic performance and international pressure (Greskovits 1998, Stone 2002).

The constraints that come from economic reform and its underlying causes can negatively affect democratic quality. In the first place, these constraints limit politicians' room for maneuver. Because they find the coffers bare and have to engage in economic reform to receive international aid and recognition, they cannot always engage in policies that the public desires. It is difficult for them to slow down or stop privatization and liberalization when they become unpopular. Similarly, the funds to maintain or increase popular programs may simply not exist. Accession to international organizations like the European Union (EU) can put similar restrictions on policy makers because it is tied to the policies that these organizations desire (Vachudova 2004). Because policy makers are constrained by the economy and international integration, they cannot allow themselves to be constrained by citizen demands.

The transition can affect quality in other ways. Some scholars have noted that policy makers are also burdened by policy overload and information constraints. Because they have to engage in so many decisions in such a short period of time about matters that they understand only dimly, they are bound to make mistakes. The rigors of the transition may also negatively affect

TABLE 8.1. *Predictions for Causes of Quality*

Theory	Types in Eastern Europe	Trend in Eastern Europe	Global
Socioeconomic modernization	Medium-to-high policy responsiveness	Constant	ED > EE > LA
Civil society	Low policy responsiveness	Constant or declining	ED > LA > EE
Institutions	Low electoral accountability	Constant	EE like proportional democracies unlike majoritarian
Communist legacies	Low mandate and policy responsiveness	Improving	ED > LA > EE
Transition constraints	Low mandate and policy responsiveness	Improving	ED > LA > EE

Note: ED, established democracies; EE, Eastern Europe; LA, Latin America.

citizens. Struggling to survive and adapt to a new political, social, and economic order, citizens may have difficulty developing opinions and engaging in politics. Solving their existential problems trumps engagement in political action. The special circumstances of the transition – or of economic difficulties even in established democracies – may thus negatively impact democratic quality; the greater these pressures, the lower the levels of democratic quality.

8.2. EASTERN EUROPE AS A WHOLE

In the following sections, I consider how well these explanations account for patterns of democratic quality within Eastern Europe and across other regions. In each section, I first lay out the predictions of the five theories for the cases at hand and then describe the reality. Table 8.1 presents the predictions for each set of cases and can be used as a guide for the analyses that follow. I begin by considering how these explanations would account for the distribution of linkages within Eastern Europe. Why did these countries have the types of linkages they did?

8.2.1. Predictions

Modernization theory would predict relatively high levels of democratic quality in Eastern Europe. If communism did achieve one thing, it was modernization. Prior to World War II, Eastern Europe was a predominantly agricultural, rural, and underdeveloped region (Berend 1996, Chirot 1989). Through forced industrialization and a universal safety net, communist regimes turned these countries into modern, albeit in respects distorted, economies. By 1989, most citizens were leading urban, middle-class lifestyles and benefited from high-quality, universal school systems. They were well equipped both materially and intellectually to be functioning democratic citizens. Moreover, equitable distribution of income meant that there was neither an underclass that could be excluded from politics nor an overclass holding the levers of power.[3] This explanation thus predicts strong linkages, particularly in policy responsiveness. It is this linkage that requires citizens who are attentive to the ebb and flow of politics, signal their views to politicians, and punish them if their views are not heeded. Socioeconomic modernization – at least in the capabilities approach advocated here – has a large effect on citizens' abilities in this respect.

The other explanations predict lower levels of quality. As Howard (2003) persuasively shows, postcommunist civil society has been extremely weak.[4] By just about any measure, Eastern Europeans were reluctant to participate in voluntary organizations.[5] In Howard's words (2003: 165), the weakness of civil society means that "not only are postcommunist citizens deprived of the opportunity of developing 'civic skills' through the participation in voluntary organizations, but their voices and views are hardly represented in the political decision-making process." These effects should again be most strongly felt in policy responsiveness, where voice is particularly important.

The authoritarian legacies and transition constraints theories concur with this conclusion. Communist regimes left an almost complete absence of political society in their wake. Communist ruling parties ruthlessly eliminated all competing political parties. Four decades of this policy meant that party organizations and even memories of parties were extremely weak after the transition (Mair 1997, Rose and Munro 2003). Communist regimes similarly emptied out the content of formal political institutions. Although parliaments, ministries, and other institutions did exist under the old regime, they had little role in politics. All decisions regarding policy and personnel were under the control of the communist party. As a result, these countries exited communism with no experience of party representation or of bargaining within formal institutions. Hierarchy and control were the key inheritances.[6] Similarly, the legacy of mass

[3] As Djilas (1983) pointed out, a new class of communist nomenklatura did enjoy many privileges, but their hold over material resources was weak and by and large they did not form an entrenched ruling class after the transition (Eyal et al. 1998).

[4] According to Howard (2003), the causes of a weak civil society were several. Because of communism's nearly complete destruction of civil society, few existing organizations had the capacities and leadership to organize demonstrations and protests. The experience of forced mobilization under communism further soured individuals on the benefits of collective action; instead it was viewed with suspicion. Finally, the persistence of friendship networks from communism provided a partial substitute for civil society and disappointment with the transition further demobilized citizens.

[5] This weakness can be attributed in large part to communism and so this explanation overlaps somewhat with the authoritarian legacies explanation.

[6] Bunce and Csanádi (1993: 260) aptly summed up worries about the new political leaders of the region, writing that they were "used to attacking governments, not representing them; clinging

mobilization under communism is said to have produced citizens who see politics as a dangerous realm that should be avoided and to have created a sense of apathy and learned helplessness (Jowitt 1992, Marody 1990). Others note that the ideological indoctrination of the old regime has led citizens to see politics as a zero-sum, winner-take-all contest (Sztompka 1991).[7] These legacies are particularly problematic for mandate responsiveness, which requires well-known parties with clear views, but even policy responsiveness should be affected because political actors viewed the public as a mass to be herded or incited rather than listened to.

Eastern European countries likewise faced stiff obstacles from the transition (Offe 1991). The scope of economic reforms required in these countries was unprecedented: they had to liberalize virtually all prices and privatize nearly the entire economy. And they had to do this under difficult macroeconomic circumstances, with GDP dropping by approximately 20% over the first years of the transition. This is not to mention the massive number of decisions confronting policy makers because every aspect of the political economy required reform. At the same time, these countries were under strong pressures from the EU to conform to European standards.[8] These constraints should limit both forms of responsiveness. Both policy and mandate responsiveness require that policy makers have flexibility in policy choices – flexibility that was precluded by the constraints of the transition.

Institutional theories yield an alternative set of predictions. Eastern European countries fall mainly in the consensus/proportional camp (Roberts 2006). All but two of them use proportional electoral rules (Hungary and Lithuania have mixed systems) and all feature multiparty systems. Single-party majority governments are virtually unknown. This institutional structure means that they should generally perform well on programmaticness (the menu of options is wide) but worse on electoral accountability (due to diminished clarity of responsibility) and mandate responsiveness (due to veto points).

8.2.2. Reality

Which of these predictions fits the region-wide results? The empirical analyses found relatively strong linkages in Eastern Europe, particularly electoral

to principles, not engaging in bargaining and making constant tradeoffs; talking and not listening; representing narrow and well-defined interests, not broad and ill-defined interests; and exercising some control over what they were doing versus being at the mercy of an extraordinarily demanding agenda."

7 Sztompka (2000) goes even farther and refers to citizens as "civilizationally incompetent."

8 This is not to say that the EU did not help to promote democracy in the region. As Vachudova (2004) has persuasively argued, it did. But the effect of the EU was entirely on formal institutions – on democracy itself. The EU helped to ensure that elections were free and fair, that civil liberties were respected, and that opposition parties could compete. But the EU had few means to improve linkages. It could not legislate that voters throw out poorly performing incumbents, that parties fulfill their promises, or that governments listen to the median voter. The EU likely did not even wish to do this.

accountability and policy responsiveness. The relative strength of linkages flies in the face of three explanations outlined earlier. The reality is inconsistent with laments that communist legacies, transition constraints, and civil society stand in the way of popular control. Although these explanations – particularly communist legacies and transition constraints – can help explain the weakness of mandate responsiveness in the region, they directly contradict the results on policy responsiveness.

But these alternatives should not be completely dismissed. The case studies did show that communist legacies and transition constraints mattered, but more for the content of policy than the strength of linkages.[9] Communist-era social and even economic policies shaped public expectations and contributed to particular choices, but they did not weaken linkages.

Institutional explanations are also less consistent with the particular results found here. This theory suggests that Eastern European countries should feature high levels of mandate responsiveness (or at least programmaticness) and low levels of electoral accountability. In fact, just the opposite holds: electoral accountability was strong and mandate responsiveness weak. Institutions do not explain the particular form that quality takes.

The strength and type of linkages in Eastern Europe are rather more consistent with explanations based on socioeconomic modernization. Although communist regimes did suffer serious economic problems, they put their countries firmly in the upper region of the middle-income countries in the world; they gave rise to citizens capable of understanding politics and acting on their understandings. Socioeconomic modernization is the only explanation that predicts the high levels of policy responsiveness found in the region. It is hard to think of a trump card these countries possessed that would lead to democratic quality besides the capabilities of their citizens.

8.3. TRENDS

These results are based on average effects across the region, but it is possible to gain additional leverage by disaggregating them. Although the sparseness of the data prevents comparisons of individual countries, it is possible to say something about trends across the region. Comparing the strength of linkages early and later in the transition provides more evidence for assessing the relative strength of the five theories.

8.3.1. Predictions

What do the five explanations imply about changes in democratic quality over time? Socioeconomic and institutional explanations predict little change. Modernization occurs very slowly and, thus, should not cause large changes in democratic quality. Similarly, insofar as countries chose a single institutional structure and did not change it radically – the modal outcome in these

[9] This is also the conclusion of Kitschelt et al. (1999).

countries – quality should also not change greatly over time.[10] It is harder to make predictions about civil society because of the lack of good measures of fluctuations over time, but Howard (2003) did find some evidence that participation in civil society has declined over time, which should lead to declining levels of citizen control.

Conversely, the authoritarian-legacy explanation predicts a rising trend in quality. Presumably, communist legacies are not permanent and should fade as citizens and politicians slough off communist indoctrination and a younger generation unaffected by legacies replaces the older generation. Similarly, transition constraints should fade over time as reforms come to a close and economies stabilize, although accession to the EU might extend these constraints further into the transition.

8.3.2. Reality

Chapters 3 and 4 explicitly considered the difference in the strength of linkages between the early and the later transition. Because of the small number of data points, these inferences are not entirely reliable. Nevertheless, the available data do allow some tentative conclusions.

The analyses in Chapter 3 showed that electoral accountability has become stronger over time, but it reached reasonably high levels even early in the transition, particularly if one considers the first free elections. Parties did not seem to become more programmatic over time, and stances toward economic reform actually became more ambiguous later in the transition (although this may be due to the declining salience of the issue). Promise fulfillment was consistently weak across the transition and may even have weakened over time. In the domains of pensions and housing, promises became clearer over time but simultaneously more generous and thus harder to fufill. The statistical results on policy responsiveness do not allow a comparison of the early and late transition, but the fact that the main evidence, both here and from Kitschelt et al. (1999), comes from the very beginning of the transition suggests that trends in policy responsiveness were not strong. The case studies, meanwhile, usually showed higher levels of responsiveness early in the transition and variable levels later on.

In general, there does not appear to be a wide gap between the degree of democratic quality in the early and later transition, which corresponds more closely with the predictions of the socioeconomic and institutional explanations than those that emphasize communist legacies, transition constraints, and civil society. Again, limits on the data should temper these findings.

8.4. GLOBAL COMPARISONS

Another source of leverage involves comparing democratic quality in Eastern Europe to other regions. Because I conducted original analyses only on Eastern

[10] It is also possible that it takes time for citizens and politicians to adjust to new political institutions. This learning process might lead to stronger institutional effects later in the transition.

Europe, I chose two other regions where linkages have already been the object of intensive study: the established democracies in Western Europe and North America and the newer democracies of Latin America. The established democracies may be taken as a baseline for democratic quality; they are the world's oldest and most stable democracies. Latin America is a useful comparator because it democratized at approximately the same time as Eastern Europe and is at a similar level of development.[11] It also differs from Eastern Europe in ways like social structure and authoritarian legacies that allow more focused comparisons. The established democracies are more systematically different from Eastern Europe.

8.4.1. Predictions

Where would the five explanations place Eastern Europe relative to the established and Latin American democracies? The authoritarian-legacies explanation sees Eastern Europe as distinctly disadvantaged relative to both groups. Although Latin American countries also faced obstacles from recent experiences with dictatorial regimes – a particular problem was reintegrating militaries into the democratic order – they boasted relatively intact party systems and political institutions, and citizens were less marked by totalitarian repression (Linz and Stepan 1996). Authoritarian legacies were even less relevant for the established democracies, whose transitions lay farther in the past.

The transition-constraints theory makes a similar prediction. Eastern European countries had to undertake far more economic reconstruction than Latin America and further faced larger burdens in integrating into the international system. Latin American countries already had more or less market economies with considerable private industry and prices at world levels. Although they did often have to undertake market reforms, they were of a qualitatively different degree than in Eastern Europe. Nor was international integration much of an issue for Latin America; these countries had not been excluded from international organizations before the democratic transition. Not surprisingly, established democracies score better on this explanation. Their prosperity and market economies left them far less constrained in policy making.

The socioeconomic modernization thesis, by contrast, predicts higher quality in Eastern Europe than in Latin America. Although Eastern European countries had levels of GDP per capita similar to that of Latin America, they performed considerably better on measures of human development such as education, life expectancy, poverty, and income equality, which endow citizens with the capabilities to control their rulers. A common measure of such capabilities is the United Nations' Human Development Index (HDI), which combines income with health and educational outcomes. In 1991, the ten Eastern European countries had an average HDI score of 0.84 (out of a maximum of 1.0) and an average global ranking of 39 versus 0.75 and 63 for ten comparable countries

[11] For these reasons many studies have compared the two regions. See Nelson (1993), Munck and Leff (1997), Karl and Schmitter (1994); but for a note of caution, See Bunce (1995).

in Latin America (United Nations 1995).[12] Whereas virtually all citizens in Eastern Europe had access to high-quality education, health services, and social safety nets, the same was far from true in Latin America.

The regions differed even more sharply on measures of income inequality. The Gini coefficient measures the degree to which income is distributed equally across the population and ranges from 0 (complete equality) to 100 (complete inequality). Gini coefficients in the 20s and low 30s are generally taken to represent relatively equal distributions of wealth. Over the period 1991–1995, the average Gini score in Eastern Europe was 29, which is close to levels in Western Europe (UNU-WIDER 2007). In ten Latin American countries, by contrast, the average Gini score was 51. Latin American societies typically featured a large urban and/or rural underclass that had difficulty becoming a full-fledged participant in political life. Not only were opportunities for forming and getting their political opinions heard weak for this lower class, but it often faced an upper class with entrenched institutional means of influencing policy (Gibson et al. 2004). The established democracies naturally surpass both regions on these measures with unequivocally higher levels of human development and income inequality at around the same level as Eastern Europe.

Civil society replicates the differences found in authoritarian legacies and transition constraints: postcommunist countries lagged behind both Latin America and, to a larger extent, the established democracies. Eastern Europeans joined about 0.84 organizations per capita versus 1.82 in other new democracies and 2.39 in established democracies (Howard 2003).[13] Finally, institutional explanations expect quality in Eastern Europe to resemble other consensus/proportional democracies, particularly in continental Europe, but to diverge from the more majoritarian democracies in most Anglo-American and Latin American countries.

8.4.2. Reality

How well do actual levels of democratic quality match these predictions? Table 8.2 presents the main results of studies of democratic quality in both regions. Comparisons among them should be taken with a grain of salt because the studies in question use different methodologies and data sources. Nevertheless, they provide a rough sense of the strength of linkages in the three groups.

Studies of electoral accountability in the established democracies have found mixed results. Aggregate studies of the type undertaken here have generally produced weak results; little relation exists between economic outcomes and

[12] The Latin American countries are Argentina, Bolivia, Brazil, Chile, Colombia, Ecuador, Paraguay, Peru, Uruguay, and Venezuela.

[13] These results on based on the World Values Survey (1995–1998) which asked citizens whether they participated in church/religious groups, sports/recreational clubs, educational, cultural or artistic organizations, environmental organizations, professional organizations, and charitable organizations.

TABLE 8.2. *Levels of Democratic Quality in Three Regions*

	Electoral Accountability	Mandate Responsiveness	Policy Responsiveness
Eastern Europe	High	Low	High
Established democracies	High in majoritarian, low in consensus	High	High
Latin America	High	Low	Medium

election results (Lewis-Beck 1988, Paldam 1991, Przeworski and Cheibub 1999).[14] Powell and Whitten (1993) do manage to find accountability, but only in majoritarian countries and only for specific combinations of party types and economic outcomes; electoral accountability is dependent on context. Studies have painted a far better picture of mandate responsiveness, where electoral manifestos, campaign promises, and general ideology serve as good predictors of behavior in office (Boix 1998, Garrett 1998, Klingemann et al. 1994, Royed 1996).[15] Studies of policy responsiveness over time have been less common, but the ones that exist do find high levels of responsiveness (Canes-Wrone and Shotts 2004, Eichenberg and Stoll 2003, Franklin and Wlezien 1997, Soroka and Wlezien 2005). Studies also find that majority opinion tends to be translated into policy on most issues (Brettschneider 1996, Brooks 1987, 1990, Monroe 1979, 1995, Petry 1999). Works that look at dyadic/party representation or the relation between the median voter and the median policy maker also find reasonably strong levels of correspondence (Miller et al. 1999, Powell 2000).[16]

Studies of Latin America are less common but still paint a fairly clear picture. Works on electoral accountability have yielded results very similar to those for Eastern Europe, with incumbents being strongly punished for poor economic performance (Remmer 1989). Mandate responsiveness, by contrast, functions poorly. In a landmark study, Stokes (2001a) found that a large number of presidents renounced their campaign promises within days of taking office.[17] Policy

[14] Works using public opinion data have found stronger confirmation that negative assessments of the economy lead voters to vote against the incumbent (Duch and Stevenson 2008).

[15] The most relevant study concluded: "First, and most important, political parties in the ten countries have been performing their functions relatively well. On average, the issue priorities in the party manifestoes predict over 50 percent of the variance in national budgetary priorities, ranging from a high of 80 percent in France to a low of 40 percent in Australia" (Klingemann et al. 1994: xxi).

[16] According to Dalton (2005: 228), "If we judge collective correspondence by substantive criteria – for example, a 10 percent difference or less in issue opinions – then citizen/elite agreement is fairly common. Most economic, security, and New Politics issues fall within the 10 percent range for the British, German, and French comparisons to the European Parliament elites."

[17] Johnson and Crisp (2003) confirm that the ideologies of presidents do not predict reform, but argue that the ideology of the legislature does.

responsiveness has been less systematically studied, although correspondence between parties and their electorates varies considerably across countries; some perform well and others poorly (Luna and Zechmeister 2005). On this score, it is also worth mentioning the massive public outcry against economic reform in Latin America, including demonstrations and riots, which suggests that governments were not responsive to the public. Such events were far less common in Eastern Europe (Greskovits 1998).

Which explanations do these results support? The authoritarian-legacies, transition-constraints, and civil-society approaches predict lower levels of quality in Eastern Europe than in the other two regions. But the evidence shows that Eastern Europe performed better than Latin America and nearly as well as the established democracies. Even with an unfavorable ancien regime and a particularly difficult post-transition environment – not to mention very weak civil societies – Eastern Europe appears to be punching above its weight. The institutional thesis suggests that Eastern Europe should resemble continental Western Europe whose consensus or proportional institutions were the inspiration for those in the East. In fact, continental Western Europe does look like the predictions of institutional theory, whereas Eastern Europe shows just the opposite set of results.

The explanation that best fits these admittedly rough comparisons is the socioeconomic modernization thesis. It explains why these countries performed better than Latin America but worse than the established democracies. It should be reemphasized here that it is not GDP per capita that is doing the work, but capabilities and agency. It is the creation of an educated, relatively egalitarian, middle-class society in Eastern Europe that distinguishes it from Latin America. (The next chapter presents more data on this point; see Section 9.3.) Less democratic countries in the postcommunist region, like Russia, bolster this conclusion. Even though they shared communist legacies and transition constraints with the Eastern European democracies, socioeconomically they resembled Latin America's higher rates of poverty and greater income inequality. Not surprisingly, they exhibited lower levels of democratic quality if they can even be considered democracies.

8.5. MAKING SENSE OF THE RESULTS

The analyses in this chapter are not rigorous tests of explanations of democratic quality. Such tests would require considerably more comparable data from a larger number of democracies over a longer time period. Nevertheless, even the limited investigation here has shed light on the plausibility of various hypotheses. It appears that socioeconomic modernization does the best job of explaining the types of and trends in linkages in Eastern Europe and the differences between Eastern Europe and other regions. Although the other explanations provide a degree of leverage on these variations, each fails at explaining the totality of the distinctions.

In a sense, these results are surprising. Existing work has paid greater attention to authoritarian legacies and transitional constraints in explaining postcommunist politics (Barany and Volgyes 1995, Linz and Stepan 1996). Yet, a careful reading of these works suggests that these factors may not be the prime determinants of democratic quality. Kitschelt et al. (1999), for example, showed persuasively that a country's particular form of communism affects its postcommunist politics, but its effects involve more the content of politics – the sorts of issues that become salient – than the nature of representation, which the authors believe is fairly consistent across different old regime types.

Studies of political behavior in fact have cast doubt on the proposed negative effects of communism. In a study comparing five postcommunist countries and the United Kingdom on a variety of attitudinal dimensions, Miller et al. (1998: 28) concluded that "in terms of democratic consolidation in the former Soviet Union/East Central Europe (FSU/ECE), political values in the early 1990s were part of the solution not part of the problem. There was no evidence that the people of the FSU/ECE were not yet ready for democracy."[18]

In fact, many aspects of political behavior in Eastern Europe can be seen precisely as a reaction against the legacies of communism. For example, the failures of the command economy helped to create citizens sympathetic to a market economy, which in turn allowed politicians to engage in economic reform in a responsive way. Similarly, the repressiveness of the old regime may have made citizens more suspicious of politicians and supportive of democracy. However, these are "backhanded legacies" – it is the reaction against communism that helped linkages rather than the inheritance of communism itself, and it was the capabilities of citizens that allowed them to recognize these legacies for what they were.

Another backhanded legacy was the absence of historical political parties. But although this absence certainly weakened mandate responsiveness, it may have helped policy responsiveness. Because parties could not count on established constituencies, they had to work even harder to win over voters by performing well. The possibility that they would not survive the "electoral lottery" of the transition only exacerbated this risk (Innes 2002). Paradoxically, the lack of fertile ground for democracy may have spurred parties to serve voters more assiduously. A final backhanded legacy was the tradition of protest voting against the single slate of communist candidates (Greskovits 1998). This tradition may have encouraged voters to practice electoral accountability in the present.

A quick glance at the transition-constraints thesis also suggests problems. Although the greatest constraint on policy makers is presumed to be economic and budgetary difficulties, one of the surprises of the transition has been

[18] They base this conclusion on the fact that liberal and democratic values were supported by large majorities and nationalistic views by only small groups. Moreover, there was little difference between these countries and the United Kingdom.

the ability of states to increase spending, even under inauspicious conditions (O'Dwyer 2006). Poland, for example, was under perhaps the greatest fiscal pressure of any country early in the transition, when it faced hyperinflation and large foreign debts, yet it simultaneously managed to massively increase social spending, as shown in Chapter 6. In general, large cuts in social expenditures have not occurred in these countries. Politicians have found room for maneuver at least as far as spending goes. Regarding international constraints, Vachudova (2005: 4) writes: "From 1989 to 1994, I demonstrate that the EU and other international actors had a negligible impact on the course of political change in [East Central European] states." Even later she finds that their impact was limited mainly to the less democratic states.

Some factors connected with the transition may even have helped citizen control, but again in a backhanded way that works through citizen capabilities. The scale and depth of changes in the transition were likely to have caught the eyes of most voters. Balcerowicz (1994) refered to the early transition as a period of "extraordinary politics." Although active participation in public affairs was low, voters could hardly be unaware of the changes taking place. This differs from the situation in most established democracies where policy changes are typically incremental and of the muddling-through variety. In fact, the World Values Survey, conducted at the turn of the millennium, found that citizens of the postcommunist democracies were more likely than those in established democracies to follow politics every day and to discuss politics with friends and as likely to be interested or very interested in politics (Rose-Ackerman 2005: 8–9). A recent study of voter turnout in Eastern Europe meanwhile found not only relatively high levels of turnout – on average 70% of registered voters – but also that voters were "discerning"; they were more likely to turn out for more important elections (Pacek et al. 2009). What is noteworthy is that these factors again highlight the capabilities of citizens.

What about civil society? Although it is certainly surprising that popular control could coexist with a weak civil society, it is also true that such a syndrome may be occurring in the established democracies, where civil society is purportedly in decline (Dalton 2005, Putnam 2000). On the influence of institutions, it may simply be too early to find them (Roberts 2006). Moser (1999) has found that electoral rules do not have their expected effects in Eastern Europe due to inchoate party systems. The uncertainty of the transition combined with the volatility of party politics meant that citizens have had to privilege certain linkages over others – they could punish parties but could not prospectively enforce their will. The lack of effects for the government type variables in Chapters 3, 4, and 5 supports this conclusion. As politics is consolidated in these countries, institutions are likely to emerge as a more potent influence on democratic quality.

Finally, other studies have come to the similar conclusion that socioeconomic modernization mattered. Thus, Elster et al. (1998) explain the weaker democratic performance of Bulgaria and Slovakia relative to the Czech Republic and Hungary as a result of late industrialization imposed on an agrarian social structure. In their words, "Bulgaria and Slovakia have great difficulties in adopting the institutions of a constitutional democracy and a market economy and to apprehend and internalize their spirit because their precipitously and coercively imposed industrialization did not go along with cultural and political modernization" (Elster et al. 1998: 305). Likewise, Tworzecki (2004) and Kitschelt et al. (1999) emphasize the ability of citizens to interpret politics in reasonable ways as standing behind strong linkages.

The results here also support two other perspectives on Eastern Europe. One emphasizes the importance of citizen mobilization in overthrowing the ancien regime – the way solidaristic citizens were able to work together in common cause to realize their preferences (Bunce 1999, Tismaneanu 1992). Although these revolutions would not have occurred without the right constellation of external forces, they also would not have taken place without concerted citizen action. Few observers could help being impressed by the way citizens spontaneously acted together to throw their rulers out (Kuran 1991). If these capabilities could produce 1989, why would they stop functioning after the revolution? This book argues that they did not stop. More evidence on this point is presented in Chapter 9 (see Section 9.3).

Similarly, the results support the scholars who, in the bleakest periods of communism, saw citizens who were adaptable, were resilient, and, in Garton Ash's (1989) phrase, had found "the uses of adversity." The very repression and bleakness of the communist era created citizens who learned how to manage in any situation and to carve out their own small spaces of freedom. Virtually all scholars of communist regimes in Eastern Europe have come away impressed by the toughness and intelligence of their citizens. This may explain how they were able to overcome the negative legacies of communism, not to mention the hardships of the transition.

8.6. CREATING HIGH-QUALITY DEMOCRACIES

What do these results imply for improving democratic quality? Although the present conclusions should be taken with a large grain of salt given the preliminary and sometimes rudimentary nature of the previous analysis, they do suggest that, to strengthen linkages, societies should focus on improving citizen capabilities. This approach would raise income levels while ensuring that income is equitably distributed, provide existential security for citizens, and improve educational opportunities. It is these factors that appear to have helped Eastern Europe to produce high-quality democracies.

It is less clear that attempts to promote political party and institutional development or to encourage civil society would improve democratic quality. However, such efforts are not necessarily misguided; their effects may be felt in other areas besides linkages. In fact, the bang for the buck from these sources of support could be more than that for improvements in socioeconomic modernization given the difficulties in the latter. This fact particularly applies to foreign aid, where development assistance has not always produced the desired results (Easterly 2006). Nevertheless, as Carothers (2004) points out, the promotion of democracy ignores the structural conditions of societies at its peril.

As Section 1.3 made clear, it is not obvious that creating high-quality democracies should be the goal of public policy. A trade-off may exist between strong linkages and good policy (see Section 9.4). But to the extent that democratic quality is a goal, this chapter argues that the way to achieve it is to improve citizen capabilities, which can promote popular rule even in the absence of other prerequisites. Insofar as capabilities are an important goal on their own merits, this may be a case of two for the price of one (Nussbaum and Sen 1993).

9

Conclusions

The study of democratic quality has exploded in recent years. A search of scholarly papers for the phrases "democratic quality" and "quality of democracy" reveals more than 1,000 hits for the former and more than 2,000 for the latter.[1] And this interest is new. As Chapter 1 showed, the phrase was rarely used in scholarly articles before 1999, but has become common currency since then. This outpouring of work suggests that scholars have identified a real empirical phenomenon which has not yet been adequately addressed by political science.

The phenomenon is the performance of new democracies. After studying democratization for two decades, scholars came to realize that the new democracies which emerged from the Third Wave deserved to be studied not only as outcomes or temporary outcomes of a democratization process, but as democratic systems in their own right. When they undertook such studies, they often noticed that these democracies did not resemble the established democracies (or their idealized picture of those democracies). Political life in these countries was not as rosy as they hoped with such flaws as high levels of conflict, dishonest politicians, and dismal economic performance becoming the order of the day. It was disappointment at these failings that has justifiably inspired the field of democratic quality.

Yet, this emerging literature suffers from two problems – one conceptual and one empirical. In the first place, the concept of democratic quality has become vague and all-encompassing. Most of the works on the subject have emerged from a disquiet about the performance of new democracies, but the result is that any and all shortcomings in these new democracies – from high levels of corruption to broken campaign promises to low civic participation – are grouped under the rubric of democratic quality. Extant works on quality provide lists of potential failings or conversely desiderata rather than a

[1] Searches conducted in Google Scholar and phrases entered in quotation marks.

fully formed conception of democratic quality. In short, the concept has been stretched to become a shorthand for all good or bad things about a society.

On the empirical side, much of the research on democratic quality has relied on anecdotal evidence about how new democracies function and has not systematically compared these countries with established democracies. As a result, it is difficult to determine the extent to which skepticism about their performance is justified. Philippe Schmitter (2005: 21) in fact writes about "the unquestioned assumption that all or most neodemocracies are inferior in quality, whether considered absolutely or in relation to older democratic regimes" and argues that the assumption is mistaken on both counts. Indeed, it is easy to find faults similar to those chalked up to new democracies in the presumably high quality democracies of Western Europe and North America. Only systematic study of new democracies preferably in comparison with established democracies can determine whether these doubts are warranted. Although several such studies exist, they are still more the exception than the rule.

This book has tried to remedy these shortcomings. It has undertaken two major projects. The first was to delineate a concept of democratic quality. It has argued that democratic quality is best characterized as the strength of linkages between citizens and policy makers. Linkages best capture the fundamental democratic principle of citizen rule. Each of the three linkages analyzed here – electoral accountability, mandate responsiveness, and policy responsiveness – describes a means through which citizens can make their preferences felt.

The second and larger part of the book assessed the quality of democracy in Eastern Europe according to this conceptual scheme. The main message that emerged from these investigations is that democratic quality is in general higher than expected but with variations across types of linkages and policy areas. The statistical analysis finds that politicians have usually been held accountable for performance at elections and responded to public opinion, but have been less consistent in presenting and following through on clear campaign promises. The case studies largely support these conclusions but with several nuances that I discuss in Section 9.2.

Does this mean that these countries deserve to be called high-quality democracies? I am not willing to go so far yet. In the first place, the comparisons with other regions are rudimentary and do not say exactly where these countries lie on the continuum of quality. Similarly, the results are bound by the focus on a limited number of policy areas and countries over a relatively short period of time. What I would emphasize is that citizens in Eastern Europe do appear to have reasonable means of controlling politicians. Although a final judgment awaits both criticism of the present analysis and further research, this study does come down on the side of optimism. Just a decade and a half after exiting brutal dictatorships, these countries look much like their Western European neighbors, an accomplishment that few foresaw.

What allowed strong linkages to emerge? The previous chapter argued that, despite a lack of experience with democracy and established means of interest intermediation, citizens had the skills, desire, and capacity to enforce accountability and responsiveness. They had learned from adversity. Indeed, some of the negative legacies of communism served as "backhanded" spurs to democratic quality by creating a reaction against the old regime or forcing parties to work harder to gain the support of voters. Just as the Velvet Revolutions would not have taken place without massive, spontaneous commitment on the part of citizens, democratic linkages would not have emerged without a citizenry that was able to hold rulers accountable for their actions.

These results, however, leave open a number of questions that I pursue in this concluding chapter. These questions include the interactions between linkages, the conceptual validity and pathways of policy responsiveness, the degree to which linkages produce substantive representation, and various objections to my arguments.

9.1. INTERACTIONS BETWEEN LINKAGES

In Chapter 2, I noted that the three linkages that make up democratic quality are not independent of one another; trade-offs or complementarities may exist between them. Ultimately, the strength of these interactions is an empirical question. One cannot say a priori whether complementarities will dominate trade-offs or vice versa (Powell 2000). Only studies of all three linkages in tandem can say how they interact in practice. Although the research in this book was not specifically designed to investigate these interactions, a broad-brush look at the findings can provide a sense of how these linkages interact. I focus on the aggregate results from the first half of the book because of the many nuances in the case studies which are discussed in the next section.

There do appear to be both complementarities and tradeoffs in Eastern Europe. Arguably the strongest linkage in Eastern Europe is electoral accountability. There are good reasons to expect this linkage to drive the others. In the first place, it is the clearest connection between citizens and policy makers. It is clearer than either the public opinion that drives policy responsiveness or the choice among party platforms that drives mandate responsiveness. More important, if one assumes that politicians value staying in office above all, then it is this electoral verdict which should be foremost in their minds.

Given the threat of punishment, there are two actions that incumbents could take to win elections. One is to be responsive to the public. By producing policies that the public wants, incumbents can hope to maintain their popularity. Although rotely following public opinion can have adverse effects – politicians may be perceived as weak leaders or the policies preferred by the public may produce negative outcomes – staying close to the public on the broad contours of policy should help the reelection prospects of incumbents. This would imply that electoral accountability produces strong policy responsiveness.

A second means that incumbents have to win reelection is their election campaigns. By promising what voters want, incumbents may be able to win support beyond what their records deserve. This could entail two possibilities. One is to support popular policies and remain vague on controversial ones. Another is to promise voters the moon. There is a strategic element to both options. Vagueness and overpromising by incumbents should lead to the same behavior by challengers. Both actions would produce weak mandate responsiveness. Parties with vague platforms on some of the controversial issues of the day and broadly similar programs on popular policies deprive voters of clear and distinct choices. Parties who overpromise meanwhile find it difficult to meet their promises. This corresponds with the results in Chapter 4. In short, there is a trade-off between electoral accountability and mandate responsiveness.

The interaction may work in the opposite direction as well. Given weak mandate responsiveness, citizens should concentrate more effort on electoral accountability. If they cannot control their representatives ex ante by choosing policy directions, then they should try to influence them ex post. It is likely that the link from electoral accountability to mandate responsiveness is stronger than in the opposite direction – because it is easier to explain why voters punish politicians than why politicians break their promises – but there may also be a vicious circle between the two where causality is blurred. In short, there is complementarity between electoral accountability and policy responsiveness, but a trade-off between electoral accountability and policy responsiveness.[2] Not all good things go together, but some of them do.

9.2. TYPES OF POLICY RESPONSIVENESS

In Chapter 1, I described the ways that case studies can complement statistical analyses. One of their main advantages is in developing better concepts. Not surprisingly, the case studies of pension and housing policy do provide evidence for a more nuanced concept of policy responsiveness than the one used in the statistical analysis. Responsiveness is not so simple as policy changes following or not following public opinion. In particular, the case studies showed five possible ways in which politicians may respond to the public.

A number of policies demonstrated what may be called *strong public-initiated responsiveness*. In these cases, demands for a policy emerged directly from the public and politicians heeded these preferences. The large majority of citizens in Eastern Europe needed no prodding in opposing cuts in pensions or increases in the retirement age or in desiring (or not desiring) housing privatization. Politicians usually followed these preferences. An idealized view of the democratic process sees most policies following this scheme – an informed and

[2] What about other possible interactions? It is possible that the negative correlation between policy and mandate responsiveness implies a trade-off – changing public opinion may produce a dilemma for politicians who must choose between following through on promises and reacting to current preferences. Studies of public opinion, however, do not find large and rapid changes (Rose et al. 1998, Tworzecki 2004). Could policy responsiveness be driving electoral accountability? It is not clear how responsive policy making could make citizens more or less capable of holding politicians accountable.

activated public telling politicians the policies they desire and politicians then implementing them.

But this is not the only way that politicians can respond. In several policy areas, politicians responded to activated and attentive publics who, however, were not broadly representative of society. This situation characterized the struggle over pension privileges, rent control, and inherited housing loans where a fairly small group of affected individuals got their way. In most of these cases, the remainder of the public did not oppose policies which these groups demanded and often sympathized with them. Occasionally the majority did oppose them, which may move these situations into nonresponsiveness. But where an attentive public existed and cared about an issue and did not face strong opposition, a diminished type of responsiveness obtains (Arnold 1990). I refer to *weak public-initiated responsiveness* where politicians respond to a strongly interested minority but not a relatively indifferent majority.

There are also situations where even attentive publics do not have strong opinions. Citizens are often uninformed about the variety of policy options and may not express clear opinions. This can lead to a second-best form of responsiveness where politicians provide citizens with a policy agenda and citizens acquiesce to their choices. I call this type *elite-initiated* or *entrepreneurial responsiveness*. Such a situation could be said to characterize pension privatization in Hungary and Poland. Initially, only small groups in both countries pushed for privatization. Citizens wanted a fairer, more sustainable pension system, but had few clear ideas about how this should be achieved. Politicians sensed this dissatisfaction and looked for ways to address it. Privatization was one such policy and, after public debate, it commanded reasonable levels of public support. The policy was initiated and framed by elites, but it struck enough of a chord with the public that I classify it as a form of responsiveness.

This differs from a fourth type that I call *elite-manipulated responsiveness*. In this type, political elites give the public misleading or one-sided information about policy choices and thus move public opinion in the direction of the policies they favor. The difference between elite-manipulated and elite-initiated responsiveness lies in an evaluation of several factors. Did citizens receive a reasonable amount of information about the variety of policy options and their likely consequences? Were alternative points of view allowed free expression? Was there a reasonable amount of public discussion on the issue? Did the government conduct propaganda on behalf of a particular policy option? There is debate about whether pension privatization in Hungary and Poland fit this image (Ferge 1999). I have argued that the degree of manipulation in these cases was small enough to classify it as elite-initiated responsiveness, though informed observers may differ here.

I would now point to a fifth sort of relation that may not count as responsiveness, but nevertheless indicates that politicians are concerned with public reactions. This is *blame avoidance politics* (Weaver 1986). In these cases, politicians know and care about mass preferences, but for a variety of reasons cannot or do not respond to them. Instead of directly contradicting the public, they craft policies that are designed not to antagonize. The policy may be introduced gradually or postponed into the future; the changes may be complicated enough that most citizens cannot follow their consequences; policies may be sweetened with safety nets or packaged with other more popular policies. Such tactics were common in Eastern Europe as they are in established democracies (Pierson 1994). Most cuts in pension and housing benefits follow this logic. These policies were not policy responsive, but they did show a real relation between citizens and policy makers. Their frequency in established democracies suggests that they are a natural part of the democratic process.[3]

One may argue that they could be avoided by politicians explaining to the public the necessity of their actions. But governing politicians are not the only ones trying to persuade the public. Rather they must contend with opposition politicians who would just as assiduously try to persuade citizens that such policies are unnecessary and hurtful as a way to improve their own electoral fortunes. Perhaps a more consensus-oriented political culture would limit this threat, but the image of the government and opposition cooperating to sell unpopular policies challenges the idea of democracy as competition over office and leads to its own dangers.

The real question is whether policies introduced in this way provide substantive representation or not. Are politicians cutting benefits because they want to avoid a fiscal crisis or because they want to channel more resources to their own supporters? In general, politicians in Eastern Europe have worked hard to avoid benefit cuts and have usually been forced to engage in them by economic pressures. Politicians typically used blame avoidance techniques because they were trying to balance the economic harms of not cutting benefits with the political costs of cutting them.

Blame avoidance thus differs from what may be called *classic nonresponsiveness* where politicians know the public's preferences, but nevertheless introduce policies at odds with them. Such a situation is said to characterize policy making in new democracies where autonomous executives enact unpopular policies at will (Bates and Krueger 1993, Haggard and Kaufman 1995, Williamson 1994). I found little evidence of this sort of policy making in Eastern Europe which can be counted a success for democratic processes. Politicians in the region were rarely forced or tempted to ignore the public altogether.[4] Such a finding, however, may indicate that politicians are not representing if unpopular policies are in the true best interests of citizens. I consider this possibility in Section 9.4.

[3] More controversially, one may suggest that if citizens do not vociferously object to a policy, then they support it. Although this goes too far, I would still argue that citizens often prefer policies with blame avoidance elements to those without them. For example, they prefer a retirement age increase to be introduced gradually rather than immediately and this is a real policy difference.

[4] It is true, however, that I did not look in depth at a number of economic reforms like price liberalization that caused considerable social pain. Some have argued that the public did accept even these reforms at least when they were first introduced (Przeworski 1993, Weyland 1998).

These five types of responsiveness constitute a broader palette for assessing the relation between citizens and politicians than the concept implied in the statistical analysis. Indeed, most of these subtleties of responsiveness would not have emerged from a simple examination of public opinion and policy choices. This expanded typology thus illustrates the way that case studies can produce better concepts.

9.3. MECHANISMS OF POPULAR CONTROL

Given high levels of policy responsiveness, what are the mechanisms through which it works? How exactly are public preferences translated into policy? These questions were addressed in passing in the empirical chapters, but deserve more concentrated theoretical attention. One mechanism has already been discussed. The threat of punishment at election time provides politicians with a strong incentive to stay close to the public. This is the interaction between electoral accountability and policy responsiveness described in Section 9.1. The case studies moreover showed considerable evidence that politicians worried about elections. They frequently timed policies with elections in mind – avoiding unpopular policies in preelectoral periods and pursuing popular ones in those same periods.

But is this the only message that catches politicians' attention? Another pathway for representation is through parties. Citizens may exert strong control over parties who go on to represent citizen opinion. To a certain extent this is the model of mandate responsiveness which appears to function only weakly in the region. But other points can be made against this mechanism.

First are the relatively low rates of party membership in these countries (Kostelecky 2002, Lewis 1996, 2000). As Table 9.1 shows, only about 5% of Eastern European citizens claimed to be members of parties versus three times that number in other democracies. Few citizens were participating actively in party politics by paying party dues or regularly attending party meetings. As a result, they had few means to directly influence the behavior of parties. Second, parties in the region tend to be organized hierarchically with relatively little movement of opinion up through parties; they have been called "couch" parties because the important players could fit on a single couch (Lewis 1996). Finally, parties were relatively transient. Even today rates of volatility are high with new parties continually joining the political scene and old ones disappearing (Birch 2003, Rose and Munro 2003). If voters do not expect parties to be around for a long time, they are unlikely to participate in party activities and lobby the party leadership. In fact, the volatility of parties may be a consequence of their weak representational capacities.

Citizens may also influence policy through various forms of interest intermediation. In Western Europe, labor unions have considerable power and when they are encompassing may be a driver of policy responsiveness. In Eastern Europe, previously high rates of membership in labor unions declined

TABLE 9.1. *Participation in Parties, Unions, and Civil Society*

Countries	Party Member	Union Member	Average Number of Organizations
Eastern Europe	5.3%	16.6%	0.84
Established democracies	16.6%	32.2%	2.39
Other new democracies	16.1%	12.8%	1.82

Note: Figures are unweighted averages of country averages. They refer to the percentage of citizens who were members of a political party or labor union and the average number of civil society organizations to which they belonged. Established democracies are Australia, Finland, Japan, Norway, Sweden, Switzerland, United States, and West Germany. Other new democracies are Argentina, Bangladesh, Brazil, Chile, Philippines, South Africa, South Korea, Spain, Uruguay, and Venezuela.
Source: Howard (2003: 65–66) from the World Values Survey conducted in 1995–1998.

precipitously after the transition (Crowley and Ost 2001, Kubicek 1999).[5] Table 9.1 shows that union membership in Eastern Europe averaged 17% of the population in the mid-1990s, about half the level of the established democracies and nearly the same as other new democracies. This level moreover is likely overstated because it captures the inertia of extremely high rates of membership under communism and the existence of many retired members (Kubicek 1999). Even if some unions are having an impact on policy, it is unlikely that they are representative of public opinion generally.

Corporatism, the formal representation of business and labor in government, presents a similar picture. Ost (2000) refers to corporatism in Eastern Europe as "illusory." Though tripartite institutions existed in all ten countries, their effect on policy was small, in part because of the weakness of unions. An equally large obstacle was the absence of organizations representing employers due to the pervasiveness of state-ownership and the changes induced by privatization. Fiscal constraints and international pressures further stood in the way of corporatist deals. Ost (2000: 515) thus observes "a consistent pattern of belittling of unions, nonbinding agreements, restrictions to the state sector, and general tripartite impotence." Although unions and corporatism may have achieved some victories (Iankova 1998, Orenstein and Hale 2001), it is improbable that they were responsible for the strong connections between the government and the public.

5 The forces driving down unionization are multiple (Kubicek 1999). Employment dropped in the manufacturing sectors of the economy traditionally most inclined to unionization, whereas the new dynamic sectors – especially services – were small, fragmented, and often on the margins of the formal economy. New foreign firms could use the threat of exit to discourage unionization. Unions had also discredited themselves by their perceived collaboration with the communist regime. Finally, the forces of globalization that weakened unions in the West were at work in the East as well.

TABLE 9.2. *Levels of Contentious Politics*

Region	Petition	Boycott	Lawful Demonstration	Unofficial Strike	Occupying Building/Factory
Eastern Europe	20.8	5.0	12.9	3.5	1.2
Established democracies	57.8	15.9	19.1	4.2	1.2
Latin America	26.3	3.6	13.0	5.3	3.0

Note: Figures are the percentage of citizens who have participated in the given activity. They are unweighted averages of country average. Established democracies are Australia, Finland, Japan, New Zealand, Norway, Spain, Sweden, Switzerland, the United States, and West Germany. Latin American states are Argentina, Brazil, Chile, Colombia (an average of two surveys), Peru, Uruguay, and Venezuela.
Source: World Values Survey conducted in 1995–1998.

Another mechanism of responsiveness is civil society. A strong civil society gives citizens the power to make their views heard (Putnam 1992). As described in the previous chapter, Eastern Europeans were far less inclined to join civil organizations than citizens in established democracies or other new democracies (see Table 9.1). These low levels imply that voluntary organizations are not a strong conduit for representation.

A less formal means of influence on politics is contentious collective action. This ranges from such innocent activities as petition campaigns to participating in demonstrations and strikes. All of these activities should signal to politicians that citizens care about an issue. They should also encourage politicians to follow the public either because they signal a loss of electoral support or because civil and economic unrest detract from politicians' appearance of competence and control.

What is noteworthy in Eastern Europe is that these activities were relatively uncommon. Table 9.2 presents data from the World Values Survey on the percentage of respondents who participated in various forms of collective action. Only about one in five Eastern European citizens has even signed a petition, only one in eight has attended a lawful demonstration, and very low numbers have participated in boycotts, unofficial strikes, or factory occupations. In the case of the three lawful forms of protest – petition, boycott, and demonstration – these countries show considerably less activity, by about half, than the established democracies. They are, however, comparable to the new democracies in Latin America in the reluctance of citizens to participate actively.

Other evidence suggests that Eastern Europeans were even more quiescent than citizens of Latin America. Although economic reforms in Latin America were frequently accompanied by protests and riots, such activities were almost nonexistent in the postcommunist democracies (Greskovits 1998). Most studies have emphasized the quiescence of losers from economic reform in Eastern Europe rather than their activity (Crowley 2003, Ekiert and Kubik 1999). The paradox of Eastern Europe is the high degree of patience among citizens who suffered considerable pain from income drops and job loss.[6] The case studies in fact showed limited evidence of contentious collective action producing responsiveness.

In short, it appears that neither parties, corporatism, civil society, nor contentious collective action were the main transmission belts for responsiveness. Rather fear of electoral retribution was the strongest force confronting politicians. But how did politicians find out what the public wants if these other mechanisms are weak? Opinion polls were a prime means of information (Henn 1998). Conducted at least weekly in these countries, they provided politicians with both horserace information about their electoral prospects as well as evidence of attitudes on a variety of specific policy issues. Politicians could also extend their antennae in other directions, seeking out information from the organized activity that did exist. Because most of these countries are fairly small and homogeneous, the search for information was not too onerous.

Citizens for their part do pay close attention to politics and are therefore likely to develop relatively informed and precise opinions. According to the World Values Survey of 1999–2001, 49% of citizens identified themselves as interested or very interested in politics which is exactly equal to the percentage in established democracies and higher than the 30% in Latin America.[7] Fifty-percent of Eastern Europeans claimed to follow political news every day compared to 46% in established democracies and 39% in Latin America. These are good reasons to believe that citizens knew what politicians were doing and politicians knew that citizens knew.

In these ways, Eastern European politics has come to resemble the established democracies. Although responsiveness once occurred mainly through strong parties built from the bottom up and publics who participated actively in party and union organizations, it is increasingly the case that parties have become professional, campaign organizations dependent on money more than members and citizens interact with politics more through their televisions and polls than collective channels (Dalton 2005). If this is the new face of democracy in the established democracies, it is also the face of democracy in the postcommunist democracies. These countries have skipped the mass participation, mass parties stage and jumped directly to the poll- and media-driven modern era. Whether this is a good thing remains to be seen (Pharr and Putnam 2000).

9.4. ASSESSING SUBSTANTIVE REPRESENTATION

The hope of all democrats is that strong linkages lead to substantive representation, to policies that are in citizens' best interests. Is this the case in

[6] Greskovits (1998) argues that a number of region-specific factors account for this phenomenon. Eastern Europeans often had alternative sources of income that they could turn to, for example, subsistence plots of land and jobs in the gray or black economy. Eastern European populations were also older and more secure than in Latin America; and there were fewer young, urban poor who are most likely to protest.

[7] Again, these are averages of country averages.

Eastern Europe? Did popular rule mean good rule? The difficulty in answering this question is in determining what citizens' best interests are. If one does not accept citizens' own evaluations of policy – the standard of democratic quality – whose should replace them? One may make simple assumptions: that citizens prefer more income to less, a clean environment to a dirty one. But how should one deal with conflicts or trade-offs between these values? How should one aggregate opinions and weight their intensity? And given the diversity of policies and the mutual interactions between them, how can one measure the final effects of any one policy change much less a multitude of changes? Although methods exist to make such judgments, they are far from foolproof.[8]

Despite these caveats it remains important to ask whether governments in the region have acted in the best interests of citizens. To do this I consider whether policies produced the societal outcomes they were intended to produce without undue negative consequences elsewhere. Did economic reforms lead to higher growth and lower inflation? Did pension reforms protect the elderly? Did housing reforms improve the accessibility, affordability, and quality of housing? I also consider whether better policy choices for achieving these outcomes were available but ignored.

9.4.1. Economic Reforms

I begin with the basic economic reforms considered in Chapters 3, 4, and 5. Simple bivariate relations show that thorough and speedy economic reform were associated with a variety of positive outcomes whether higher growth, lower inflation, and even greater democracy (Frye and Commander 1999). The clearest evidence of this proposition is the large difference in economic outcomes between countries that pursued comprehensive economic reforms as in all of the countries considered here and those who conducted only partial or halting reforms as in the other former Soviet republics and parts of the Balkans. The democratic countries in Eastern Europe could thus be said to have achieved substantive representation by pursuing economic reform.

This is not to say that reforms have been perfect. In the first place, several countries lagged in enacting key reforms and suffered economically for it. Bulgaria and Romania typify this failing. Furthermore, all countries suffered through very serious transformational recessions with GDP dropping by 15 to 30% (Kornai 1994). The universality of these drops suggests that they were unavoidable. In many cases, however, there is evidence either that reformers overshot their targets (Kołodko 2000) or that they neglected key institutional reforms which hurt growth in the medium term (Orenstein 2001, Stiglitz 2000).

Sophisticated studies of the relation between reform and economic outcomes using panel data from the entire region present nuanced results. Early studies showed that faster reform unequivocally improved growth rates (e.g., de Melo et al. 1996, Fischer et al. 1996, Havrylyshyn and Rooden 2000, Selowsky and

[8] This is the aim of standard cost-benefit analysis.

Martin 1997). Other studies using somewhat different controls and methods have shown that too rapid reforms or reforms without the proper institutional context may have smaller or even negative effects (Aslund et al. 1996, Godoy and Stiglitz 2006, Heybey and Murrell 1999, Krueger and Ciolko 1998, Popov 2000). Although it is undoubtedly true that nonreformers did not do well, there are still many outstanding issues about the proper speed and sequencing of reforms.

These results suggest a qualified positive assessment. Most governments did reform in a way that benefited citizens if not in the short run, then more clearly in the medium and long run. Yes, problems existed, and even the democratic countries could have done better, but in global comparison their experience looks positive.

9.4.2. Pensions

The main goal of the pension system is to prevent poverty among the elderly. Before modern pension systems, the lives of many elderly could be described in Hobbesian terms as "nasty, brutish, and short" (Costa 1998, Graebner 1980). The elderly, moreover may be expected to suffer under the new market capitalism in Eastern Europe. They were not encouraged to save under communism and thus possessed few resources to survive without state aid. They also had few skills that were marketable in the new economy.

Postcommunist pension policies did a good job of sheltering the elderly from poverty. The Czech Republic, Hungary, and Poland had considerably lower rates of elderly poverty than richer and more established democracies. They ranked first, second, and fifth in the expanded EU with elderly poverty rates below 10% in all of them versus an average of 19% in the preexpansion EU 15.[9] Poverty rates in fact dropped during the transition in both Hungary and Poland where comparative data is available (Speder 2000: 90, Szulc 2000: 131). The case studies in Chapter 6 confirmed that policy makers worked to keep benefit levels relatively high. Cutbacks, however, were often postponed to the future leading to the real possibility that poverty rates would rise in these countries.

All, however, is not sweetness and light. Although pension systems managed to keep elderly poverty low, there were costs to these policies. The states of the ten new EU members spent slightly more on pensions as a percentage of GDP than the established EU 15 – 10.9 versus 10.6% (Zaidi 2005). And this higher spending was for a group of pensioners which was smaller – those aged 65 or more made up 17% of population in the EU 15 but only 14% in the new members – and had a shorter life expectancy – by about six years.

It is therefore likely that more efficient policies could have prevented poverty at a lower cost. Indeed, considerable evidence exists of poor targeting of

[9] Poverty is measured as incomes less than 60% of the median (Zaidi 2005). The average for the eight states admitted to the EU in 2004 is 9%.

spending and extra privileges for already secure groups. Furthermore, these relatively generous pension systems required high payroll taxes which are associated with higher unemployment rates. Moreover, the resources used for the pension system were resources that could not be used elsewhere. The trend in poverty among unmarried mothers or ethnic minorities like the Roma, for example, was far less positive than for the elderly (Ringold et al. 2005).[10]

An additional question is whether the pension privatizations in Hungary and Poland benefited citizens. Many of the supposed benefits of privatization did not in fact materialize (Andrews 2006). Privatization did not improve the fiscal situation in either country with deficits rising in both. Neither did it improve savings rates or deepen capital markets as measured by market capitalization. Since many benefits take time to appear, however, a full evaluation of these reforms will require a longer time horizon.

9.4.3. Housing

The conventional standard for assessing housing policy is whether it leads to abundant and well-equipped housing that citizens can rent or purchase at a reasonable price. Communist regimes fell short on this standard. Housing was in short supply, of low quality, and poorly allocated, though thanks to regulation rents were low (Renaud 1990).

How well did the three states address these problems? Accessibility did not improve as construction rates plummeted after the transition with partial recoveries only in the later 1990s. On the question of affordability, renters now pay more than they used to. However, this was mainly a consequence of artificially low rents and utility costs under communism. Spending as a percentage of total consumption has now reached levels comparable to Western Europe with citizens paying between 18 and 25% of consumption on housing expenses (Housing Statistics 2004: 61). Purchasing housing presents a more negative picture. Price-to-income ratios rose to 10 to 12 years of average household income – versus 3 to 4 years in Western Europe – before declining somewhat (Hegedüs and Struyk 2005: 12).

Most quality indicators, however, showed an improvement over the course of the transition with higher percentages of units featuring running water, central heating, and indoor plumbing than before the transition (Housing Statistics 2004). This continued the trend from the communist era and reflected the higher standards of newly built housing. However, there are also indications that the public stock and some newly privatized apartment buildings are deteriorating due to lack of maintenance.

Could different policies have led to better outcomes? No clear verdict has been reached on the decision to privatize and its speed. In countries that engaged

[10] Golinowska (1999: 178) argues explicitly about Poland that "Growing pension expenditures forced health services and, to some extent, education into the market economy and decreased expenditures on family policy . . . and social assistance."

in mass privatization some flats ended up in the hands of individuals too poor to afford them, but privatization may also have led to more efficient allocation, better upkeep, and greater mobility. There are strong reasons to believe that rent regulation has had negative effects on the housing sector. Regulated rents inhibit construction, provide poor matching between housing and individuals, and limit labor mobility. This last factor may have been an important factor in high unemployment rates. Rent regulation was also not well targeted and thus benefited many tenants with high incomes at the expense of more deserving individuals.

It is unclear that large declines in housing construction could have been averted. These declines struck all countries regardless of their policy choices. Diamond (1999) further notes that the three countries under study did introduce policies to promote construction lending early in the transition, but that for reasons of both supply and demand take-up on loans was low. He suggests, however, that states should have spent more effort on educating the public about mortgage lending, put banks in private hands earlier, and developed better regulations (Diamond 1999: 25–27). Housing scholars see a great deal of inefficiency in subsidy policy (Struyk 2000: 65), however, because the total amount of subsidies remained low, the inefficiencies may not have had large effects (Hegedüs and Struyk 2005: 16). In short, these countries did remove some inherited distortions, but still fell short of success.

9.4.4. Linkages and Substantive Representation

Have strong linkages led to substantive representation? Chapter 2 outlined the necessary preconditions for linkages to produce substantive representation. For policy and mandate responsiveness to produce substantive representation, citizens must know what policies best promote their interests. Although this precondition sometimes holds in these countries – particularly impressive is popular support for economic reform – scholars have found one large bias. Citizens in the region manifest very low tax awareness (Csontos et al. 1998). They do not recognize that higher government spending requires higher taxes which may have deleterious effects. The failure to recognize the relation between taxes and spending has frequently led voters to ask governments for unsustainable policies which responsive governments have then introduced. This bias explains many of the inefficiencies in pension and housing policy.

For electoral accountability to produce representation, citizens should hold politicians to a high but achievable standard. Although it is true that voters punish politicians for poor results, they may be punishing them too much. Too-strict accountability may cause politicians to overshoot for fear of losing their jobs, which can explain the strong political business cycles in the region as well as many of the timing effects in the case studies (Hallerberg et al. 2002). The tendency of voters to punish all incumbents may have even more deleterious effects – as on corruption which is discussed in the next section.

This book has unfortunately ignored one key factor in the relation between linkages and substantive representation: the mass media. If citizens are to rule well, they must be well-informed about both policy and electoral options and their consequences. Much of this information comes from the mass media – newspapers, television, and now the internet. Citizens in Eastern Europe do follow the media closely, but it is still an open question whether the mass media is providing them with relevant, objective information that allows them to make informed choices. The answer to this question is likely to have substantial effects on substantive representation.

In sum, although democratic linkages have lead to reasonable policy choices in the region, they have sometimes produced policies that are not in the best interests of citizens. This failure stems both from a failure of citizens to know the consequences of policies and a tendency for them to judge politicians too harshly. Democratic quality does not automatically led to substantative representation, but it can have positive effects.

9.5. CORRUPTION AND QUALITY

Though this study has presented fairly positive results about democratic quality, can they be reconciled with the conventional view of the region as plagued by corruption and violations of law? Many works identify a political class willing to sell policy to the highest bidder, flouting checks on their power, and using xenophobic or populist appeals to remain in power (Karklins 2005).

It would be foolish to deny these problems. Yet, they can be consistent with the findings for democratic quality. In the first place, one of the central findings here was that mandate responsiveness was not strong in the region. This is consistent with complaints that political campaigns in the region are hazy or manipulative in an effort to cover over representational failures.

More serious is the charge that governments in these countries are hopelessly corrupt. This charge can be overstated. Treisman (2003), for example, finds that corruption in postcommunist countries is about what one would expect after controlling for their income levels. Moreover, although it has not been measured, I would argue that there was a large decline in corruption in these countries after the fall of communism. Corruption was a daily occurrence at all levels of life under the old regime; one could barely survive without it. Given this baseline, postcommunist governments may be performing relatively well.

There are also reasons to believe that corruption can be partially consistent with strong linkages. If citizens place a premium on honest officials, one would worry whether a corrupt political class can be policy responsive. But if corruption is an accepted or at least tolerated part of politics, then the two may be consistent. Citizens may place a higher value on particular policy choices – where politicians do listen to the public – than on honesty itself. Indeed, if the findings here about policy responsiveness are correct, then it is hard to argue that policy in these areas was sold to the highest bidder.

Moreover, strong linkages could in fact create corruption. The high levels of electoral punishment found in Chapter 3 may encourage politicians to both sell policy and engage in clientelistic or charismatic campaigns. The reason is that they see little prospect of reelection and thus have an incentive to profit from their office today.

Finally, circumstances in Eastern Europe posed particularly difficult problems for politicians. Converting a planned economy with near universal state ownership into a market economy with private ownership generated enormous opportunities for corruption. Even countries with strong democratic traditions would find it hard to navigate this path without malfeasance. The temptation of personal enrichment was enormous. Meanwhile, the political actors who engaged in this process had very little experience with the policies they were implementing and with democratic politics itself. One should not overlook sheer incompetence as a force behind policy failures in the region.

This is not to say that to understand all is to forgive all. Rather it is to try to explain how the relatively positive findings on the strength of linkages in Eastern Europe can coexist with more worrisome trends elsewhere. This book does not mean to claim that these countries have navigated the transition as best they could, only that the public has played a key role in the process. Interestingly, one of the most frequent criticisms of politicians in the region is their failure to exercise leadership and unwillingness to buck public opinion. This criticism supports the present findings.

9.6. PUBLIC PERCEPTIONS OF QUALITY

Another discordant note is citizens' own perceptions of how their democracy is working. Consider Figure 9.1 which presents the net percentage of citizens in each of the ten countries who were satisfied with the development of democracy in their country (the percentage satisfied minus the percentage unsatisfied) over the first eight years of the transition.[11] What is noteworthy is that virtually all of the data points are on the negative side of the figure. Over this period citizens were almost uniformly dissatisfied with the development of democracy. Generally 28% more citizens were unsatisfied than satisfied with country averages ranging from −52% in Slovakia to −8% in Poland. There was no discernible upward or downward trend in these opinions (regressing satisfaction on year yields a coefficient of −0.58 with a p-value of .63).

This dissatisfaction shows up in international comparisons as well. The World Values Survey asked citizens across the world whether they were satisfied or dissatisfied with the development of democracy in their country. The net percentage of satisfied citizens (satisfied minus dissatisfied) in Eastern Europe was −32.7 compared to +23.8 in established democracies and +5.7 in other

[11] Data are from the Central and East Eurobarometer.

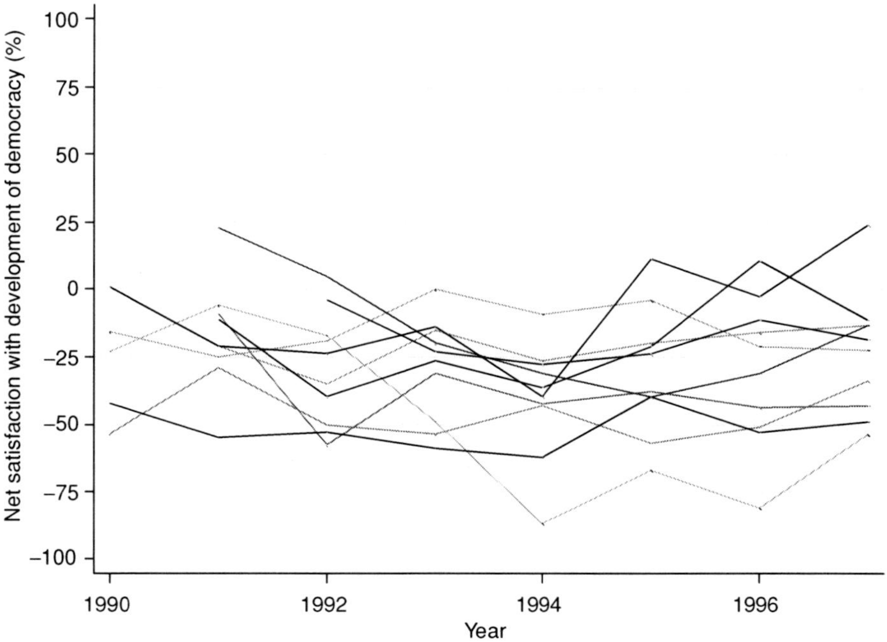

FIGURE 9.1. Satisfaction with the development of democracy.

new democracies.[12] Citizens of Eastern Europe viewed the working of democracy negatively both in absolute and relative terms.[13]

Is it possible to reconcile these mainly negative attitudes of citizens toward their own democracy with the relatively sanguine results here? Although it would be a mistake to dismiss these attitudes – the unhappiness was more than palpable as in Havel's diagnosis of a bad mood – they can be explained.

In the first place, it is unlikely that respondents are referring to the present conception of democratic quality in their evaluation of the "development of democracy." For most citizens "democracy" refers to politics as a whole and includes such phenomena as corruption, rule of law, and bureaucratic effectiveness. A citizen audit of democracy in Costa Rica, for example, found that

[12] All ten countries considered here were included in the survey. The established democracies were Austria, Belgium, Canada, Denmark, Finland, France, Germany (West), Iceland, Ireland, Italy, Japan, Luxembourg, Netherlands, Sweden, the United Kingdom, and the United States. The other democracies were Argentina, Chile, Greece, India, Korea, Malta, Mexico, Peru, Philippines, Portugal, South Africa, Spain, Turkey, and Venezuela. The survey was conducted in 1999–2001.

[13] They are considerably more sanguine about democracy in the abstract which majorities usually support. Rose et al. (1998: 109) wrote that there is "little popular endorsement of undemocratic attitudes." It is the actual practice of democracy that worries them (see also Evans and Whitefield 1995, Haerpfer 2002, Linde 2004).

one of the main complaints about democracy was that bureaucrats did not treat citizens well (Cullel 2004).

Democratic quality may indeed be low if it is conceived in such an encompassing way. Job security has disappeared, corruption has remained high, and crime has risen (Rose-Ackerman 2005). But as I argued in Chapter 2, these failures should be distinguished from failures of democratic linkages. Although these aspects of political life are far from insignificant, they are also at a considerable remove from the concept investigated here. The belief that politicians have done a bad job is separate from the belief that politicians are nonresponsive. Popular control can coexist with dissatisfaction. If citizens are demanding bad policies and politicians respond to those demands, who will be blamed for the outcomes that result? For a variety of psychological reasons citizens are more likely to blame politicians than themselves.

It is also worth noting that these negative assessments can be partially explained by economic conditions. All of these countries suffered massive recessions that surely soured citizens on even the indisputable achievements of the new democracies. Regressing satisfaction with democracy on economic variables reveals that high unemployment and low growth both have a strongly negative impact on satisfaction.[14] Although the degree of democracy measured by Freedom House scores also affects satisfaction in the expected direction – more democratic countries had higher satisfaction – its impact was smaller.

It is similarly unclear what baseline citizens are choosing in assessing the performance of democracy. Relative to what is democracy working poorly? Some scholars have argued that postcommunist citizens entered the transition with extremely high expectations that were almost bound to be disappointed (Holmes 1997). Many citizens compared their countries with their Western neighbors who had enjoyed forty years of postwar prosperity and peace. In traveling to Western Europe for the first time and watching those societies in the media, their own societies could only come up short. If they had made a more appropriate comparison to other new democracies – for example, to the new democracies of Latin America – they would probably have been more satisfied with their own democracies.[15] Although dissatisfaction was real, it does not necessarily overturn the present conclusions.

9.7. IMPLICATIONS FOR COMPARATIVE POLITICS

The findings of this study carry significant implications for comparative politics research. In the first place, they encourage a reconsideration of the prevalent pessimism about the functioning of Third Wave democracies. At least some

[14] Estimations were conducted with panel corrected standard errors and are available from the author.

[15] In analyzing pension privatization, Orenstein (2000) and Müller (1999) note that reformers avoided comparisons with Latin America because those countries were viewed by the public as inferior.

new democracies have attained a level of responsiveness and accountability comparable with the established democracies and have done so in an extremely short time.[16] Although the picture is not all positive, there are indications that democratic processes are working as theory predicts. This development should encourage comparativists to treat new democracies not as a separate category of countries in transition, but as democracies in their right that deserve to be studied in the same way as the established democracies.

Another contribution of this work is to bring the public back into the study of policy making. Much of comparative politics is elite-based, finding the causes of political outcomes in political parties, institutions, or the ideologies of public officials. It would be foolish to deny the importance of any of these variables, but it is curious that the impact of ordinary citizens has not played a central role in comparative politics. There are reasons for this; until recently most countries in the world were dictatorships that could ignore the desires of their citizens and there was an almost complete absence of comparative data on public opinion. Yet, both factors have been changing. More countries are democratic and we know more about the attitudes and behaviors of their citizens. This book forms part of a recent wave of studies that take seriously the impact of mass publics on politics. Among the works that take this path are Nancy Bermeo's (2003) *Ordinary People in Extraordinary Times* on the effect of the masses on democratization, Ronald Inglehart and Pippa Norris's *Rising Tide* (2003) on the importance of popular beliefs about religion and women, and Clem Brooks and Jeff Manza's (2007) *Why Welfare States Persist* on the effect of public opinion on welfare policies.

The study of democratic quality also provides a new unifying theme for comparative politics. For much of the past two decades, the quest that united comparative politics was for the determinants of democratization. Although it is premature to say that the field has answered this question, there is now a good understanding of where and when democratization takes place. It also appears that most countries in the world have sorted themselves into stable democracies, stable hybrid regimes, or stable dictatorships. At the moment few anticipate large swings in the democratic or nondemocratic direction as have occurred in the recent past, though changes on the margin are likely (Huntington 1992, Diamond 2007).

Democratic quality can provide a new unifying mission for comparative politics. In the first place, it is the logical next step from research on democratization. Once countries become democratic, what happens to them? Does democracy improve political life and policy choices as one would hope? How do politicians and citizens respond to the incentives that democratic institutions provide? Do new democracies function in the same way as older democracies or do they possess their own specificities? The study of democratic quality encompasses all of these questions.

[16] Kitschelt et al. (1999: 384) share this conclusion, noting that "citizens and politicians learn to act on well-understood self-interests in new democracies quite rapidly."

It provides a unifying theme in other ways as well. It helps to bring together studies of democracies across regions which are not usually compared (Huber 2003). The Third Wave of democracy touched all five continents and so it is natural to ask how democracies which emerged at a similar world-historical moment are functioning. Indeed, insofar as exogenous international forces pushed all of these regimes toward democracy (Whitehead 2001), these countries represent an important natural experiment that allows one to ask how different conditions – such as economic development or prior regime type – affect democratic processes (Linz and Stepan 1996).

Democratic quality similarly provides a way to bring together the multitude of studies on policy making in democracies. Most of these studies have been undertaken with the goal of understanding particular policy choices. But many can be reinterpreted in terms of democratic linkages. One can ask in each case to what extent policy follows public opinion and election promises. And having done this, it is then possible to determine which background conditions and policy characteristics promote strong linkages.

A final contribution is the linking of the usually separate fields of political behavior and political institutions. Most political scientists study either behavior – public opinion, voting, collective action – or political institutions – legislatures, executives, and policy making – but not both. By asking about the interaction between citizens and politicians, democratic quality forces scholars to study these two areas in tandem for issues that matter. In this way, democratic quality helps to unite an increasingly specialized discipline and avoid what Pierson (2004) calls the pizza pie approach to political science – slicing up politics into disconnected slices.

In short, democratic quality may be a fruitful way of at once addressing important issues and bringing under a single tent a large number of disparate fields in political science. This is not to say that it is the be-all and end-all of political science. Its greatest shortcoming is that it provides little help in understanding the dictatorial regimes under which much of humanity still lives. Nevertheless, it does serve to redirect the attention of comparativists to questions of clear importance that still lack good answers and contributes to a constructive dialogue among them.

9.8. FUTURE DIRECTIONS

Where should scholars go from here? Although this book has focused on the nature of linkages in Eastern Europe across several policy areas, it is important to expand this work both spatially and substantively. Though there have been some studies of linkages in Eastern Europe and Latin America (Kitschelt et al. 1999, Stokes 2001a, 2001b, Luna and Zechmeister 2005, Remmer 1989), there is still much work to be done on all regions. Indeed, only such cross-regional comparative work can identify the factors that underlie the strength of linkages. I have speculated on these factors in Chapter 8, but only systematic comparisons of countries with strong and weak linkages will confirm or disconfirm these speculations. Only then can we determine whether and how to promote democratic quality.

The analyses here also suggest that there is room for pushing the study of individual linkages forward. The study of electoral accountability has long been a mainstay of political science, but its focus has been curiously limited to the effect of economic conditions or perceived economic conditions on election results or vote choices. The study of accountability could be expanded on both sides of this equation. One could look both at other measures of performance besides the macroeconomy – corruption would be one important possibility – as well as other sanctions – for example, resignations amidst public scandals. These expansions would produce a more rounded concept of accountability that squares better with popular perceptions that politicians often escape accountability.

The study of mandate responsiveness has also been a staple of political science and was recently reinvigorated by the work of Stokes (2001a). What can be added are better ways to study the content of electoral campaigns and the way they are perceived by voters. Recent advances in text analysis may produce progress in this area (Laver et al. 2003) and move away from subjective judgments. These assessments could then be combined with more subtle measures of policy outcomes (another area of burgeoning research) instead of the ubiquitous spending variables.

Finally, political scientists have long studied the nature of policy responsiveness. Besides expanding this work to new democracies, it is important to begin the process of disaggregating responsiveness across policy areas and relating these variable degrees of responsiveness to characteristics of these areas (Manza and Cook 2002). Work on this issue has begun, but has mainly focused on the United States, a case in many ways anomalous. Ultimately, scholars should develop a theory of why responsiveness emerges in certain places and times rather than simply determining whether it exists or not.

More generally, research on linkages has typically viewed them in isolation. In Section 9.1, I suggested that there are interactions between these linkages. Yet, there has been little work on the trade-offs or complementarities between means of popular control. Two recent works have pointed the way in this area – Erikson, MacKuen, and Stimson's (2002) *The Macropolity* and Powell's (2000) *Elections as Instruments of Democracy*. Each comes to a different conclusion. The former finds accountability and responsiveness to be mutually supportive whereas the latter sees trade-offs between them. Continuing such work should yield considerable advances in understanding how democracy works as a system of government.

Perhaps most important is the necessity of research on the nature of public opinion in new democracies. If the public is systematically misinformed about policy, then democratic quality can truly be a curse. As one colleague remarked when I described my definition of democratic quality as popular control, "What if a country has bad citizens?" Although these issues have been studied in depth in the United States, little is still known about the nature and origins of public opinion in new democracies. It is possible that poorly informed citizens rather than corrupt elites are responsible for some of the political failures in new democracies. For strong linkages to produce substantive representation, citizens need to be fairly knowledgable about policy. More must be known about whether they possess or can acquire the knowledge they need. Only then does democracy produce policies that benefit all citizens.

In short, much research still needs to be done on the quality of democracy and many new democracies need to be studied. This book has tried to take a small first step toward elucidating what quality means and how it can studied. Future research will shed more light on perhaps the fundamental political fact of the modern world – the nature of democratic government.

Bibliography

Achen, Christopher H. 1978. "Measuring Representation." *American Journal of Political Science* 22(3): 477–510.
Achen, Christopher H. and Larry M. Bartels. 2004. "Musical Chairs: Pocketbook Voting and the Limits of Democratic Accountability." Paper presented at the Annual Meeting of the American Political Science Association, Chicago, September 1–4.
Alda, Kristina. 2006. "Rents Likely to Rise." *The Prague Post*, 4 January.
Althaus, Scott L. 2003. *Collective Preferences in Democratic Politics: Opinion Surveys and the Will of the People*. New York: Cambridge University Press.
Altman, David and Anibal Pérez-Liñán. 2002. "Assessing the Quality of Democracy: Freedom, Competitiveness, and Participation in 18 Countries." *Democratization* 9(2): 85–100.
Anderson, Leslie, Michael Lewis Beck, and Mary Stegmaier. 2003. "Post-Socialist Democratization: A Comparative Political Economy Model of the Vote for Hungary and Nicaragua." *Electoral Studies* 22(3): 469–484.
Andrews, Emily S. 2006. *Pension Reform and the Development of Pension Systems: An Evaluation of World Bank Assistance*. Washington, DC: The World Bank.
Appel, Hilary. 2004. *A New Capitalist Order: Privatization and Ideology in Russia and Eastern Europe*. Pittsburgh, PA: University of Pittsburgh Press.
Appel, Hilary. 2005. "Anti-Communist Justice and Founding the Postcommunist Order: Lustration and Restitution in Central Europe." *East European Politics and Societies* 19(3): 379–405.
Arellano, Manuel and Olympia Bover. 1995. "Another Look at Instrumental Variable Estimation of Error-Component Models." *Journal of Econometrics* 68(1): 29–51.
Arnold, R. Douglas. 1990. *The Logic of Congressional Action*. New Haven, CT: Yale University Press.
Asghar, Zaidi. 2006. "Poverty of Elderly People in EU25." Policy Brief. Vienna: European Center for Social Welfare Policy and Research.
Aslund, Anders, Peter Boone, and Simon Johnson. 1996. "How to Stabilize: Lessons from Post-communist Countries." *Brookings Papers on Economic Activity* 1: 217–313.
Bacon, Wally. 2004. "Economic Reform." In Henry F. Carey, ed., *Romania Since 1989: Politics, Economics, and Society*. Lanham, MD: Lexington Books.

Balcerowicz, Leszek. 1994. "Understanding Postcommunist Transitions." *Journal of Democracy* 5(4): 75–89.

Barany, Zoltan and Ivan Volgyes, eds. 1995. *The Legacies of Communism in Eastern Europe*. Baltimore: Johns Hopkins University Press.

Barany, Zoltan. 2002. "Bulgaria's Royal Elections." *Journal of Democracy* 13(2): 141–155.

Barber, Benjamin. 1984. *Strong Democracy: Participatory Politics for a New Age*. Berkeley: University of California Press.

Barr, Nicolas. 1998. *The Economics of the Welfare State*. Palo Alto, CA: Stanford University Press.

Bartels, Larry M. 2008. *Unequal Democracy: The Political Economy of the New Gilded Age*. Princeton: Princeton University Press.

Bates, Robert H. and Anne O. Krueger, eds. 1993. *Political and Economic Interactions in Economic Policy Reform: Evidence from Eight Countries*. Oxford: Blackwell.

Baxandall, Phineas. 2000. "The Communist Taboo Against Unemployment." *East European Politics and Societies* 14(3): 597–635.

BBC. 2006. "Excerpts: Hungarian 'Lies' Speech." Accessed at: http://news.bbc.co.uk/2/hi/europe/5359546.stm.

Beetham, David, Sarah Bracking, Iain Kearton, and Stuart Weir. 2002. *International IDEA Handbook on Democracy Assessment*. The Hague: Kluwer Law International.

Bell, Janice. 1997. "Unemployment Matters: Vote Patterns During the Economic Transition in Poland, 1990–1995." *Europe-Asia Studies* 49(7): 1263–1291.

Benoit, Kenneth and Michael Laver. 2006. *Party Policy in Modern Democracies*. London: Routledge.

Berend, Ivan T. 1996. *Central and Eastern Europe, 1944–1993: Detour from the Periphery to the Periphery*. Cambridge: Cambridge University Press.

Berg, Andrew, Eduardo R. Borensztein, Ratna Sahay, and Jeromin Zettelmeyer. 1999. "The Evolution of Output in Transition Outcomes: Explaining the Differences." IMF Working Paper, No. 73.

Berglund, Sten, Tomas Hellen, and Frank H. Aarebrot, eds. 1998. *The Handbook of Political Change in Eastern Europe*. Cheltenham: Edward Elgar.

Bermeo, Nancy. 2003. *Ordinary People in Extraordinary Times: The Citizenry and the Breakdown of Democracy*. Princeton: Princeton University Press.

Birch, Sarah. 2003. *Electoral Systems and Political Transformation in Postcommunist Europe*. New York: Palgrave Macmillan.

Blaydes, Lisa. 2007. Electoral Authoritarianism in Mubarak's Egypt. Ph.D. dissertation. University of California, Los Angeles.

Blejer, Mario I. and Fabrizio Coricelli, 1995. *The Making of Economic Reform in Eastern Europe: Conversations with Leading Reformers in Poland, Hungary, and the Czech Republic*. Cheltenham: Edward Elgar.

Blendon Robert J., John M. Benson, Mollyann Brodie, Richard Morin, Drew E. Altman, Daniel Gitterman, Mario Brossard, and Matt James. 1997. "Bridging the Gap Between the Public's and Economists' Views of the Economy." *Journal of Economic Perspectives* 11(3): 105–18.

Blinder, Alan S. 1997. "Is Government Too Political?" *Foreign Affairs* 76(6): 115–126.

Blundell, Richard and Stephen Bond. 1998. "Initial Conditions and Moment Conditions in Dynamic Panel Data Models." *Journal of Econometrics* 87(1): 115–143.

Bodnar, Judit. 2001. *Fin de Millenaire Budapest: Metamorphoses of Urban Life*. Minneapolis: University of Minnesota Press.

Boix, Carles. 1998. *Political Parties, Growth, and Equality: Conservative and Social Democratic Economic Strategies in the World Economy*. Cambridge: Cambridge University Press.

Boix, Carles and Susan C. Stokes. 2003. "Endogenous Democratization." *World Politics* 55(4): 517–549.

Bonoli, Giuliano. 2000. *The Politics of Pension Reform: Institutions and Policy Change in Western Europe*. Cambridge: Cambridge University Press.

Bouc, Frantisek. 2006. "Landlords Gain in Rent-Control Fight." *The Prague Post*, 28 June.

Bowman, Kirk, Fabrice Lehoucq, and James Mahoney. 2005. "Measuring Political Democracy: Case Expertise, Data Adequacy, and Central America." *Comparative Political Studies* 38(8): 939–970.

Bozóki, András and John T. Ishiyama, eds. 2002. *The Communist Successor Parties of Central and Eastern Europe*. Armonk, NY: M.E. Sharp.

Brady, Henry E. and David Collier, eds. 2004. *Rethinking Social Inquiry: Diverse Tools, Shared Standards*. Lanham, MD: Rowan and Littlefield.

Brom, Karla and Mitchell Orenstein. 1994. "The Privatised Sector in the Czech Republic: Government and Bank Control in a Transitional Economy." *Europe-Asia Studies* 46(6): 893–928.

Brooks, Clem and Jeff Manza. 2007. *Why Welfare States Persist: Public Opinion and the Future of Social Provision*. Chicago: University of Chicago Press.

Brooks, Joel E. 1987. "The Opinion-Policy Nexus in France – Do Institutions Make a Difference." *Journal of Politics* 49(2): 465–480.

Brooks, Joel E. 1990. "The Opinion-Policy Nexus in Germany." *Public Opinion Quarterly* 54(4): 508–529.

Brooks, Sarah. 2002. "Social Protection and Economic Integration: The Politics of Pension Reform in an Era of Capital Mobility." *Comparative Political Studies*, 35(5): 491–523.

Brooks, Sarah. 2005. "Interdependent and Domestic Foundations of Policy Change: The Diffusion of Pension Privatization Around the World." *International Studies Quarterly* 49(2): 273–294.

Budge, Ian, Hans-Dieter Klingemann, Andrea Volkens, Judith Bara, Eric Tannenbaum, Richard Fording, Derek Hearl, Hee Min Kim, Michael McDonald, and Silvia Mendes. 2001. *Mapping Policy Preferences: Parties, Electors and Governments: 1945–1998*. Oxford: Oxford University Press.

Bugajski, Janusz. 2002. *Political Parties of Eastern Europe: A Guide to Politics in the Postcommunist Era*. Armonk, NY: M.E. Sharpe.

Bunce, Valerie. 1995. "Should Transitologists Be Grounded?" *Slavic Review* 54(1): 111–127.

Bunce, Valerie. 1999. *Subversive Institutions: The Design and Destruction of Socialism and the State*. New York: Cambridge University Press.

Bunce, Valerie. 2001. "Democratization and Economic Reform." *Annual Review of Political Science* 4: 43–65.

Bunce, Valerie and Mária Csanádi. 1993. "Uncertainty in Transition: Postcommunism in Hungary." *East European Politics and Societies* 7(2): 240–276.

Butler, Stuart and Peter Germanis. 1984. "Achieving Social Security Reform: A Leninist Strategy." *Cato Journal* 3: 547–556.

Cain, Michael J. G. And Aleksander Surdej. 1999. "Transitional Politics or Public Choice? Evaluating Stalled Pension Reforms in Poland."In Linda J. Cook, Mitchell A.

Orenstein, and Marilyn Rueschemeyer, eds. *Left Parties and Social Policy in Post-communist Europe*. Boulder, CO: Westview Press.

Campos, Nauro F. and Roman Horvath. 2006. "Reform Redux: Measurement, Determinants, and Reversals." Center for Economic Policy Research, Working Paper No. 5673.

Canes-Wrone, Brandice. 2006. *Who Leads Whom? Presidents, Policy, and the Public*. Chicago: University of Chicago Press.

Canes-Wrone, Brandice and Kenneth W. Shotts. 2004. "The Conditional Nature of Presidential Responsiveness to Public Opinion." *American Journal of Political Science* 48(4): 690–706.

Caplan, Bryan. 2006. *The Myth of the Rational Voter*. Princeton: Princeton University Press.

Carothers, Thomas. 2004. *Critical Mission: Essays on Democracy Promotion*. Washington, DC: Carnegie.Endowment for International Peace.

Chan, Kenneth Ka-Lok. 1998. "The Polish General Election of 1997." *Electoral Studies* 17(4): 561–567.

Chirot, Daniel, ed. 1989. *The Causes of Backwardness in Eastern Europe: Economics and Politics from the Middle Ages until the Early Twentieth Century*. Berkeley: University of California Press.

Chlon, Agniezska. 2000. "Pension Reform and Public Information in Poland." Social Protection Discussion Paper No. 0019. Washington, DC: World Bank.

Chlon, Agnieszka, Marek Góra, and Michal Rutkowski. 1999. "Shaping Pension Reform in Poland." Social Protection Discussion Paper No. 9923. Washington, DC: World Bank.

Chlon-Dominczak, Agnieszka and Marek Mora. 2003. "Commitment and Consensus in Pension Reform." In Robert Holzmann, Mitchell Orenstein, and Michal Rutkowski, eds., *Pension Reform in Europe: Process and Progress*. Washington, DC: World Bank.

Chua, Amy. 2003. *World on Fire: How Exporting Free Market Democracy Breeds Ethnic Hatred*. New York: Doubleday.

Clapham, David and Keith Kintrea. "Analyzing Housing Privatization." In David Clapham, Joszef Hegedüs, Keith Kintrea, Iván Tosics, and Helen Kay, eds., *Housing Privatization in Eastern Europe*. Westport, CT: Greenwood Press.

Clark, Terry D. and Nerijus Prekevičius. 2003. "Explaining the 2000 Lithuanian Parliamentary Elections: An Application of Contextual and New Institutionalist Approaches." *Slavic Review* 62(3): 548–569.

Commander, Simon and Timothy Frye. 1999. "The Politics of Postcommunist Economic Reform." *Transition Report 1999*. London: EBRD.

Conley, Patricia Heidotting. 2001. *Presidential Mandates: How Elections Shape the National Agenda*. Chicago: University of Chicago Press.

Cook, Linda. 1993. *The Soviet Social Contract and Why It Failed: Welfare Policies and Workers' Politics from Brezhnev to Yeltsin*. Cambridge, MA: Harvard University Press.

Cook, Linda J., Mitchell A. Orenstein, and Marilyn Rueschemeyer, eds. 1999. *Left Parties and Social Policy in Postcommunist Europe*. Boulder, CO: Westview Press.

Cook, Linda J. and Mitchell A. Orenstein. 1999. "The Return of the Left and Its Impact on the Welfare State in Russia, Poland, and Hungary." In Linda J. Cook, Mitchell A. Orenstein, and Marilyn Rueschemeyer, eds. *Left Parties and Social Policy in Postcommunist Europe*. Boulder, CO: Westview Press.

Cook, Linda J., Mitchell A. Orenstein, and Marilyn Rueschemeyer. 1999. "Conclusions." In Linda J. Cook, Mitchell A. Orenstein, and Marilyn Rueschemeyer, eds. *Left Parties and Social Policy in Postcommunist Europe.* Boulder, CO: Westview Press.

Costa, Dora L. 1998. *The Evolution of Retirement: An American Economic History, 1880–1990.* Chicago: Chicago University Press.

Crowley, Stephen. 2003. "Explaining Labor Quiescence in Postcommunist Europe: Historical Legacies and Comparative Perspective." Central and Eastern European Working Paper No. 56. Minda de Gunzberg Center for European Studies, Harvard University.

Crowley, Stephen and David Ost, eds. 2001. *Workers after Workers' States: Labor and Politics in Postcommunist Europe.* Lanham, MD: Rowan and Littlefield.

Csontos, László, Janos Kornai, and István György Tóth. 1998. "Tax Awareness and Reform of the Welfare State: Hungarian Survey Results." *Economics of Transition* 6(2): 287–312.

Cullel, Jorge Vargas. 2004. "Democracy and the Quality of Democracy: Empirical Findings and Methodological and Theoretical Issues Drawn from the Citizen Audit of the Quality of Democracy in Costa Rica." In Guillermo O'Donnell, Jorge Vargas Cullel, and Osvaldo M. Iazzetta, eds., *The Quality of Democracy: Theory and Applications.* South Bend: University of Notre Dame Press.

Curry, Jane L. 1995. "The Sociological Legacies of Communism." In Zoltan Barany and Ivan Volgyes, eds., *The Legacies of Communism in Eastern Europe.* Baltimore: Johns Hopkins University Press.

Czepulis-Rutkowska, Zofia. 1999. "The Polish Pension System and its Problems." In Katharina Müller, Andreas Ryll, and Hans-Jürgen Wagener, eds., *Transformation of Social Security: Pensions in Central-Eastern Europe.* Heidelberg: Physica-Verlag.

Dahl, Robert. 1971. *Polyarchy: Participation and Opposition.* New Haven, CT: Yale University Press.

Dahl, Robert. 1989. *Democracy and Its Critics.* New Haven, CT: Yale University Press.

Dahl, Robert. 1990. "The Myth of the Presidential Mandate." *Political Science Quarterly* 105: 355–372.

Dahl, Robert. 1998. *On Democracy.* New Haven, CT: Yale University Press.

Dalton, Russell. 2005. *Citizen Politics.* Washington, DC: Congressional Quarterly Press.

Danics, Viktoria. 1998. The Hungarian Pension Reform: How Could the Government Do It in 18 Months? M.A. Thesis, Central European University, Budapest.

De Deken, Johan Jeroen. 1994. "Social Policy in Postwar Czechoslovakia. The Development of Old-Age Pensions and Housing Policies During the Period 1945–1989." European University Institute Working Paper SPS No. 94/13.

Delli Carpini, Michael X. and Scott Keeter. 1996. *What Americans Know About Politics and Why It Matters.* New Haven, CT: Yale University Press.

de Melo, Martha, Cevdet Denizer, and Alan Gelb. 1996. "Patterns of Transition from Plan to Market." *The World Bank Economic Review* 10(3): 397–424.

de Melo, Martha, Cevdet Denizer, Alan Gelb, and Stoyan Tenev. 1997. "Circumstance and Choice: The Role of Initial Conditions and Policies in Transition Economies." World Bank Working Paper series No. 1866. Washington, DC: World Bank.

DeMelo, Mathias, Calvo Denizer, and Alan Gelb. 1996. "From Plan to Market: Patterns of Transition." World Bank Policy Research Working Paper No. 1564.

Diamond, Douglas B. 1999. *The Transition in Housing Finance in Central Europe and Russia, 1989–1999.* Washington, DC: The Urban Institute.

Diamond, Larry. 2002. "Thinking About Hybrid Regimes." *Journal of Democracy* 13: 21–35.

Diamond, Larry. 2007. *The Spirit of Democracy: The Struggle to Build Free Societies Around the World*. New York: Henry Holt.

Diamond, Larry and Leonardo Morlino, eds. 2005. *Assessing the Quality of Democracy*. Baltimore: Johns Hopkins University Press.

Dimitrov, Vesselin. 2001. *Bulgaria: The Uneven Transition*. London: Routledge.

Djilas, Milovan. 1983. *The New Class: An Analysis of the Communist System*. San Diego: Harcourt Brace Jovanovich.

Doling, J. F. 1997. *Comparative Housing Policy: Government and Housing in Advanced Industrialized Countries*. New York: St. Martin's Press.

Dovi, Suzanne. 2007. *The Good Representative*. Oxford: Blackwell.

Downs, Anthony. 1957. *An Economic Theory of Democracy*. New York: Harper and Row.

Drazen, Allen and Vittorio Grilli. 1993. "The Benefits of Crises for Economic Reform." *American Economic Review* 83(3): 598–607.

Dreifelds, Juris. 1996. *Latvia in Transition*. Cambridge: Cambridge University Press.

Druckman, James and Andrew Roberts. 2005. "Context and Coalition Bargaining: Comparing Portfolio Allocation in Eastern and Western Europe."*Party Politics* 11(5): 535–555.

Duch, Raymond. 1995. "Economic Chaos and the Fragility of Democratic Transition in Former Communist Regimes." *Journal of Politics* 57(1): 121–158.

Duch, Raymond. 2001. "A Developmental Model of Heterogeneous Economic Voting in New Democracies." *American Political Science Review* 98(4): 895–910.

Duch, Raymond M. and Randolph T. Stevenson. 2008. *The Economic Vote: How Political and Economic Institutions Condition Election Results*. New York: Cambridge University Press.

Dvořák, Ivan. 1997. "Analýza kapitálového trhu a jeho možných vývojových trendu z hlediska potřeb transformace důchodového pojištěni." Prague: Czechoslovak Commercial Bank.

Easterly, William. 2006. *The White Man's Burden: Why the West's Efforts to Aid the Rest Have Done So Much Ill and So Little Good*. New York: Penguin.

EBRD. 1995–2009. *Transition Report*. London: European Bank for Reconstruction and Development.

Eddy, Kester. 2006. "Fidesz: Government Economic Policy is 'Populist.'" *Budapest Sun*, XIV/7, 16 February.

Eichenberg, Richard and Richard Stoll. 2003. "Representing Defense: Democratic Control of the Defense Budget in the United States and Western Europe." *Journal of Conflict Resolution* 47(4): 399–423.

Ekiert, Grzegorz. 1996. *The State Against Society: Political Crises and Their Aftermath in East Central Europe*. Princeton: Princeton University Press.

Ekiert, Grzegorz and Jan Kubik. 1999. *Rebellious Civil Society: Popular Protest and Democratic Consolidation in Poland, 1989–1993*. Ann Arbor: University of Michigan Press.

Elster, Jon, Claus Offe, and Ulrich Preuss, eds. 1998. *Institutional Design in Post-communist Societies: Rebuilding the Ship at Sea*. Cambridge: Cambridge University Press.

Erikson, Robert S., Michael MacKuen, and James A. Stimson. 2002. *The Macro Polity*. New York: Cambridge University Press.

Esping-Andersen, Gøsta. 1990. *The Three Worlds of Welfare Capitalism*. Princeton: Princeton University Press.

Evans, Geoffrey and Stephen Whitefield. 1995. "The Politics and Economics of Democratic Commitment: Support for Democracy in Transition Societies." *British Journal of Political Science* 25(4): 485–514.

Evans, Martin C. 1999. *Change and Choice in Social Protection: The Experience of Central and Eastern Europe*. Phare Consensus Programme, European Commission, ADECRI.

Eyal, Gil, Ivan Szelenyi, and Eleanor Townsley. 1998. *Making Capitalism Without Capitalists: The New Ruling Elites in Eastern Europe*. London: Verso.

Falcetti, Elisabetta, Martin Raiser, and Peter Sanfey. 2002. "Defying the Odds: Initial Conditions, Reforms, and Growth in the First Decade of Transition." *Journal of Comparative Economics* 30(2): 229–251.

Feldstein, Martin. 1997. "The Case for Privatization." *Foreign Affairs* 76(4): 24–38.

Ferejohn, John. 1999. "Electoral Accountability and the Control of Politicians: Selecting Good Types Versus Sanctioning Poor Performance." In Adam Przeworski, Susan C. Stokes, and Bernard Manin, eds., *Democracy, Accountability and Representation*. Cambridge: Cambridge University Press.

Ferge, Zsuzsa. 1999. "The Politics of the Hungarian Pension Reform." In Katharina Müller, Andreas Ryll, and Hans-Jürgen Wagener, eds., *Transformation of Social Security: Pensions in Central-Eastern Europe*. Heidelberg: Physica-Verlag.

Fidrmuc, Jan. 2000a. "Political Support for Reforms: Economics of Voting in Transition Countries." *European Economic Review* 44(8): 1491–1513.

Fidrmuc, Jan. 2000b. "Economics of Voting in Postcommunist Countries." *Electoral Studies* 19(2/3): 199–217.

Fink-Hafner, Danica. 1997. "Development of a Party System." In Danica Fink-Hafner and John R. Robbins, eds., *Making a New Nation: The Formation of Slovenia*. Aldershot: Dartmouth.

Fischer, Stanley, Ratna Sahay, and Carlos Vegh. 1998. "Stabilization and Growth in Transition Economies: The Early Experience." *Journal of Economic Perspectives* 10(2): 45–66.

Fish, M. Steven. 1998. "The Determinants of Economic Reform in the Postcommunist World." *East European Politics and Societies* 12(1): 31–78.

Fish, M. Steven. 2005. *Democracy Derailed in Russia: The Failure of Open Politics*. New York: Cambridge University Press.

Fishel, Jeff. 1985. *Presidents and Promises: From Campaign Pledge to Presidential Performance*. Washington, DC: Congressional Quarterly Press.

Fitzmaurice, John. 1993. "The Estonian Elections of 1992." *Electoral Studies* 12(2): 168–173.

Fitzmaurice, John. 1995. "The Slovak Election of September 1994." *Electoral Studies* 14(2): 203–206.

Fitzmaurice, John. 1997. "The Slovenian Parliamentary Elections of 10 November 1996." *Electoral Studies* 16(3): 403–407.

Fitzmaurice, John. 1999. "The Slovak Elections of 25th and 26th September 1998." *Electoral Studies* 18(2): 290–296.

Fitzmaurice, John. 2001. "The Parliamentary Election in Estonia, March 1999." *Electoral Studies* 20(1): 141–146.

Franklin, Mark and Christopher Wlezien. 1997. "The Responsive Public, Issue Salience, Policy Change, and Preferences for European Unification." *Journal of Theoretical Politics* 9(3): 247–263.

Freedom House. 2005. *Freedom in the World.* New York: Freedom House.

Frye, Timothy. 2002. "The Perils of Polarization: Economic Performance in the Post-communist World." *World Politics* 54(4): 308–337.

Gál, Robert I. 1999. "Hungarian Old-Age Security Prior to the 1998 Reform." In Katharina Müller, Andreas Ryll, and Hans-Jürgen Wagener, eds., *Transformation of Social Security: Pensions in Central-Eastern Europe.* Heidelberg: Physica-Verlag.

Gandhi, Jennifer. 2004. Political Institutions Under Dictatorship. Ph.D. Dissertation. New York University.

Garrett, Geoffrey. 1998. *Partisan Politics in the Global Economy.* Cambridge: Cambridge University Press.

Garton Ash, Timothy. 1989. *The Uses of Adversity: Essays on the Fate of Central Europe.* New York: Random House.

Gati, Charles. 1996. "If Not Democracy, What? Leaders, Laggards, and Losers in the Postcommunist World." In Michael Mandelbaum, ed., *Postcommunism: Four Perspectives.* New York: Council on Foreign Relations.

Geddes, Barbara. 1999. "What Do We Know About Democratization After Twenty Years." *Annual Review of Political Science* 2: 115–144.

George, Alexander L. and Andrew Bennett. 2005. *Case Studies and Theory Development in the Social Sciences.* Cambridge, MA: MIT Press.

Gerring, John. 2004. "What Is a Case Study and What Is It Good For." *American Political Science Review* 98(2): 341–354.

Gesell, Rainer, Katharina Müller, and Durck Süss. 1999. "Social Security Reform, Privatization, and the Promise of Uwlaszczenie: An Analysis of Competing Proposals." In Jerzy Schroeder, ed., *From Plan to Market: Selected Problems of the Transition.* Poznan: Poznan University of Economics.

Gibson, Edward, Ernesto Calvo, and Tulia Falleti. 2004. "Reallocative Federalism." In Edward Gibson, ed., *Federalism and Democracy in Latin America.* Baltimore: Johns Hopkins University Press.

Gilens, Martin. 2005. "Inequality and Democratic Responsiveness." *Public Opinion Quarterly* 69(5): 778–796.

Godoy, Sergio and Joseph Stiglitz. 2006. "Growth, Initial Conditions, Law and Speed of Privatization in Transition Countries: 11 Years Later." NBER Working Paper Series No. 11992.

Goertz, Gary. 2006. *Social Science Concepts: A User's Guide.* Princeton: Princeton University Press.

Golinowska, Stanisława. 1999. "Political Actors and Reform Paradigms in Old-Age Security in Poland." In Katharina Müller, Andreas Ryll, and Hans-Jürgen Wagener, eds., *Transformation of Social Security: Pensions in Central-Eastern Europe.* Heidelberg: Physica-Verlag.

Gow, James and Cathie Carmichael. 2000. *Slovenia and the Slovenes: A Small State and the New Europe.* London: Hurst and Company.

Graebner, William. 1980. *A History of Retirement: The Meaning and Function of an American Institution, 1885–1978.* New Haven, CT: Yale University Press.

Greskovits, Bela. 1998. *The Political Economy of Protest and Patience: East European and Latin American Transformations Compared.* Budapest: Central European University Press.

Gross, Jan. 1990. *Revolution from Abroad: The Soviet Conquest of Western Ukraine and Western Byelorussia.* Princeton: Princeton University Press.

Grzymala-Busse, Anna. 2002. *Redeeming the Communist Past: The Regeneration of Communist Parties in East Central Europe*. Cambridge: Cambridge University Press.

Grzymala-Busse, Anna. 2003. "Political Competition and the Politicization of the State in East Central Europe." *Comparative Political Studies* 36(10): 1123–1147.

Györi, Peter and Eva Matern. 1997. "Housing Movements in Budapest." In Katy Lang-Pickvance, Nick Manning, and Chris Pickvance, eds., *Environmental and Housing Movements: Grassroots Experience in Hungary, Russia, and Estonia*. Aldershot, UK: Avebury.

Haberlová, Věra and Jan Hartl. 1998. "Současnost a budoucnost důchodového zabezpečení v České republice." Prague: Konsorcium VÚPSV a STEM.

Hacker, Jacob S. 2006. *The Great Risk Shift: The Assault on American Jobs, Families, Health Care, and Retirement and How You Can Fight Back*. Oxford: Oxford University Press.

Haerpfer, Christian W. 2002. *Democracy and Enlargement in Postcommunist Europe: The Democratisation of the General Public in Fifteen Central and Eastern European Countries, 1991–1998*. London: Routledge.

Haggard, Stephan, and Robert R. Kaufman. 1995. *The Political Economy of Democratic Transitions*. Princeton: Princeton University Press.

Hall, Peter and Rosemary Taylor. 1996. "Political Science and the Three New Institutionalisms." *Political Studies* 44(5): 935–957.

Hallerberg, Mark, Lúcio Vinhas deSouza, and William Roberts Clark. 2002. "Political Business Cycles in EU Accession Countries." *European Union Politics* 3(2): 231–250.

Hanson, John Mark. 1991. *Gaining Access: Congress and the Farm Lobby, 1919–1981*. Chicago: University of Chicago Press.

Harper, Marcus A.G. 2000. "Economic Voting in Postcommunist Eastern Europe. *Comparative Political Studies* 33(9): 1191–1227.

Hausner, Jerzy. 2001. "Security Through Diversity: Conditions for a Successful Reform of the Pension System in Poland." In Janos Kornai, Stephan Haggard, and Robert P. Kaufman, eds., *Reforming the State: Fiscal and Welfare Reform in Post-Socialist Countries*. Cambridge: Cambridge University Press.

Havel, Václav. 1999. *Projevy a jiné texty z let 1992–1999*. Praha: Torst.

Havrylyshyn, Oleh and Ron vonRooden. 2000. "Initial Conditions Matter in Transition, But So Do Policies." International Monetary Fund Working Paper 00/07.

Hegedüs, József and Eszter Somogyi. 2005. "An Evaluation of the Hungarian Mortgage Program, 2000–2004." In József Hegedüs and Raymond J. Struyk, eds. *Housing Finance: New and Old Models in Central Europe, Russia, and Kazakhstan*. Budapest: Open Society Institute.

Hegedüs, József and Iván Tosics. 1996. "The Disintegration of the East European Housing Model." In David Clapham, Joszef Hegedüs, Keith Kintrea, Ivan Tosics, and Helen Kay, eds., *Housing Privatization in Eastern Europe*. Westport, CT: Greenwood Press.

Hegedüs, József and Iván Tosics. 1998. "Rent Reform – Issues for the Countries of Eastern Europe and the Newly Independent States." *Housing Studies* 13(5): 657–678.

Hegedüs, József and Raymond J. Struyk. 2005. "Divergences and Convergences in Restructuring Housing Finance in Transition Countries." In József Hegedüs and Raymond J. Struyk, eds. *Housing Finance: New and Old Models in Central Europe, Russia, and Kazakhstan*. Budapest: Open Society Institute.

Hegedüs, József, Katharine Mark, and Iván Tosics. 1996. "Uncharted Territory: Hungarian Housing in Transition." In Raymond Struyk, ed., *Economic Restructuring of the Former Soviet Bloc: The Case of Housing*. Washington, DC: The Urban Institute Press.

Hegedüs, József, Katharine Mark, Raymond Struyk, and Iván Tosics. 1993. "Local Options for Transforming the Public Rental Sector: Empirical Results from Two Cities in Hungary." *Cities* 10(3): 257–271.

Hegedüs, József, Stephen K. Mayo, and Iván Tosics. 1996. "Transition of the Housing Sector in the East Central European Countries." *Review of Urban and Regional Development Studies* 8: 101–136.

Hejduk, Henryk. 1996. "Poland." In Paul Balchin, ed., *Housing Policy in Europe*. London: Routledge.

Hellman, Joel. 1996. "Winners Take All: The Politics of Partial Reform in Postcommunist Transitions." *World Politics* 50(2): 203–234.

Hellwig, Timothy and David Samuels. 2007. "Electoral Accountability and the Variety of Democratic Regimes." *British Journal of Political Science* 38(1): 1–26.

Henderson, Karen. 2002. *Slovakia: The Escape from Invisibility*. Amsterdam: Harwood Academic Publishers.

Henn, Matt. 1999. "Polls and the Political Process: The Use of Opinion Polls by Political Parties and Mass Media Organizations in European Post-Communist Societies (1990–1995)." *Journal of Communist Studies and Transition Politics* 13(3): 127–147.

Heybey, Berta and Peter Murrell. 1999. "The Relationship between Economic Growth and the Speed of Liberalization during Transition." *Journal of Policy Reform* 3: 121–137.

Hill, Kim Quaile and Patricia Hurley. 1999. "Dyadic Representation Reappraised." *American Journal of Political Science* 43(1): 109–137.

Holbrook, Thomas and James Garand. 1996. "Homo Economus? Economic Information and Economic Voting." *Political Research Quarterly* 49(2):351–375.

Holmes, Leslie. 1997. *Post-Communism: An Introduction*. Cambridge: Polity Press.

Holmes, Stephen. 1996. "Cultural Legacies or State Collapse? Probing the Postcommunist Dilemma." In Michael Mandelbaum, ed., *Postcommunism: Four Perspectives*. New York: Council on Foreign Relations.

Housing Statistics in the European Union 2004. 2005. Karlskrona: Boverket.

Howard, Marc Morjé. 2002. *The Weakness of Civil Society in Post-Communist Europe*. New York: Cambridge University Press.

Huber, Evelyn. 2003. "The Role of Cross-Regional Comparison." *Comparative Politics Newsletter* 13: 1–6.

Huber, Evelyne and John D. Stephens. 2001. *Development and Crisis of the Welfare State: Parties and Policies in Global Markets*. Chicago: University of Chicago Press.

Huber, John D. and G. Bingham Powell. 1994. "Congruence Between Citizens and Policymakers in Two Visions of Liberal Democracy." *World Politics* 46(3): 291–326.

Huntington, Samuel P. 1991. *The Third Wave: Democratization in the Late Twentieth Century*. Norman, OK: University of Oklahoma Press.

Husák, Petr. 1997. *Budování kapitalismu v Čechách: Rozhovory s Tomášem Ježkem*. Prague: Volvox Globator.

Hutcheson, Derek and Elena A. Korosteleva, eds. 2005. *The Quality of Democracy in Post-Communist Europe*. London: Routledge.

Iankova, Elena A. 1998. "The Transformative Corporatism of Eastern Europe." *East European Politics and Societies* 12(2): 222–264.

Inglehart, Ronald and Pippa Norris. 2003. *Rising Tide: Gender Equality and Cultural Change around the World.* Cambridge: Cambridge University Press.

Inglot, Tomasz. 1995. "The Politics of Social Policy Reform in Postcommunist Poland: Government Responses to the Social Insurance Crisis during 1989–1993." *Communist and Post-Communist Studies* 28(3): 361–373.

Inglot, Tomasz. 2003. "Historical Legacies, Institutions, and the Politics of Social Policy in Hungary and Poland, 1989–1999." In Grzegorz Ekiert and Stephen Hanson, eds., *Capitalism and Democracy in Central and Eastern Europe: Assessing the Legacy of Communist Rule.* Cambridge: Cambridge University Press.

Inglot, Tomasz. 2008. *Welfare States in East Central Europe, 1919–2004.* New York: Cambridge University Press.

Innes, Abby. 2002. "Party Competition in Postcommunist Europe: The Great Electoral Lottery." *Comparative Politics* 35(1): 85–105.

Jackson, John E., Jacek Klich, and Krystyna Poznańska. 2005. *The Political Economy of Poland's Transition: New Firms and Reform Governments.* New York: Cambridge University Press.

Jacobs, Lawrence. 1993. *The Health of Nations: Public Opinion and the Making of American and British Health Policy.* Ithaca: Cornell University Press.

Jacobs, Lawrence R. and Robert Y. Shapiro. 1994. "Studying Substantive Democracy: Public Opinion, Institutions, and Policymaking." *PS; Political Science and Politics* 27(1): 9–17.

Jacobs, Lawrence R. and Robert Y. Shapiro. 2000. *Politicians Don't Pander: Political Manipulation and the Loss of Democratic Responsiveness.* Chicago: University of Chicago Press.

Janos, Andrew. 1996. "What Was Communism: A Retrospective in Comparative Analysis." *Communist and Postcommunist Studies* 29(1): 1–24.

Jelínek, Tomáš and Ondřej Schneider. 1999. "An Analysis of the Voluntary Pension Fund System in the Czech Republic." In Katharina Müller, Andreas Ryll, and Hans-Jürgen Wagener, eds., *Transformation of Social Security: Pensions in Central-Eastern Europe.* Heidelberg: Physica-Verlag.

Johnson, Gregg B. and Brian F. Crisp. 2003. "Mandates, Powers, and Policies." *American Journal of Political Science* 47(1): 127–141.

Jowitt, Ken. 1992. *New World Disorder: The Leninist Extinction.* Berkeley: The University of California Press.

Kalogeropoulou, Efthalia. 1989. "Election Promises and Government Performance in Greece: PASOK's Fulfilment of Its 1981 Election Pledges." *European Journal of Political Research* 17(3): 289–311.

Karklins, Rasma. 2005. *The System Made Me Do It: Corruption in Post-Communist Societies.* Armonk, NY: M.E. Sharpe.

Karl, Terry. 1986. "Imposing Consent? Electoralism versus Democratization in El Salvador." In Paul Drake and Edward Silva, eds. *Elections and Democratization in Latin America.* San Diego: Center for Iberian and Latin American Studies.

Kay, Stephen. 1999. "Unexpected Privatizations: Politics and Social Security Reforms in the Southern Cone." *Comparative Politics* 31(4): 403–422.

Kedar, Orit. 2005. "When Moderate Voters Prefer Extreme Parties: Policy Balancing in Parliamentary Elections." *American Political Science Review* 99(2): 185–199.

Kelley, Stanley, Jr. 1983. *Interpreting Elections.* Princeton: Princeton University Press.

Kemeny, Jim. 1981. *The Myth of Home-Ownership: Private Versus Public Choices in Housing Tenure*. London: Routledge.

Kenway, Peter and Eva Klvačová. 1996. "The Web of Cross-Ownership Among Czech Financial Intermediaries: An Assessment." *Europe-Asia Studies* 48(5): 797–809.

Kessel, John H. 1972. "Comment: The Issues in Issue Voting." *American Political Science Review* 66(2): 459–465.

Kim, Byung-Yeon and Jukka Pirttila. 2006. "Political Constraints and Economic Reform: Empirical Evidence from the Postcommunist Transition in the 1990s." *Journal of Comparative Economics* 34(3): 446–466.

King, Gary and Michael Laver. 1993. "Party Platforms, Mandates, and Government Spending." *American Political Science Review* 87(3): 744–747.

Kingsley, G. Thomas and Maris Mikelsons. 1996. "The Czech and Slovak Republics: Housing as a 'Second Stage' Reform." In Raymond Struyk, ed., *Economic Restructuring of the Former Soviet Bloc: The Case of Housing*. Washington, DC: The Urban Institute Press.

Kitschelt, Herbert. 2000. "Linkages Between Citizens and Politicians in Democratic Polities." *Comparative Political Studies* 33(6–7): 845–879.

Kitschelt, Herbert. 2003. "Accounting for Postcommunist Regime Diversity: What Counts as a Good Cause?" In Grzegorz Ekiert and Stephen Hanson, eds., *Capitalism and Democracy in Central and Eastern Europe: Assessing the Legacy of Communist Rule*. Cambridge: Cambridge University Press.

Kitschelt, Herbert, Radoslaw Markowski, Zdenka Mansfeldova, and Gabor Tóka. 1999. *Postcommunist Party Systems: Competition, Representation, and Inter-Party Cooperation*. Cambridge: Cambridge University Press.

Klaus, Václav. 1997. *Renaissance: The Rebirth of Liberty in the Heart of Europe*. Washington, DC: Cato Institute.

Klingemann, Hans-Dieter, Richard I. Hofferbert, and Ian Budge with Hans Kelman. 1994. *Parties, Policies, and Democracy*. Boulder, CO: Westview Press.

Klingemann, Hans-Dieter, Andrea Volkens, Judith Bara, Ian Budge, and Michael McDonald. 2006. *Mapping Policy Preferences II: Estimates for Parties, Electors, and Governments in Eastern Europe, European Union, and OECD 1990–2003*. Oxford: Oxford University Press.

Kołodko, Grzegorz W. 1993. "Strategy for Poland." Working Paper No. 40. Warsaw: Institute of Finance.

Kołodko, Grzegorz W. 2000. *From Shock to Therapy: The Political Economy of Post-socialist Transformation*. Oxford: Oxford University Press.

Kornai, Janos. 1994. "Transformational Recession: The Main Causes." *Journal of Comparative Economics* 19(3): 39–63.

Körösenyi, András. 1999. *Government and Politics in Hungary*. Budapest: Central European University Press.

Kostadinova, Petia. No date. "Measuring Economic Reform: An Innovative Approach and New Dataset." Working Paper, Department of Political Science, University of Florida.

Kostelecky, Tomas. 2002. *Political Parties after Communism: Developments in East Central Europe*. Washington, DC: Woodrow Wilson Center Press.

Kozlowski, Edward. 1996. "Poland." In David Clapham, Joszef Hegedüs, Keith Kintrea, Ivan Tosics, and Helen Kay, eds. *Housing Privatization in Eastern Europe*. Westport, CT: Greenwood Press.

Krastev, Ivan. 2004. *Shifting Obsessions: Three Essays on the Politics of Anticorruption*. Budapest: Central European University Press.

Krause, Kevin Deegan. 2003. "Slovakia's Second Transition." *Journal of Democracy* 14(2): 65–79.

Krause, Kevin Deegan. 2006. *Elected Affinities: Democracy and Party Competition in Slovakia and the Czech Republic*. Palo Alto, CA: Stanford University Press.

Krečck, Stanislav and Saša Procházková. 2000. "Deregulace nájemného má smysl, až budou mít lide možnost volby." *ZN Zemské noviny* 10/40, 17 February.

Krueger, Gary and Marek Ciolko. 1998. "A Note on Initial Conditions and Liberalization During the Transition." *Journal of Comparative Economics* 26(4): 718–734.

Krugman, Paul. 2001. "2016 and All That." *The New York Times*, 22 July.

Krukones, Michael G. 1984. *Promises and Performance: Presidential Campaigns as Polity Predictors*. Lanham, MD: University Press of America.

Krupavičius, Algis. 1997. "The Lithuanian Parliamentary Elections of 1996." *Electoral Studies* 16(4): 541–549.

Kubicek, Paul. 1999. "Organized Labor in Post-Communist States: Will the Western Sun Set on It Too." *Comparative Politics* 32(1): 83–102.

Kuran, Timur. 1991. "Now Out of Never: The Element of Surprise in the East European Revolution of 1989." *World Politics* 44(1): 7–48.

Laakso, Markku and Rein Taagepera. 1979. "Effective Number of Parties: A Measure with Application to West Europe." *Comparative Political Studies* 12(1): 3–27.

Lane, Thomas. 2001. *Lithuania: Stepping Westward*. London: Routledge.

Lasagabaster, Esperanza, Roberto Rocha, and Patrick Wiese. 2002. Czech Pension System: Challenges and Reform Options. World Bank Social Protection Discussion Paper No. 0217. Washington, DC: World Bank.

Laver, Michael, Kenneth Benoit, and John Garry. 2003. "Estimating the Policy Positions of Political Actors Using Words as Data." *American Political Science Review* 97(2): 311–331.

Levitsky, Steven and Lucan Way. 2002. "The Rise of Competitive Authoritarianism." *Journal of Democracy* 13: 51–65.

Lewis, Paul G. 2000. *Political Parties in Postcommunist Eastern Europe*. London: Routledge.

Lewis, Paul G., ed. 1996. *Party Structure and Organization in East-Central Europe*. Cheltenham: Edward Elgar.

Lewis-Beck, Michael S. 1988. *Economics and Elections: The Major Western Democracies*. Ann Arbor: University of Michigan Press.

Lewis-Beck, Michael S. and Mary Stegmaier. 2000. "Economic Determinants of Electoral Outcomes." *Annual Review of Political Science* 3: 183–219.

Lijphart, Arend. 1984. *Democracies: Patterns of Majoritarian and Consensus Government in Twenty-one Countries*. New Haven: Yale University Press.

Lijphart, Arend. 1999. *Patterns of Democracy: Government Forms and Performance in Thirty-Six Countries*. New Haven, CT: Yale University Press.

Lin, Ann C. and Kenyatha Loftis. 2005. "Mixing Qualitative and Quantitative Methods in Political Science: A Review." Presented at the American Political Science Association Annual Meeting. Washington, DC, September.

Linde, Jonas. 2004. *Doubting Democrats? A Comparative Analysis of Support for Democracy in Central and Eastern Europe*. Örebro: Örebro University.

Linz, Juan and Alfred Stepan. 1996. *Problems of Democratic Transition and Consolidation: Southern Europe, South America, and Postcommunist Europe.* Baltimore: Johns Hopkins University Press.

Lipset, Seymour Martin. 1959. "Some Social Requisites of Democracy: Economic Development and Political Legitimacy." *American Political Science Review* 53(1): 69–105.

Lipset, Seymour Martin. 1994. "The Social Requisites of Democracy Revisited." *American Sociological Review* 59(1): 1–22.

Lipsmeyer, Christine. 2000. "Reading Between the Welfare Lines: Politics and Policy Structure in Postcommunist Europe." *Europe-Asia Studies* 52(7): 1191–1211.

Lipsmeyer, Christine. 2002. "Parties and Policy: Evaluating Economic and Partisan Influences on Welfare Policy Spending during the European Postcommunist Transition." *British Journal of Political Science* 32(4): 641–661.

Lipsmeyer, Chrstine. 2003. "Welfare and the Discriminating Public: Explaining Entitlement Attitudes in Postcommunist Europe." *Policy Studies Journal* 31(4): 445–464.

Luna, Juan P. and Elizabeth J. Zechmeister. 2005. "Political Representation in Latin America: A Survey of Elite-Mass Congruence in Nine Countries." *Comparative Political Studies* 38(4): 388–416.

Lupia, Arthur and Matthew D. McCubbins. 1998. *The Democratic Dilemma: Can Citizens Learn What They Need to Know?* Cambridge: Cambridge University Press.

Lux, Martin, ed. 2003. *Housing Policy: An End or a New Beginning.* Budapest: Open Society Institute.

MacDonald, Stuart, George Rabinowitz, and Ola Listhaug. 1995. "Political Sophistication and Models of Issue Voting." *British Journal of Political Science* 25(4): 453–483.

Macha, Martin. 1999. "Political Actors and Reform Paradigms in Czech Old-Age Security." In Katharina Müller, Andreas Ryll, and Hans-Jürgen Wagener, eds., *Transformation of Social Security: Pensions in Central-Eastern Europe.* Heidelberg: Physica-Verlag.

MacKuen, Michael B., Robert S. Erikson, and James A. Stimson. 1992. "Peasants or Bankers? The American Electorate and the U.S. Economy." *American Political Science Review* 86(3): 597–611.

Madison, James, Alexander Hamilton, and John Jay. 1987. *The Federalist Papers.* Harmondsworth: Penguin.

Madrid, Raúl. 2003. *Retiring the State: The Politics of Pension Privatization in Latin America and Beyond.* Palo Alto, CA: Stanford University Press.

Mainwaring, Scott. 2003. "Introduction: Democratic Accountability in Latin America." In Scott Mainwaring and Christopher Welna, eds., *Democratic Accountability in Latin America.* Oxford: Oxford University Press.

Mair, Peter. 1997. *Party System Change: Approaches and Interpretations.* New York: Oxford University Press.

Mair, Peter and Cas Mudde. 1998. "The Party Family and Its Study." *Annual Review of Political Science* 1: 211–229.

Manin, Bernard, Adam Przeworski, and Susan C. Stokes. 1999. "Elections and Representation." In Adam Przeworski, Susan C. Stokes, and Bernard Manin, eds., *Democracy, Accountability, and Representation.* New York: Cambridge University Press.

Mansbridge, Jane. 2003. "Rethinking Representation." *American Political Science Review* 97(4): 515–528.

Mansbridge, Jane. 2004. "Representation Revisited: Introduction to the Case against Electoral Accountability." *Democracy and Society* 2(1): 12–13.

Manza, Jeff and Fay Lomax Cook. 2002. "A Democratic Polity? Three Views of Policy Responsiveness to Public Opinion in the United States." *American Politics Research* 30(6): 630–667.

Marody, Miroslawa. 1990. "Perceptions of Politics in Polish Society." *Social Research* 57(2): 257–274.

Marshall, Monty G. and Keith Jaggers. 2001. *Polity IV Project: Political Regime Characteristics and Transitions 1800–1999*. University of Maryland.

Mayhew, David. 1992. *Divided We Govern: Party Control, Lawmaking and Investigations, 1946–1990*. New Haven, CT: Yale University Press.

McAdam, Doug, Sidney Tarrow, and Charles Tilly. 2001. *Dynamics of Contention*. New York: Cambridge University Press.

Merlevede, Bruno. 2003. "Reform Reversals and Output Growth in Transition Economies." *Economics of Transition* 11(4): 597–651.

Merrill, Sally R., Rebecca Lawrence, Harry Garnett, Wanda Urbanska, Edward Kozlowski, and Jacek Laszek. 1998. *Local Government Rent Policy and Best Practice in Poland: The Need for Rent Reform and an Improved Housing Allowance Program*. Washington, D.C.: The Urban Institute.

Michalovic, Peter. 1996. "Czechoslovakia." In David Clapham, József Hegedüs, Keith Kintrea, and Iván Tosics, eds., *Housing Privatization in Eastern Europe*. Westport, CT: Greenwood Press.

Milanović, Branko. 1995. "Poverty, Inequality, and Social Policy in Transition Economies." Policy Research Working Paper 1530. Washington, DC: World Bank.

Millard, Frances. 1999. *Polish Politics and Society*. London: Routledge.

Miller, Warren E. and Donald E. Stokes. 1963. "Constituency Influence in Congress." *American Political Science Review* 57(1): 45–56.

Miller, Warren E., Roy Pierce, Jacques Thomassen, Richard Herrera, Soren Homberg, Peter Esaiasson, and Bernhard Wessels. 1999. *Policy Representation in Western Democracies*. Oxford: Oxford University Press.

Miller, William L., Stephen White, and Paul Heywood. 1998. *Values and Political Change in Postcommunist Europe*. New York: St. Martin's Press.

Monroe, Alan D. 1979. "Consistency Between Public Preferences and National Policy Decisions." *American Politics Quarterly* 7(1): 3–19.

Monroe, Alan D. 1995. "Public Opinion and Public Policy, 1980–1993." *Public Opinion Quarterly* 62(1): 6–28.

Moreno, Erika, Brian F. Crisp, and Matthew Soberg Shugart. 2003. "The Accountability Deficit in Latin America." In Scott Mainwaring and Christopher Welna, eds., *Democratic Accountability in Latin America*. Oxford: Oxford University Press.

Moser, Robert G. 1999. "Electoral Systems and the Number of Parties in Postcommunist States." *World Politics* 51(3): 359–384.

Mueller, John. 1996. "Democracy, Capitalism, and the End of Transistion." In Michael Mandelbaum, ed., *Postcommunism: Four Perspectives*. New York: Council on Foreign Relations.

Müller, Katharina, Andreas Ryll, and Hans-Jürgen Wagener, eds. 1999. *Transformation of Social Security: Pensions in Central-Eastern Europe*. Heidelberg: Physica-Verlag.

Müller, Katherina. 1999. *The Political Economy of Pension Reform in Central-Eastern Europe*. Cheltenham, UK: Edward Elgar.

Müller-Rommel, Ferdinand, Katja Fettelschoss, and Philipp Harfst. 2004. "Party Government in Central and Eastern European Democracies: A Data Collection (1990–2003)." *European Journal of Political Research* 43(6): 869–893.

Munck, Gerardo L. 2001. "The Regime Question: Theory Building in Democracy Studies." *World Politics* 54(1): 119–144.

Munck, Gerardo L. and Carol Skalnik Leff. 1997. "Modes of Transition and Democratization: South America and Eastern Europe in Comparative Perspective." *Comparative Politics* 29(3): 343–362.

Munck, Gerardo L. and Jay Verkuilen. 2002. "Conceptualizing and Measuring Democracy: Evaluating Alternative Indices." *Comparative Political Studies* 35(1): 5–34.

Murrell, Peter. 1996. "How Far Has the Transition Progressed?" *Journal of Economic Perspectives* 10(2): 25–44.

Muzioł-Węclawowicz, Alina. 1996. "Poland Housing in Transition, 1990–1994." In Raymond Struyk, ed., *Economic Restructuring of the Former Soviet Bloc: The Case of Housing*. Washington, DC: The Urban Institute Press.

Nannestad, Peter and Martin Paldam. 2002. "The Cost of Ruling: A Foundation of Stone for Two Theories." In Han Dorussen and Michael Taylor, eds., *Economic Voting*. London: Routledge.

Nelson, Joan M. 1993. "The Politics of Economic Transformation: Is Third World Experience Relevant in Eastern Europe." *World Politics* 45(3): 433–463.

Nelson, Joan. 2001. "The Politics of Pension and Health Care Reforms in Hungary and Poland." In Janos Kornai, Stephan Haggard, and Robert P. Kaufman, eds., *Reforming the State: Fiscal and Welfare Reform in Post-Socialist Countries*. Cambridge: Cambridge University Press.

Nørgaard, Ole. 1996. *The Baltic States After Independence*. Cheltenham, England: Edward Elgar.

Norpoth, Helmut. 1996. "Presidents and the Prospective Voter." *Journal of Politics* 58(3): 776–792.

Nussbaum, Martha and Amartya Sen, eds. 1993. *The Quality of Life*. Oxford: Clarendon Press.

O'Donnell, Guillermo. 1998. "Horizontal Accountability in New Democracies." *Journal of Democracy* 9(3): 112–126.

O'Donnell, Guillermo. 2004. "Human Development, Human Rights, and Democracy." In Guillermo O'Donnell, Jorge Vargas Cullel, and Osvaldo M. Iazzetta, eds., *The Quality of Democracy: Theory and Applications*. Notre Dame, IN: University of Notre Dame Press.

O'Donnell, Guillermo, Jorge Vargas Cullel, and Osvaldo M. Iazzetta, eds. 2004. *The Quality of Democracy: Theory and Applications*. South Bend, IN: University of Notre Dame Press.

O'Dwyer, Conor. 2006. *Runaway State-Building: Patronage Politics and Democratic Development*. Baltimore: Johns Hopkins University Press.

Offe, Claus. 1991. "Capitalism by Democratic Design? Democratic Theory Facing the Triple Transition in East Central Europe." *Social Research* 58(4): 865–892.

Olson, David M. and William E. Crowther, eds. 2002. *Committees in Postcommunist Democratic Parliaments: Comparative Institutionalization*. Columbus: Ohio State University Press.

Olson, Mancur. 1965. *The Logic of Collective Action: Public Goods and the Theory of Groups*. Cambridge, MA: Harvard University Press.

Orenstein, Mitchell. 1998. "Václav Klaus: Revolutionary and Parliamentarian." *East European Constitutional Review* 7: 46–55.

Orenstein, Mitchell. 1999. "A Political-Institutional Analysis of Pension Reform in Postcommunist Countries." World Bank Policy Research Working Paper No. 2310. Washington, DC: World Bank.

Orenstein, Mitchell A. 2001. *Out of the Red: Building Capitalism and Democracy in Postcommunist Europe.* Ann Arbor: University of Michigan Press.

Orenstein, Mitchell. 2003. "Mapping the Diffusion of Pension Innovation." In Robert Holzmann, Mitchell Orenstein, and Michal Rutkowski, eds., *Pension Reform in Europe: Process and Progress.* Washington, DC: World Bank.

Orenstein, Mitchell. 2008. *Privatizing Pensions: The Transnational Campaign for Social Security Reform.* Princeton: Princeton University Press.

Orenstein, Mitchell and Martine Haas. 2000. "The Global Politics of Attention and Social Policy Transformation in East Central Europe." Paper presented to the American Association for the Advancement of Slavic Studies Annual Conference, 9–12 November, Denver.

Orenstein, Mitchell and Lisa E. Hale. 2001. "Corporatist Renaissance." In Christopher Candland and Rudra Sil, eds., *The Politics of Labor in a Global Age: Continuity and Change in Late-Developing and Post-Socialist Economies.* Oxford: Oxford University Press.

Orszag, Peter R. and Joseph E. Stiglitz. 1999. "Rethinking Pension Reform: Ten Myths About Social Security Systems." Presented at the New Ideas About Old Age Security, 14–15 September. Washington, DC: World Bank.

Ost, David. 2000. "Illusory Corporatism in Eastern Europe: Neoliberal Tripartism and Post-communist Class Identities." *Politics and Society* 28(4): 503–530.

Pabriks, Artis and Aldis Purs. 2001. *Latvia: The Challenges of Change.* London: Routledge.

Pacek, Alexander C. 1994. "Macroeconomic Conditions and Electoral Politics in East Central Europe." *American Journal of Political Science* 38(3): 723–744.

Pacek, Alexander C., Grigore Pop-Eleches, and Joshua A. Tucker. 2009. "Disenchanted or Discerning: Voter Turnout in Postcommunist Countries." *Journal of Politics* 71(2): 473–491.

Page, Benjamin I. 1978. *Choices and Echoes in Presidential Elections: Rational Man and Electoral Democracy.* Chicago: University of Chicago Press.

Page, Benjamin I. 2002. "The Semi-Sovereign Public." In Jeff Manza, Fay Lomax Cook, and Benjamin Page, eds., *Navigating Public Opinion: Polls, Policy and the Future of American Democracy.* Oxford: Oxford University Press.

Page, Benjamin I. and Marshall M. Bouton. 2006. *The Foreign Policy Disconnect: What Americans Want from Our Leaders But Don't Get.* Chicago: University of Chicago Press.

Page, Benjamin I. and Robert Y. Shapiro. 1983. "Effects of Public Opinion on Policy." *American Political Science Review* 77(1): 175–190.

Page, Benjamin I. and Robert Y. Shapiro. 1992. *The Rational Public: Fifty Years of Trends in Americans' Policy Preferences.* Chicago: Chicago University Press.

Palacios, Robert and Roberto Rocha. 1998. "The Hungarian Pension System in Transition." In Lajos Bokros and Jean-Jacques Dethier, eds., *Public Finance Reform During the Transition: The Experience of Hungary.* Washington, DC: World Bank.

Paldam, Martin. 1991. "How Robust Is the Vote Function? A Study of Seventeen Nations over Four Decades." In Helmut Norpoth, Michael S. Lewis-Beck, and Jean-Dominque Lafay, eds., *Economics and Politics: The Calculus of Support.* Ann Arbor: University of Michigan Press.

Palmer, Edward. 2007. "Pension Reform and the Development of Pension Systems: An Evaluation of World Bank Assistance. Background Paper: Hungary Country Study." Washington, DC: World Bank.

Persson, Torsten and Guido Tabellini. 2003. *The Economic Effects of Constitutions.* Cambridge, MA: MIT Press.

Pharr, Susan J. and Robert D. Putnam, eds. 2000. *Disaffected Democracies: What's Troubling the Trilateral Countries.* Princeton: Princeton University Press.

Pickvance, C.G. 1994. "Housing Privatization and Housing Protest in the Transition from State Socialism: A Comparative Study of Budapest and Moscow." *International Journal of Urban and Regional Research* 18: 433–450.

Pierson, Paul. 1994. *Dismantling the Welfare State? Reagan, Thatcher, and the Politics of Retrenchment.* Cambridge: Cambridge University Press.

Pierson, Paul, ed. 2001. *The New Politics of the Welfare State.* Oxford: Oxford University Press.

Pierson, Paul. 2004a. "Why Americanists Should Be Buyers in the Marketplace of Ideas." *APSA-CP Newsletter* 15: 6–8.

Pierson, Paul. 2004b. *Politics in Time: History, Institutions, and Social Analysis.* Princeton: Princeton University Press.

Pierson, Paul and R. Kent Weaver. 1993. "Imposing Loses in Pension Policy." In R. Kent Weaver and Bert Rockman, eds., *Do Institutions Matter? Government Capabilities in the U.S. and Abroad.* Washington, DC: Brookings Institution.

Pitkin, Hanna Finchel. 1967. *The Concept of Representation.* Berkeley: University of California Press.

Plato. 1966. *The Republic.* Translated by Benjamin Jowett. New York: Random House.

Polívka, Milan. 1998. "Debate on the Social Laws." Prague: START Foundation.

Pomper, Gerald M. and Susan S. Lederman. 1980. *Elections in America: Control and Influence in Democratic Politics*, 2nd edition. New York: Longman.

Popescu, Marina. 2003. "The Parliamentary and Presidential Elections in Romania, November 2000." *Electoral Studies* 22(2): 325–335.

Powell, G. Bingham. 2000. *Elections as Instruments of Democracy: Majoritarian and Proportional Visions.* New Haven, CT: Yale University Press.

Powell, G. Bingham. 2004. "Political Representation in Comparative Politics." *Annual Review of Political Science* 7: 273–296.

Powell, G. Bingham. 2005. "The Chain of Responsiveness." In Larry Diamond and Leonardo Morlino, eds., *Assessing the Quality of Democracy.* Baltimore: Johns Hopkins University Press.

Powell, G. Bingham and Guy D. Whitten. 1993. "A Cross-National Analysis of Economic Voting: Taking Account of Political Context." *American Journal of Political Science* 37(2): 391–414.

Powers, Denise V. and James H. Cox. 1997. "Echoes from the Past: The Relationship Between Satisfaction with Economic Reforms and Voting Behavior in Poland." *American Political Science Review* 91(3): 617–633.

Poznanski, Kazimierz. 1996. *Poland's Protracted Transition: Institutional Change and Economic Growth, 1970–1994.* Cambridge: Cambridge University Press.

Project on Political Transformation and the Electoral Process in Postcommunist Europe. University of Essex, www.essex.ac.uk/elections.

Przeworski, Adam. 1991. *Democracy and the Market: Political and Economic Reforms in Eastern Europe and Latin America.* Cambridge: Cambridge University Press.

Przeworski, Adam. 1993. "Economic Reforms, Public Opinion, and Political Institutions: Poland in Eastern European Perspective." In Luiz Carlos Bresser Pereira, José María Maravall, and Adam Przeworski, eds., *Economic Reforms in New Democracies: A Social-Democratic Approach.* Cambridge: Cambridge University Press.

Przeworski, Adam. 1996. "Public Support for Economic Reforms in Poland." *Comparative Political Studies* 29(5): 520–543.

Przeworski, Adam and Jose Antonio Cheibub. 1999. "Democracy, Elections, and Accountability for Economic Outcomes." In Adam Przeworski, Susan C. Stokes, and Bernard Manin, eds., *Democracy, Accountability, and Representation.* New York: Cambridge University Press.

Przeworski, Adam and Fernando Limongi. 1993. "Political Regimes and Economic Growth." *Journal of Economic Perspectives* 7(3): 51–69.

Przeworski, Adam, Susan C. Stokes, and Bernard Manin, eds. 1999. *Democracy, Accountability, and Representation.* New York: Cambridge University Press.

Przeworski, Adam, Michael E. Alvarez, Jose Antonio Cheibub, and Fernando Limongi. 2000. *Democracy and Development: Political Institutions and Well-Being in the World, 1950–1990.* New York: Cambridge University Press.

Putnam, Robert D. 2000. *Bowling Alone: The Collapse and Revival of American Community.* New York: Simon and Schuster.

Putnam, Robert D., with Robert Leonardi, and Raffaella Y. Nanetti. 1994. *Making Democracy Work: Civic Traditions in Modern Italy.* Princeton: Princeton University Press.

Rallings, Colin. 1987. "The Influence of Election Programs: Britain and Canada 1945–1976." In Ian Budge, David Robertson, and Derek Hearl, eds., *Ideology, Strategy, and Party Change.* Cambridge: Cambridge University Press.

Remmer, Karen L. 1989. "The Political Impact of Economic Crisis in Latin America in the 1980s." *American Political Science Review* 85(3): 777–800.

Renaud, Bertrand. 1991. "Housing Reform in Socialist Economies." World Bank Discussion Paper No. 125. Washington, DC: World Bank.

Radio Free Europe–Radio Liberty. 2001. "Polish President Vetoes Mass Privatization Bill." Radio Free Europe-Radio Liberty, 11 September.

Riker, William. 1982. *Liberalism against Populism: A Confrontation Between the Theory of Democracy and the Theory of Social Choice.* Prospect Heights, IL: Waveland Press.

Ringold, Dena, Mitchell A. Orenstein, and Erika Wilkens. 2005. *Roma in an Expanding Europe: Breaking the Poverty Cycle.* Washington, DC: World Bank.

Roberts, Andrew. 2003. "Demythologizing the Czech Opposition Agreement." *Europe-Asia Studies* 55(8): 1273–1303.

Roberts, Andrew. 2004. "The State of Socialism: A Note on Terminology." *Slavic Review* 63(2): 349–366.

Roberts, Andrew. 2006. "What Kind of Democracy Is Emerging in Eastern Europe." *Post-Soviet Affairs* 22(1): 37–64.

Roberts, Andrew. No date-a. "Pension Privatization in Eastern Europe and Beyond." Working Paper, Northwestern University.

Roberts, Andrew. No date-b. "Campaign Promises in a New Democracy." Working Paper, Northwestern University.

Rocha, Roberto, and Dimitri Vittas. 2002. "The Hungarian Pension Reform: A Preliminary Assessment of the First Years of Implementation." In Martin Feldstein and Horst Siebert, eds., *Social Security Pension Reform in Europe.* Chicago: University of Chicago Press.

Rodrik, Dani. 1996. "Understanding Economic Policy Reform." *Journal of Economic Literature* 34(1): 9–41.

Roper, Steven D. 2000. *Romania: The Unfinished Revolution*. Amsterdam: Harwood Academic Publishers.
Rose, Richard. 1984. *Do Parties Make a Difference?* Chatham, MA: Chatham House.
Rose, Richard and Toni Makkai. 1995. "Consensus or Dissensus About Welfare in Postcommunist Societies." *European Journal of Political Research* 28(2): 203–224.
Rose, Richard and Neil Munro. 2003. *Elections and Parties in New European Democracies*. Washington, DC: Congressional Quarterly Press.
Rose, Richard, William Mishler, and Christian Haerpfer. 1998. *Democracy and Its Alternatives: Understanding Postcommunist Societies*. Baltimore: Johns Hopkins University Press.
Rose-Ackerman, Susan. 2005. *From Elections to Democracy: Building Accountable Government in Hungary and Poland*. Cambridge: Cambridge University Press.
Royed, Terry J. 1996. "Testing the Mandate Model in Britain and the United States: Evidence from the Reagan and Thatcher Eras." *British Journal of Political Science* 26(1): 45–80.
Sachs, Jeffrey. 1993. *Poland's Jump to the Market Economy*. Cambridge: MIT Press.
Sakwa, Richard. 1999. *Postcommunism*. Buckingham: Open University Press.
Sartori, Giovanni. 1970. "Concept Misinformation in Comparative Politics." *American Political Science Review* 64(4): 1033–1053.
Sartori, Giovanni. 1976. *Parties and Party Systems: A Framework for Analysis*. Cambridge: Cambridge University Press.
Saxonberg, Steven. 1999. "Václav Klaus: The Rise and Fall and Re-emergence of a Charismatic Leader." *East European Politics and Societies* 13(2): 391–418.
Schaffer, Frederic Charles, ed. 2007. *Elections for Sale: The Causes and Consequences of Vote Buying*. Boulder, CO: Lynne Rienner.
Schmitter, Philippe C. 2005. "The Ambiguous Virtues of Accountability." In Larry Diamond and Leonardo Morlino, eds., *Assessing the Quality of Democracy*. Baltimore: Johns Hopkins University Press.
Schmitter, Philippe C. and Terry Lynn Karl. 1991. "What Democracy Is . . . and Is Not." *Journal of Democracy* 2(3): 75–89.
Schmitter, Philippe C. and Terry Lynn Karl. 1994. "The Conceptual Travels of Transitologists and Consolidolgists: How Far to the East Should They Attempt to Go?" *Slavic Review* 53(1): 173–185.
Schöpflin, Geroge. 1993. "Culture and Identity in Postcommunist Europe." In Stephen White, Judy Batt, and Paul Lewis, eds., *Developments in Eastern European Politics*. London: Macmillan.
Schrooten, Mechthild, Timothy M. Smeeding, and Gert C. Wagner. 1999. "Distributional and Fiscal Consequences of Social Security Reforms in Central-Eastern Europe." In Katharina Müller, Andreas Ryll, and Hans-Jürgen Wagener, eds., *Transformation of Social Security: Pensions in Central-Eastern Europe*. Heidelberg: Physica-Verlag.
Schumpeter, Joseph. 1943. *Capitalism, Socialism, and Democracy*. New York: Harper.
Seleny, Anna. 1999. "Old Political Rationalities and New Democracies: Compromise and Confrontation in Hungary and Poland." *World Politics* 51(4): 484–519.
Seleny, Anna. 2006. *The Political Economy of State-Society Relations in Hungary and Poland: From Communism to the European Union*. Cambridge: Cambridge University Press.
Selowsky, Marcelo and Ricardo Martin. 1997. "Policy Performance and Output Growth in Transition Economies." *American Economic Review* 87(2): 349–353.

Shabad, Goldie and Kazimierz M. Slomczynski. 1999. "Political Identities in the Initial Phase of Systemic Transformation in Poland." *Comparative Political Studies* 32(6): 690–723.

Shapiro, Robert Y. and John T. Young. 1989. "Public Opinion and the Welfare State: The United States in Comparative Perspective." *Political Science Quarterly* 104(1): 59–89.

Simonovits, András. 1999. "The New Hungarian Pension System and Its Problems." In Katharina Müller, Andreas Ryll, and Hans-Jürgen Wagener, eds., *Transformation of Social Security: Pensions in Central-Eastern Europe*. Heidelberg: Physica-Verlag.

Simonovits, András. 2000. "Partial Privatization of a Pension System: Lessons from Hungary." *Journal of International Development* 12(4): 519–529.

Smith, David J. 2001. *Estonia: Independence and European Integration*. London: Routledge.

Snyder, Jack L. 2000. *From Voting to Violence: Democratization and Nationalist Conflict*. New York: Norton.

Snyder, Jack and Karen Ballentine. 1996. "Nationalism and the Marketplace of Ideas." *International Security* 21(2): 5–41.

Soroka, Stuart N. and Christopher Wlezien. 2004. "Opinion Representation and Policy Feedback: Canada in Comparative Perspective." *Canadian Journal of Political Science* 37(3): 531–559.

Soroka, Stuart N. and Christopher Wlezien. 2005. "Opinion-Policy Dynamics: Public Preferences and Public Expenditure in the United Kingdom." *British Journal of Political Science* 35(4): 665–689.

Spéder, Zsolt. 2000. "Hungary: Getting Better and Becoming Dissimiliar." In Tine Stanovnik, Nada Stropnik, and Christopher Prinz, eds., *Economic Well-Being of the Elderly: A Comparison Across Five European Countries*. Aldershot: Ashgate.

Stanovnik, Tine, Nada Stropnik, and Christopher Prinz, eds. 2000. *Economic Well-Being of the Elderly: A Comparison Across Five European Countries*. Aldershot: Ashgate.

Stark, David and László Bruszt. 1998. *Postsocialist Pathways: Transforming Politics and Property in East Central Europe*. Cambridge: Cambridge University Press.

Stiglitz, Joseph E. 2000. "Whither Reform? – Ten Years of the Transition." Proceedings of the Annual World Bank Conference on Development Economics. Washington, DC: World Bank.

Stimson, James A., Michael B. MacKuen, and Robert S. Erikson. 1995. "Dynamic Representation." *American Political Science Review* 89(3): 543–565.

Stokes, Susan. 2001a. *Mandates and Democracy: Neoliberalism by Surprise in Latin America*. Cambridge: Cambridge University Press.

Stokes, Susan, ed. 2001b. *Public Support for Market Reforms in New Democracies*. New York: Cambridge University Press.

Stone, Randall W. 2002. *Lending Credibility: The International Monetary Fund and the Postcommunist Transition*. Princeton: Princeton University Press.

Struyk, Raymond. 1996. "The Long Road to the Market." In Raymond Struyk, ed., *Economic Restructuring of the Former Soviet Bloc: The Case of Housing*. Washington, DC: The Urban Institute Press.

Struyk, Raymond. 2000. "A Regional Policy Report." In Raymond Struyk, ed. *Homeownership and Housing Finance Policy in the Former Soviet Bloc: Costly Populism*. Washington, DC: The Urban Institute Press.

Surowiecki, James. 2004. *The Wisdom of Crowds: Why the Many Are Smarter Than the Few and How Collective Wisdom Shapes Business, Economics, Societies, and Nations*. London: Little, Brown.

Sýkora, Luděk. 1998. "Housing System, Housing Policy and House Building in the Czech Republic and Prague." Accessed at www.natur.cuni.cz/~sykora/text/housing.htm.

Sýkora, Luděk. 2003. "Between the State and Market: Local Government and Housing in the Czech Republic." In Martin Lux, ed., *Housing Policy: An End or a New Beginning*. Budapest: Open Society Institute.

Szczerbiak, Aleks. 2003. "Old and New Divisions in Polish Politics: Polish Parties' Electoral Strategies and Bases of Support." *Europe-Asia Studies* 55(5): 729–746.

Szelenyi, Iván. 1983. *Urban Inequalities Under State Socialism*. Oxford: Oxford University Press.

Sztompka, Piotr. 1991. "The Intangibles and Imponderables of the Transition to Democracy." *Studies in Comparative Communism* 24(3): 295–311.

Sztompka, Piotr. 2000. "Civilisational Incompetence: A Prerequisite of Postcommunist Transition." Jagellonian University: Center for European Studies.

Szulc, Adam. 2000. "Poland: Transition Gainers with an Uncertain Future." In Tine Stanovnik, Nada Stropnik, and Christopher Prinz, eds., *Economic Well-Being of the Elderly: A Comparison Across Five European Countries*. Aldershot: Ashgate.

Taagepera, Rein. 1995. "Estonian Parliamentary Elections, March 1995." *Electoral Studies* 14(3): 328–331.

TÁRKI. 1996. "Changes in Attitudes to Pensions and to the Pension System: Report 1/5 for the Ministry of Finance." Budapest: TÁRKI.

Telgarsky, Jeffrey P., G. Thomas Kingsley, and Peter Tatian. 1992. "Housing Allowances and Czechoslovakia's Social Safety Net." Urban Institute Project Report 6127–96. Washington, DC: The Urban Institute.

Thelen, Kathleen. 1999. "Historical Institutionalism in Comparative Politics." *Annual Review of Political Science* 2: 369–404.

Thomson, Robert. 2001. "The Programme to Policy Linkage: The Fulfillment of Election Pledges on Socio-economic Policy in the Netherlands, 1986–1998." *European Journal of Political Research* 40(2): 171–197.

Tismaneanu, Vladimir. 1992. *Reinventing Politics: Eastern Europe from Stalin to Havel*. New York: Free Press.

Tokes, Rudolf L. 1996. *Hungary's Negotiated Revolution: Economic Reform, Social Change, and Political Succession, 1957–1990*. Cambridge: Cambridge University Press.

Treisman, Daniel. 2003. "Postcommunist Corruption." In Jan Fidrmuc and Nauro Campos, eds., *Political Economy of Transition and Development: Institutions, Politics, and Policies*. Norwell, MA: Kluwer Academic Publishers.

Tsebelis, George. 2002. *Veto Players: How Political Institutions Work*. Princeton: Princeton University Press.

Tucker, Joshua. 2006. *Regional Economic Voting: Russia, Poland, Hungary, the Czech Republic, and Slovakia, 1990–1999*. Cambridge: Cambridge University Press.

Tworzecki, Hubert. 1994. "The Polish Parliamentary Elections of 1993." *Electoral Studies* 13(2): 180–185.

Tworzecki, Hubert. 1996. *Parties and Politics in Post-1989 Poland*. Boulder, CO: Westview Press.

Tworzecki, Hubert. 2003. *Learning to Choose: Electoral Politics in East-Central Europe*. Palo Alto, CA: Stanford University Press.

Uchman, Ryszard and Jerzy Adamski. 2003. "How to Meet the Market Rules and Social Goals for Housing? Local Government and Housing in Poland." In Martin Lux, ed., *Housing Policy: An End or a New Beginning*. Budapest: Open Society Institute.

United Nations. 1995. *Human Development Report*. New York: Oxford University Press.

UNU-WIDER. 2007. *World Income Inequality Database V 2.0b*. Accessed at http://www.wider.unu.edu/wiid/wiid.htm.

USAID. 1998. *Handbook of Democracy and Governance Program Indicators*. Washington, DC: USAID.

Vachudova, Milada Anna. 2005. *Europe Undivided: Democracy, Leverage, and Integration After Communism*. Oxford: Oxford University Press.

Vachudova, Milada Anna, and Tim Snyder. 1997. "Are Transitions Transitory?: Two Types of Political Change in Eastern Europe Since 1989." *East European Politics and Societies* 11(1): 1–35.

Vanhuysse, Pieter. 2006. *Divide and Pacify: Strategic Social Policies and Political Protests in Postcommunist Democracies*. Budapest: Central European University Press.

Večerník, Jiří. 2002. *The Pension System in the Czech Republic: From Reform to Non-Reform*. Prague: Institute of Sociology, Czech Academy of Sciences.

Vittas, Dimitri. 1996. "Private Pension Funds in Hungary: Early Performance and Regulatory Issues." Policy Research Working Paper No. 1638. Washington, DC: World Bank.

Voinovich, Vladimir. 1977. *The Ivankiad: Or, The Tale of the Writer Voinovich's Installation in His New Apartment*. New York: Farrar, Straus and Giroux.

VÚPSV. 2002. "Social Dialogue on Pension Reform in EU Applicant Countries." Prague: Research Institute of the Ministry of Labor and Social Affairs.

Weaver, R. Kent. 1986. "The Politics of Blame Avoidance." *Journal of Public Policy* 6(4): 371–398.

Weaver, R. Kent. 1998. "The Politics of Pensions: Lessons from Abroad." In R. Douglas Arnold, Michael J. Graetz, and Alicia Munnell, eds., *Framing the Social Security Debate*. Washington, DC: National Academy of Social Insurance.

Weyland, Kurt. 1998. "Swallowing the Bitter Pill: Sources of Popular Support for Neoliberal Reform in Latin America." *Comparative Political Studies* 31(5): 539–568.

Whitefield, Stephen, ed. 1993. *The New Institutional Architecture of Eastern Europe*. New York: St. Martin's Press.

Whitehead, Laurence, ed. 2001. *The International Dimensions of Democratization: Europe and the Americas*. Oxford: Oxford University Press.

Whitten, Guy and Harvey D. Palmer. 1999. "Cross-National Analysis of Economic Voting." *Electoral Studies* 18(1): 49–77.

Wilkin, Sam, Brandon Haller, and Helmut Norporth. 1997. "From Argentina to Zambia: A World-wide Test of Economic Voting." *Electoral Studies* 16(3): 301–316.

Williamson, John. 1989. "What Washington Means by Policy Reform." In John Williamson, ed., *Latin American Readjustment: How Much Has Happened?* Washington, DC: Institute for International Economics.

Williamson, John, ed. 1994. *The Political Economy of Policy Reform*. Washington, DC: Institute for International Economics.

Wilson, James Q. and John DiIulio, Jr. 1998. *American Government: Institutions and Policies*. Boston: Houghton Mifflin.

Wittenberg, Jason. 2006. *Crucibles of Political Loyalty: Church Institutions and Electoral Continuity in Hungary*. Cambridge: Cambridge University Press.

Wlezien, Christopher. 2004. "Patterns of Representation: Dynamics of Public Preferences and Policy." *Journal of Politics* 66(1): 1–24.

World Bank. 1994. *Averting the Old Age Crisis: Policies to Protect the Old and Promote Growth*. Washington, DC: Oxford University Press.

World Bank. 2000. *Balancing Protection and Opportunity: A Strategy for Social Protection in Transition Economies*. Washington, DC: World Bank.

World Bank. 2006. *World Development Indicators* (CD-ROM). Washington, DC: World Bank.

World Values Survey. 1995–1998. Accessed at www.worldvaluesurvey.org. on June 1, 2008.

Zakaria, Fareed. 2003. *The Future of Freedom: Illiberal Democracy at Home and Abroad*. New York: W.W. Norton.

Zaller, John R. 1992. *The Nature and Origins of Mass Opinion*. Cambridge: Cambridge University Press.

Żukowski, Maciej. 1999. "The New Polish Pension Laws." In Katharina Müller, Andreas Ryll, and Hans-Jürgen Wagener, eds., *Transformation of Social Security: Pensions in Central-Eastern Europe*. Heidelberg: Physica Verlag.

Index

Lightning Source UK Ltd.
Milton Keynes UK
UKOW02f0214120914

238353UK00019B/208/P

9 781107 417571